V

CLOUGH

CONFIDENTIAL

BY DAVE ARMITAGE

Hot Air Publishing Ltd

A CIP catalogue record for this book is available from the British Library.

ISBN 978-0-9552466-9-2

Published by

Hot Air Publishing Ltd,
10 Marigold Court,
Red Lake, Telford,
Shropshire TF1 5ZN

DEDICATION

To my dad Ray

who spent so many hours kicking, throwing or hitting a
ball with me and died far too young.

It would have been sometime just before Christmas 1976 when he walked
into a shop and bought a copy of 'The Best of Wooldridge' for his fledgling
sports writer son. I read every word and still treasure the somewhat stained and
battered book. I had the good fortune to spend a little time in the company
of the Daily Mail's late legendary columnist Ian Wooldridge.
Not long after my dad died I was in the middle of the desert in Dubai
covering a snooker tournament when I heard a voice.

'David, are you going to join me for a drink?'

It was Wooldridge, who I had been in the company of at the Open golf that
summer. I readily accepted and stood by the bar and chatted with him. I didn't
tell him the book story for fear of embarrassing him - sometimes now, I wish I
had. As I stood by Ian, a short head away physically but five furlongs away
professionally, I still couldn't help reflecting just how far I'd come.
And somewhere in that desert sky I hoped my dad could see me.
It was the same feeling I got when I sat down with Cloughie,
which I was lucky enough to on many occasions.

And if someone bought this book for a loved one for Christmas and they
had half the pleasure I did from mine, it would all be worthwhile.

My dad encouraged me to be a reporter or do anything that he felt
would give me an interesting working life.
I thank him for that.

Wooldridge said:
*'Sportswriting is an equitable arrangement under which a
newspaper pays you for doing what you would have done
anyway had you been born rich.'*

Dad, Brian, Ian . . . I'll raise a glass to that

ACKNOWLEDGEMENTS

I'm indebted, yet again, to
Phil Shaw for the hours he put in on the book
along with his expertise, guidance and attention to detail.
Special thanks also to
Steve Mitchell of the Nottingham Post,
Steve Nicholson of the Derby Evening Telegraph and
Nottingham Forest official photographer John Sumpter
for all their help providing pictures.
Huge thanks also to both of those publications for their help and support.

A special mention also to legendary commentator
John Motson and Tim Crane
for their unselfish help and encouragement.
Thanks to Jo for her ideas and input and all the work that
goes on long after a book has hit the shelves.

Finally, to all of Cloughie's ex-players and close friends who
happily handed over their recollections and trusted me
with their safe keeping.

Typography by Alison Smith, Justified Design - 01952 246174

Printed by TJ International Ltd, Padstow, Cornwall PL28 8RW

CONTENTS

THE SALOON DOORS SWING OPEN

When Brian Clough rode into town, the crackle of expectation fizzed through the air. Some would run for cover, some would stick around and wait to see what happened. One thing was certain – there was bound to be some action.

Top radio commentator Darren Fletcher, who became very close to Cloughie, prompted the analogy (see Chapter 92) as he describes a quite remarkable confrontation with the then Defence Secretary Geoff Hoon. He sets the scene of Cloughie entering the room like a Western baddie, with everyone's eyes fixed on the man in black and no one daring to say a word.

It wasn't the first time he'd seen that and certainly not the last. I've witnessed it too as has anyone lucky enough to have spent any time in the great man's company. He was the 'baddie' with a heart of gold. Capable of astonishing acts of kindness and generosity, there would also be casualties along the way. Clough sprayed verbal bullets at will and anyone unable or unwilling to put up a defence was in danger of being mown down in the crossfire.

Clough grew up watching Western films and never hid his love for them. You can't help thinking that, in his own mind, maybe he saw himself as the hardened poker player. A man who wanted to win, but win fairly. A man who despised the cheats be they in the opposition camp or his own. Cloughie played life and football like a poker champion.

He developed a knack of knowing when to hold 'em and when to fold 'em but like all gamblers, sometimes he lost heavily. To his dying day, he regretted taking on Derby chairman Sam Longson and losing his job and it was also a crying shame that his last season at Nottingham Forest was stained by relegation.

But along the way, there was a string of quite remarkable winning hands, stunningly played by a man who captured the hearts of the entire nation. The affection for Brian Howard Clough stretched way beyond the boundaries of the East Midlands. In the 1970s he became the darling of the masses for his brash swagger, comic delivery and his forthright opinions. His regular appearances on chat shows like Parkinson and TV football panels quickly established him as a national icon. Everyone knew his face and his distinctive voice, manner and a delivery the like of which had never been seen before quickly ensured he became a national treasure. When top impressionist Mike Yarwood added him to his elite list of subjects, Clough's place in the fabric of 70's Britain was assured. The working man loved Cloughie and he loved the working man. He told them that he was the best and then vowed to go on and prove it clashing with authority and those who dared challenge him along the way.

Several years after his death in 2004, it might have made him smile to know that in a survey of 3,000 people to try and establish Britain's top all-time wits, he came ninth. He certainly hadn't been forgotten. God forbid! For the record, Oscar

Wilde, another man hardly known for his modesty, topped the list. One of the Dublin-born playwright's gems might have been hand-crafted for Cloughie himself – 'Whenever people agree with me, I always think I'm wrong!'

To set the scene, I was a football-mad teenager in the early 70s and Cloughie was already making his mark on what was to be a quite incredible decade. How could I have known then that I would even get to meet him let alone enjoy a drink in the beer garden of his local pub or visit his house? Clough came to the fore as a manager in the days of Tupperware, K-Tel, Ronco and Action Man. It was an era of lime green fluorescent socks, Cresta pop, ridiculous platform heels, glam rock, cheesecloth and bright yellow Ford Capris – and that was just Frank Worthington and Rodney Marsh.

When Cloughie took his family to the Scilly Isles in May 1972, it wasn't just to escape the Royal Scots Dragoon Guards sitting at No 1 in the charts. Just like Amazing Grace, Derby County were never going to be fashionable but they were heading for the No1 spot as well.

Not then the 'fair' finish of the post-Sky TV era with every team kicking off at exactly the same time on the last day. Derby's 1-0 victory over Liverpool in their last game saw them leading the table by one point with title rivals Leeds and Liverpool still to play.

But Liverpool drew 0-0 with Arsenal and Leeds United, who had won the FA Cup final just two days earlier, went down 2-1 at Wolves to hand the crown to Clough and his men.

And it's against this backdrop that the almost-comic TV Clough persona was born.

Cloughie was already in the public's psyche after appearances on the ITV's revolutionary 1970 World Cup panel. Now he was set to explode on to the scene. Once Yarwood featured him wagging that accusing finger and saying 'Hey, young man!' he became TV gold. He'd arrived – and he certainly wasn't going away.

Classic one-liners and a unique delivery made him the outspoken darling of the nation. Simon Cowell was still at school. Clough was the original. In fact, the comparison bears closer analysis. Because when the visionary Jimmy Hill decided that TV's football coverage had gone rather stale and needed an injection of vitality, he came up with what has become a classic formula. Stick four pundits on a panel and make sure one or a couple of them have a real edge. And so the likes of Clough, Ian St John, Derek Dougan, Pat Crerand, Bob McNab and the flambouyant Malcolm Allison really came to the fore – and all for the princely sum of £500 each.

Hill's perception gets far too little credit. The Mexico World Cup saw ITV spank the BBC's backside heavily. The independent network headed the ratings for the first time and the Corporation's stranglehold had gone for ever.

And it was largely down to Jimmy Hill who insisted on one or two extraverts to spice things up. It did that, alright. When cigar-chomping, fedora-wearing Big Mal casually suggested the Russians and Romanians were all 'peasants' the ITV switchboard was jammed.

Suddenly football had been given an almighty kick in the pants. Cloughie and Ian St John were more occasional guests in the studio for the Mexico spectacle but by 1974 they were firmly at the forefront.

Football had suddenly got its fizz back after the rather staid 60s. We might have won the World Cup but Alf Ramsey's work ethic and his decision to ditch wingers and flair players was in danger of sending the nation to sleep. George Best, Marsh and Stan Bowles had been virtual lone standard bearers for the rebels when suddenly they were joined by the likes of Worthington, Alan Hudson and Charlie George.

Winning the World Cup had certainly grabbed the nation's attention but, just like Jimmy the Chin had recognised, there was a desperate need for entertainers. And so, as glam rock was set to dominate one of the most bizarre, but enjoyable, decades of all time, along came a new band of glam footballers in flash cars and invariably with a glass in hand or a gorgeous bird on the arm – quite often both.

It was never going to be easy for the managers to follow suit. They had to still have that parental edge to them but the age of the showman boss was dawning. The genuinely trendy teacher was with us and the likes of Cloughie and Allison were shaking the perception of the modern soccer boss. Bertie Mee, Sir Matt Busby, Joe Mercer and Co were not about to silence these young bucks and the era of the celebrity manager dawned.

And right at the top of it was Cloughie. Gobby, opinionated, arrogant and never wrong! It could have been a formula for disaster but a slightly shocked nation loved it and came back for more. But what really set him apart from most of the others was that he was a winner. The fact that he so often backed up his outrageous claims, made him all the more endearing. By the mid-70s he was the stand-out public favourite to be England manager and by the turn of the decade he was just about to win his second European Cup with unfashionable Nottingham Forest.

Martin O'Neill describes Cloughie as England's very own version of Muhammad Ali – and it stands up to scrutiny. Outlandish predictions and a machine-gun delivery of classic putdowns made him compulsive viewing. Sitting rooms and bars suddenly dropped silent when Clough appeared on the screen. What ever would he say this time?

And so as I entered the 70s and 'big' school, I was weaned on the likes of Ali and Clough and the more my gran shook her head in disbelief at their arrogance, the more I liked them. My dad thought he was fantastic and would alert me when he was on the TV.

And so as Cloughie found himself a welcome guest in our modest semi-detached house, how could me a wide-eyed teenager have ever guessed that a few years on I would be walking into Brian Clough's living room?

My dad was fascinated as I recounted sitting in the beer garden of the Joiners Arms in Quarndon doing a column with the great man.

My dad had died by the time I last saw Clough, but he would certainly have been touched by what brought the meeting about. I'd been unceremoniously put out of work by the Sunday Mirror and Cloughie had heard about it on the grapevine. He was kind enough to contact me and invited me over to his beautiful country home to do an interview with him and make myself 'a few bob.'

I took him up on it and went over armed with a CD box set of Frank Sinatra's hits during his years at Capitol as a thank you.

When I got there he was clearly not himself. He was watching cricket in the large backroom which overlooked the garden but he wasn't well and looked really tired.

His wife Barbara put one of the CDs on at his request and as he asked me how things were going he mouthed the words of the songs even though it was clear he was in his own words 'knackered.'

After a while, I motioned to Barbara that it might be better if I called back some other time and she nodded. He gave me a brief hug, thanked me for coming and said not to leave it so long next time. There wasn't a next time.

Later that night, the phone rang and my partner at the time answered it and was quickly engaged in conversation with the caller.

She mouthed to me that it was Cloughie and carried on talking, with me urging her to pass the phone over. After a good 20 minutes she told him I was there to speak to him before ending the call with 'Oh, okay I'll tell him.'

The phone plonked back on the receiver. He had phoned to thank me for the CD's, asked where I'd got them from because he wanted to get a similar set for a friend of his.

On being informed that I was there just across the room to take the call, he'd said: 'It's okay. I don't talk to journalists – and you might be best advised to do the same!'

He became ill and eventually the day came when a colleague called to say Cloughie had died. It was going to be a whole lot quieter around the place and a lot less eventful.

Years later I decided to try and make a collection of some of the great Clough stories that did the rounds among Press colleagues and former players. And so '150 BC: Cloughie The Inside Stories' was born and went on to be extremely well received.

There was never a plan for a second volume until the stories kept coming in and I was asked why I hadn't included the tale about . . . .

Forest legend Kenny Burns kindly took time to tell me he felt it was the best book on Clough he had ever read. That's some compliment from a man who was one of his greatest ever players and idolised his mentor. A number of people who knew Cloughie exceptionally well took pains to say how much they had enjoyed it and were happy to give up even more of their memories.

And so, enough said, I hope you enjoy this second volume. There will be no more. But hopefully 'CLOUGH: Confidential' and '150 BC' will ensure that in years to come the legendary anecdotes are there recorded for people to enjoy for many years to come.

Thanks Brian.

Nottingham Forest keeper CHRIS WOODS was a regular squash partner of Cloughie's and was used to odd requests. But he reveals how one day he got a a real eye-opener during a game when his manager floored him with a really off-the-wall request.

1

THE GLASS EYE

CHRIS WOODS

I only ever said 'no' to the gaffer once and, believe you me, it is an occasion I will remember to my dying day.

I played quite a lot of squash when I was younger and though I can't quite remember how it came about, I became one of the boss's regular squash partners.

I must have said that I played or he got to hear about it and eventually our Friday morning squash sessions became something of a ritual. I wasn't in the first team at the time, so my preparation for the weekend started with a highly competitive runaround with the boss.

It is a wonder the first team lads didn't have a whip round and give me a few quid to make sure I lost because the outcome of our games often dictated the mood he would be in when he got back to the ground.

The first teamers reckoned they could always tell exactly how things had gone by his manner when he returned to the City Ground.

On one occasion I had to turn him down for a game because I was actually training and he ended up giving me a right rollicking!

Like virtually everyone, I inevitably ended up answering any of the gaffer's requests with a 'yes.' If he called for a let during the game, I'd let him have one.

But there was the one occasion when I stood my ground and steadfastly refused to go along with him. It's one of those situations that is so comical, people could be forgiven for thinking that you had made it up.

We were in the middle of one of our games when the former England cricketer Colin Milburn started to watch us from the spectators' gallery above.

Just for the benefit of those unfamiliar with Milburn, he was a giant of a man who carved out his reputation at county cricket with Northampton.

He then became known to a much wider audience when he made his mark as an England cricketer of some renown. He might not have looked the most athletic of types but he was a batsman capable of producing sparkling centuries.

Unfortunately his top flight career was cut short when he lost his left eye in a car crash. Anyway, I'm guessing he must have been over at Trent Bridge cricket ground in some capacity and had come over to see the gaffer.

The boss absolutely loved cricket and was big mates with England legend Geoffrey Boycott. He was just as happy talking about cricket as he was football, in fact sometimes I think he preferred to switch off by chatting away about something other than the game where he earned his living. But for now it was squash that was foremost in his thoughts. Well, until . . .

All of a sudden there was a clatter at the back of the court followed quickly by an apology from the slightly embarrassed batting legend. We looked at each other wondering just what had happened when the mystery unravelled.

'Sorry Brian, I've dropped my glass eye,' said a voice from on high.

'Can you pick it up and go and give it him back?' Cloughie said.

I told him he had to be joking. There was absolutely no chance of me doing that – gaffer or not.

In fairness to him and to avoid any embarrassment, Cloughie picked up the false eye and duly returned it to its flustered owner.

That is the first and last time I ever defied him.

❝ When I joined Forest we barely had a player in the first team who I thought could play. I even had to teach one of them how to take a throw-in. I had to teach them how to dress smartly, take their hands out of their pockets and stop slouching ❞

Brian Clough was sporting royalty and not carrying any money around with him was no stumbling block when he fancied treating his Forest kids to a fish and chip supper. Former youth team manager JOHN PERKINS saw him come up with a solution.

2

A FISHY TALE

JOHN PERKINS

The gaffer was a great support to the youth team, and if it was humanly possible he would be on the sidelines giving the benefit of his experience to the players and myself whenever he could.

The youth team had been drawn away to Peterborough United in the Midland Youth Cup and the game was to be played at their London Road ground. It was an evening kick-off and in the afternoon the gaffer called for me and asked for the arrangements for the match. So I informed him of the schedule, including the departure time of the team coach. The gaffer's reply was 'Pal, save me my seat on the coach,' then a thirty second delay came, and in a much louder voice he said 'because . . . I'M COMING"

So the coach left on time, with BC aboard. The game was played and we ended up losing but the gaffer was different class to me and the rest of the players. He was very supportive throughout the entire game even though we had not played very well. So I was quite prepared for a blast or something similar.

Once everybody was on board, I instructed our coach driver Albert to get going. Just a few yards into the journey the gaffer turned to me and said: 'Have we got anything to eat on here?'

I told him we had some sandwiches but he replied: 'That is no good to me or the players. Albert, stop at the nearest fish and chip shop, as quick as you can.'

So within ten minutes of the journey, Albert had found a chippy, and parked the coach right outside. The gaffer turned to me and asked if I'd got any money with me. I shook my head.

There was a brief delay before he said: 'Well I haven't got a penny on me either, so you had best come in with me and we'll see what we can do.'

So, we both got off the bus and went into a back street fish and chip shop. Behind the counter was a lady you would not want to argue with, big, strong and wearing glasses as thick as the bottom of a milk bottle. The gaffer turned on the charm.

'Hello darling, my name is Brian Clough and we would like twenty fish and chips, please. But we do have a slight problem . . . I haven't got any money!' This was followed by perhaps one of his more unusual requests.

'But darling, if you could be good enough to give us twenty fish and chips, I will send you a cheque in the morning, if that is ok.'

The lady looked on in amazement, raised her eyebrows and then picked up her chip scoop saying: 'I'll trust you Mr. Clough.'

So she gave us the twenty portions of fish and chips, the gaffer thanked her, and off we went. As we were getting back on the coach he said to me: 'It is your job to remind me to send the cheque to the lady in the morning. Don't forget!'

So the following day I went over to remind him to send the cheque. I knocked on his office door and he called me in. 'Gaffer, I just wanted to remind you to send the cheque to the lady for the fish and chips.'

'Oh yes, how much was it pal?'

'Sixty two pounds,' I replied.

So he wrote a cheque and gave it to me. When I looked at the amount I could see it had been made out for £90 and accompanying it was a note.

'Thank you darling. Treat yourself. Be good – Brian Clough'

On the way out he called out to me in a loud voice.

'Hey, by the way, the next time your team play like that, you can pay for the bloody fish and chips!' Class.

' I can't promise to give my team talks in Welsh but from now on I will be taking my holidays in Porthcawl and I've bought a complete set of Harry Secombe albums '
– on interest in becoming Wales boss

When PETE MASTERS came to the rescue of an exhausted canary, little did he know his act of kindness would bring him up close and personal with one of his heroes. How could he have known this particular bird had friends in high places?

3

TARZAN THE CANARY

PETE MASTERS

A tale about Cloughie, a dusty student and a missing canary . . . well, you couldn't make it up could you?

During my holidays from university in the scorching summer of 1976, I landed a splendid job putty bashing at Arbo Sealants, in Belper. For non-locals, Arbo is the biggest putty factory in the world.

One tea-time I was making my way home, as white and dusty as a flour grader, when I spotted something bright yellow on the pavement. A closer inspection revealed it to be a rather exhausted canary. It was lying on its side and breathing rather heavily because of the heat.

I carried the little chap home as gently as I could and my mum took it under her wing, so to speak. After a few days of seed and water, he had executed a remarkable recovery.

I made several enquiries as to who might be the bird's rightful owner but without joy.

By now the little fellow was sort of outstaying his welcome. Such was his recovery that he was throwing husk and seed all over the place and my mum was giving me terrible earache over the mess he was making.

I approached a guy down the road who kept them as a hobby and he dismissed my new found friend saying that he wouldn't entertain taking it because it could be diseased. How dare he? I ended up defending it nobly.

Mum gave me an ultimatum that the little fella had to go and I managed to fix him up with my mate's mum Mrs Grout, who said she would take it.

But later that same day, in the lost and found column of the Derby Evening Telegraph, was an ominous inclusion. 'Lost – one canary, Ferrers Way area.'

That was where I had found it. So, I rang the number and the man said he would be around straight away. Within minutes, a Merc pulled up and a man and three children were making their way down the front path rather briskly. I couldn't believe it. It was Brian Clough with Simon, Elizabeth and Nigel in tow. I'd been a Derby County supporter all my life, so there was no mistaking the celebrity caller.

'That's Tarzan,' one of them said

excitedly, identifying their lost pet.

Tarzan? I'd have thought it might have been named Hector or Hinton – or perhaps even Taylor . . .

I'd refused to name it for fear of any bonding going on, while Mrs Grout would have had that privilege had it not been snatched from her grasp so quickly.

Cloughie thanked us very much for our efforts and they made their way off, delighted that Tarzan's luck had swung him in the direction of me rather than the afterlife.

Now I had to tell Mrs Grout that she was not about to be the proud owner of the chirpy little chap now known to be Tarzan Clough.

My friend's mum gracefully declined my offer to buy her a replacement bird and I thought that was the end of the story.

However, a couple of nights later, Brian appeared at our front door again with a large box of Milk Tray for my mum, who has dined out for years on the tale of how we found Brian Clough's canary!

6 In the North East, the front step of your house was important. It had to be so spotless that you could have eaten your Sunday dinner off it. Ours was – it was the best in the street. It gave our mam a great deal of pride 9

Top football commentator CLIVE TYLDESLEY will never be found not wearing a tie on duty. And he admits it might well have something to do with getting tied up in knots on a Forest trip when Cloughie decided to make a point.

4

KNOTTY PROBLEM

CLIVE TYLDESLEY

The day of August 21, 1976 is one that will stick with me for ever. It was the opening game of Nottingham Forest's promotion season away at Fulham.

I was a year out of university in my first ever job at Radio Trent and I had reported on some Forest games towards the back end of the previous season.

Basically, I was the rookie reporter who, during the summer, had then been assigned to cover Forest home and away the following season.

This was the first time Radio Trent had been allocated a place with the official Forest party. It was a bright, sunny, typical opening day of the season. A beautiful August day and I was embarking on my first 'proper' trip with Nottingham Forest for the match at Craven Cottage.

Because it was my first trip, I was comfortably the first person to arrive at Nottingham railway station. I had my ticket for Forest's private carriage and so I took my seat and sat there reading the newspapers, waiting for the rest of the party to arrive.

They came in dribs and drabs and about 15 minutes before we were due to leave, Cloughie appeared in his smart blue-cloth blazer with the club emblem on it.

He said a hearty 'Good morning' to everyone before moving towards me, sitting on my own at a small table. He slowly put his hand out as he addressed me.

'Young man, you are very welcome to join the official Nottingham Forest party today but when you join the official Nottingham Forest party, you should wear a tie.'

I was only a year out of university with hair possibly too long to get me in the Forest team. But I had been around socially, to golf clubs and such-like, with my dad so I had a sense of what attire should be acceptable.

I was wearing a nice double-breasted blazer, a pair of grey slacks and a smart light-blue shirt with a button-down collar. Accordingly, my casual black shoes had a healthy shine too.

I looked at him and apologised for the slip and assured him it wouldn't happen again. But he didn't move. He just stood over my table and repeated the same words.

'Young man, you are very welcome to join the Nottingham Forest official party today, but when you join the Nottingham Forest official party, you should wear a tie."

By now I was blushing and apologising profusely and I promised him that as soon as we got to London, I would find a shop and purchase a tie.

He paused, but didn't move and, for the third time, said exactly the same thing he had said before.

'Young man, you are very welcome to join the official Nottingham Forest party today but when you join the official Nottingham Forest party, you should wear a tie.'

Now, at this point, he puts his hand in his pocket, pulls out a £5 note and slaps it into my hand.

'The train leaves in 10 minutes young man!'

So, I ran down the platform and, as chance would have it, there was a gentleman's outfitters just outside the station. It was around 9.15 am and it had just about opened.

I dashed in, thrust the fiver into this guy's hand and blurted 'I need a tie!'

He started to try and direct me towards a large rack, but there was no time for that. I just grabbed one and said 'Is this okay?' He sort of nodded and looked on in amazement as I rushed out to get back on the train.

I was now sweating and looking considerably less presentable than I had done 10 minutes earlier. About five minutes after the train pulled out, Cloughie came down past my table and glanced across at me.

'Very smart, young man,' he said with an approving nod.

Typical Clough and a moment in my career that I will never forget. There is a nice postscript to this story which underlines the effect a brief moment in the presence of someone like Clough can have.

I think the only time I have not worn a tie to cover a football match since that day was for the 1994 World Cup final in Pasadena when the temperature was around 100 degrees.

I still wore a proper shirt. I'm sure I was still half-looking around fearing he would suddenly appear around the corner pointing a finger at me . . .

**❛ I regularly scored 40 goals a season and it certainly wasn't luck.
I don't mean that conceitedly, but you can't get lucky 40 times a year.
You can get lucky five times but not 40 ❜**

*Controversy was never too far away when ref
CLIVE 'THE BOOK' THOMAS was around. But the former
top FIFA official reveals even he couldn't believe what he was
hearing when Cloughie told him to play it strictly by the book.*

5

BY THE BOOK

CLIVE THOMAS

Brian rarely had a problem with me booking his players – in fact on one occasion he actually encouraged it.

The player in question was Kenny Burns, a talented but ferocious competitor who was known to step over the mark on occasions.

Make no mistake, Burns could play, but he combined a fierce Scottish winning mentality with a tackle like a man-trap that you had to watch out for as a ref. It certainly wasn't a case of singling anyone out for special attention, but you do have to be aware of just what you are getting with a player like Burns.

'You book him. Don't ever be afraid to book him any time you like,' Brian assured me, happy to let me decide where the cut-off point was.

Burns would sometimes commit offences off the ball and if I saw them, I would obviously have a word.

There were many times when I could have booked him, but my view was better to fire a player a warning shot and then step in with the book only if absolutely necessary.

'I saw that . . . behave yourself,' I would say. I took the view most players appreciated that kind of approach. If you were to give them a precautionary word of warning, they only had themselves to blame if they didn't heed it.

Kenny would invariably say 'thanks' and that would be the end of it, but if I had to take further action at least he couldn't say he wasn't warned.

I have nothing but total respect for Brian and the team he put out. They were a credit to him, the club and football in general. As a referee, you could genuinely enjoy officiating knowing that at least one of the sides would behave themselves – by and large!

Forest tried to play football the way it was meant to be but they weren't all shrinking violets and in the likes of Burns and Larry Lloyd they had two ferocious central defenders who could rough things up as and when required.

I was in Brian's office after one game and he quizzed me over my reasons for booking his full back.

'How were my players? You cautioned one of the boys – Viv Anderson. It was a decision I couldn't really understand, Clive. Why did you do that?'

'Well, it's a funny one really. I gave a decision he didn't agree with and he just looked down at me,' I said.

'So, you're telling me Clive, that you booked one of my players because you didn't like the expression on his face?'

'That's right.'

'Hey, well I'll fine him for that as well then,' he said.

He never wavered in showing me that kind of respect and I will always be grateful to him for that.

Brian was a stickler for discipline, how refreshing when there was no shortage of players more than happy to bend the rules or test the boundaries at any given opportunity.

' When Stuart Pearce got his England call-up, I said to him that I didn't actually think he was good enough for international football. I was just trying to make sure we didn't have a cocky bastard on our hands for the next month '

When Cloughie decided to blood an unknown youngster there were one or two raised eyebrows in the dressing room. But as former Forest defender BRIAN LAWS reflects, this kid was on his way to becoming one of the greatest players of his generation.

6

ROY'S THE BOY

BRIAN LAWS

If anyone ever needed an insight into the brilliant footballing brain of Brian Clough then they need look no further than one night at Anfield back in 1990.

That's when Clough decided there was no better time to blood a raw, completely untried young kid against defending champions Liverpool.

Is there ever a good time to chance such a thing? Throwing a rookie player into the heat of battle at Anfield is the kind of thing only a genius or a madman would dare consider.

Can you imagine it? An 18-year-old lad who only thought he was on the trip to help out with the kit, was about to be tossed in for his first ever game against the likes of John Barnes and Co. The gaffer must have seen something . . . and the rest is history. That fresh-faced boy was Roy Keane.

Had Roy wilted under the pressure that night it could have set him back beyond belief. But the gaffer knew exactly what the kid was made of and obviously believed he was destined for greatness. He wasn't wrong there.

I'd never seen the lad before. I'd never spoken to him. No one in the team had heard about him. We just thought he was some youngster pushing the skips and helping out with the kit!

And then, with just over an hour to go before kick-off, the boss told Roy matter-of-factly to just put the number seven shirt on and see what he looked like.

Roy put it on and the gaffer said: 'You look a million dollars son. In fact, you look that good, you're playing! We all started laughing and thinking it was a bit of a wind-up until he said: 'I'm serious. You're playing son.'

Then he pointed at me and said: 'And you're looking after him!'

Roy was playing on the right wing. I'm playing against John Barnes who is in absolutely tip-top form, so I had more than enough on my plate without having to act as minder for a young kid I didn't even know making his debut.

But, let me tell you, after 10 minutes of that game, you knew just what Roy was all about. He put John Barnes on his backside within five minutes and then had the nerve to tell him what he was going to do to him!

I just thought 'This boy's a winner.' And he helped me do my job very well, thank you. That was the best game I played against John Barnes.

It was an absolutely incredible debut. You just never see that kind of thing happen in football. Prior to that this fresh-faced teenager had played just 45 minutes for the reserves.

He had that aggression and anger in him along with lashings of drive and determination. It was just so refreshing to see it. At 18, nothing fazed him and didn't throughout his career. From that very first glimpse of him you just suspected that you were in the presence of someone who was going to go on and be a massive name in the game. Roy, of course, went on to become an Old Trafford legend after a brilliant career under Sir Alex Ferguson at Manchester United.

It's nice to know your instincts are right because from the very start everything told me he was going to be an absolutely massive player.

❝ At Hartlepool, I cut the grass, cleaned the drains and even mopped the dressing room floor. We travelled all packed into our own cars. Fifteen of us went to Barnsley once for £22 – petrol, meals, the lot ❞

Former Forest and Manchester United legend ROY KEANE reveals how passing tests with Clough wasn't restricted to the pitch. When the master manager issued instructions, sometimes it was a case of just swallowing it - quite literally . . .

7

MADE OF THE WHITE STUFF

ROY KEANE

I ended up at the manager's house on the way to Anfield because the first team had gone up the night before and I was playing for the reserves so he brought me up that day with Ron Fenton and Phil Starbuck and we picked the gaffer up at his house in Derby. I was sent to ring the doorbell.

'Irishman, how are you doing?'

'Fine, boss.' He was putting out the milk bottles when he produces a three-quarters full bottle.

'Here, Irishman, get that down you.'

'I don't like milk, boss'

'You'd better drink it because I am putting the bottles out.' Trust me . . . I drank it!

I was just sitting in his house thinking 'What's going on?' It was all very strange.

There was no indication I was going to play against Liverpool. I was going up there to watch the game simply because I had played 10 minutes as a sub the night before for the reserves. I had been out like I always did after reserve matches. Several pints later I slumped into bed. It must have been close to 2am

An hour before the kick-off and Anfield is humming. Liverpool were the aristocrats of the game.

I was making myself useful helping the kitman when Cloughie came over.

'Irishman, what are you doing?'

'Helping.'

'Well , get hold of the No7 shirt – you're playing.'

During the warm-up I am still answering the question 'What's your name, son?'

'Roy,' I tell them. They were great and everyone wished me luck!

Strangely enough, I was calm leaving the dressing room. Clough had been daring and clever. There was no pressure on me. We lost 2-0 but we had given it our best shot. If the guys didn't know my name at the start of the match, I felt they knew it now.

❛ Some might have thought No.11 Valley Road, the end of the terrace, was just another council house, but to me it was heaven ❜

13

Commentating legend JOHN MOTSON learnt right from the very outset of his distinguished career that dealing with Clough could be an unpredictable business. But his words of wisdom haven't been forgotten after all these years.

8

JUST RELAX

JOHN MOTSON

I first met Clough when he was a young, brash manager of Derby County in 1969. It was my first year in BBC Radio and Derby had just been promoted from the Second Division. They had beaten Crystal Palace 1-0 at Selhurst Park – Dave Mackay had been awesome for Derby – and I was detailed to interview Clough for *Sports Report*.

He came in wearing a grey checked overcoat. I told him there would be a short delay while they read the results. He smiled and said he was happy to wait.

The results took longer than I expected and I was worried that Clough would walk away. He detected my anxiety. 'Just relax, young man,' he said. 'You can't do anything unless you are relaxed.'

It was the first of many interviews I did with him over the next 20 years. My first season with *Match of the Day* saw Derby win the First Division championship. Clough and Taylor had built a team around Roy McFarland and Colin Todd at the back; Archie Gemmill and Alan Durban in midfield; John O'Hare and Kevin Hector up front; and Alan Hinton providing inch-perfect crosses from the left wing.

Clough, meanwhile, was making a name for himself as a TV pundit and, still in his mid-thirties, knew exactly how to play to camera. After one game I was passed a message telling me to ask Clough about George Best, who had gone missing.

'Has Frank found him yet?' jeered Clough, targeting the beleaguered Manchester United manager Frank O'Farrell. From their little office at Derby, Clough and Taylor could access the Press room within seconds.

'What are we going to do about Toddy?' asked Clough of the journalists one day, after Sir Alf Ramsey had ignored Colin Todd because he had refused to go on a summer tour. Todd later won 27 caps as an accomplished defender.

❝ No one ever really gets the hang of me. I don't want them to – I like to keep people guessing ❞

*When Brighton Evening Argus sports writer JOHN VINICOMBE took
a quick toilet break how was he to know that life as he knew it was
about to change forever? Could it really be true? Was Brian
Clough really about to dip his feet in the water at the seaside?*

9

A WEE STORY

JOHN VINICOMBE

The start of my relationship with Cloughie could hardly have been more bizarre. How could I have known when I walked into the gents' toilets at Hereford's Edgar Street ground that my journalistic life was about to change for ever?

My entire world was turned upside down for a while as the charismatic whirlwind that was Brian Clough swept through unannounced.

As I walked into that urinal, the last thought on my mind was that I was about to be handed one of the biggest stories of my life.

In my career as football writer on the Brighton Evening Argus from 1962 to when I retired in 1994 I obviously have a lot of memories stashed away. Some take a little longer to recall than others, but that day at Hereford is something of a watershed if you will excuse the pun.

Brighton were in a dreadful position just before Cloughie took over – 20th in the old Third Division with home gates having fallen to around 6,000.

These were the old days of three o'clock kick-offs and so on Saturday, October 27, 1973 at a few minutes past 3.45pm I would be given the tip of all tips that suddenly things around Brighton would never be quite the same again.

Brighton were trailing 2-0, so nothing unusual there then, when I went downstairs from the Press Box to the toilet, which was also used by directors and their guests.

As I was standing there going about my business, Brighton's vice-chairman Harry Bloom came in and stood next to me.

'Hey John, you'll never guess who we are going to see tonight?'

I wouldn't have guessed in a million years to be fair. How could I have done? But for the fact that Harry was clearly in a quite agitated and excited state, I would have thought it was a wind-up. But the thing was, I'd known Harry for many years. I'd bought my cars off him and so our relationship was a little more than just football club director/local hack. This was clearly no wind-up, even though the magnitude of it was hard to digest.

'Go on,' I prompted him.

'Brian Clough!'

'What?'

'Brian Clough.'

'You going over to Derby?'

'No, he's coming down to us. You can use that John.'

My God!!!! How the hell was I going to get this over to my desk to get it into the Saturday night sports paper without everyone else in that crowded press box hearing?

You have to bear in mind that in those days there were no such things as mobile phones. How I could have done with one that day, so I could have nipped somewhere out of earshot and delivered my stunning tip-off to my desk. Neither was there anything like the laptop computers we all take for granted and which would have also been an absolute godsend that day.

I was trying to whisper to my copy-taker at the other end and not alert the rest of my colleagues in the box. At this particular moment I was the only one who knew all our lives were about to change and I wasn't about to tell them . . . well, not just yet anyway.

* * *

Brian Clough could spot a phoney a mile off. He was deeply suspicious of players and anyone who wasn't straight with him. My first face-to-face meeting with him was slightly different, to say the least, but it set the tone for what was to become a reasonably harmonious relationship.

He had the red-carpet treatment and a terrific reception when he was unveiled to the fascinated Brighton public at his first Press conference but that hadn't offered me an opportunity to speak with him one-on-one.

Pretty soon I would go down to the ground virtually every day without fail and it was a few days before I met him properly for the first time.

I was invited into his office where he was sat in a chair with his feet up on his desk. The first thing he did was to inform me as to how tired he was after running around on the pitch during a strenuous training session that had just finished.

'Hey, I'm knackered,' he said, presumably trying to impress me.

'Just a minute,' I said. 'There isn't a bead of sweat on you and there's not a bit of mud on the bottom of your boots!'

'You c***,' he replied, clearly realising he had been rumbled.

'Takes one to know one,' I countered and from that point on I don't think there was ever a cross word between us.

I was a few years older than Brian, so I wasn't scared of him and I wasn't about to suddenly start bowing down at his feet – muddied or not! I like to think he respected me for that and we got on well from that point onwards.

There was such candour about him that I think he respected it back sometimes. Make no mistake, if you were in the wrong he would slaughter you, but on this occasion, he hadn't really got an answer.

He was feeling his way with me and by being straight, I definitely got the impression that I had passed my first test.

It was obvious right from the start that Clough's approach to dealing with players and getting to know exactly what made them tick was completely different to anything I had ever witnessed. He came in at a completely different angle to anyone I had ever seen – and that's what made it so fascinating.

I recall a striker called Ronnie Howell scoring a hat-trick at Charlton and the Press all wanted to interview him.

'What do you want to talk to him for?' Clough asked in a disarmingly matter-of-fact fashion.

'Well, you've won 4-0 and he's scored three of them,' someone dared to observe.

'I know. He did exactly what he's paid for. You lot will give him a swollen head asking him to talk you through it!'

And so the request was turned down even though Ronnie, understandably, was over the moon and would quite happily have let us interview him.

But by far the most fascinating insight into how Cloughie tried to evaluate people came a couple or three days after he was officially installed as the new manager at The Goldstone Ground.

He took all the players out to dinner at a very swish hotel called the White Hart at Lewes. If the players thought it was purely an introductory get-together then more the fools them. Cloughie was sizing them up and watching how they behaved both in a group and as individuals. I only found that out when I dared to quiz him over why he would take a bunch of footballers to such a posh place by way of a social introduction.

'Hey, I'll tell you exactly why young man. I wanted to watch which ones ate peas with their knife . . . '

I must have looked slightly surprised, but he hadn't finished.

'And I wanted to watch which ones ogled the waitress or pinched her bum. That's why,' he continued.

'That's how you really learn about them."

❛ I've never seen the point in arguing with officials or giving them a hard time. Tell me, when was the last time you saw a referee put his notebook away and tell a player that perhaps they had got it spot on and that he, the ref, was wrong! ❜

Forget the multi-million pound signing on fees some current day footballers can command. As former Forest keeper STEVE SUTTON explains, the rewards for throwing his lot in at the City Ground weren't quite so grand.

10

PHONE TERMS

STEVE SUTTON

My first signing on 'fee' was having the phone put in at my parents' house. That's what happens when your dad acts as unofficial agent and is a fully paid up member of the Brian Clough Fan Club!

My father Jack is a dyed-in-the wool Derby County fan and so the boss was an absolute legend in his eyes. Cloughie could do no wrong and the only surprise is that he didn't come away from those talks having agreed for me to play for nothing on a 10-year deal. Only joking.

I was about 15 and I had played for Derbyshire Schools and been in county squads when Peter Taylor came to watch me. A report had gone in on me, but it all seemed to go a bit quiet. Then one day Cloughie took me by surprise saying: 'When are you going to sign for me young man?'

'As soon as you like,' came the reply.

'Right, well I understand you have got a very nice pub in your village. I will bring the family across and we will all go out and have Sunday lunch.'

Dad had to pinch himself. There we all were – our family, dining out with Brian Clough, his wife Barbara and the three kids. Nigel, who would one day become a team mate of mine was only a nipper – maybe eight or nine at most.

We went back to the house and the gaffer said: 'Right, leave me and your dad to it.'

I went upstairs while Cloughie and dad had a good chat and thrashed out the deal!

So, it was me going one way . . . and a brand new trimphone (remember them?) coming the other way. It was a big event back then having the phone put in.

It was a meeting that would change my life.

I wonder what the modern day player would think of that?

❝ Don't walk on my pitch with your high heels on. Mind you, they go with your earrings ❞

– to a bunch of fashion-conscious opposition players

11

TROON TRIP

TREVOR BARTLETT

When Forest played Celtic in 1984 they were famously up against it after drawing in the first leg 0-0 at the City Ground. The general feeling was that the Scottish side had done enough and that Cloughie and his players had good cause to be anxious. Perhaps someone should have told them!

We had flown up there and were staying in a posh place called The Marine Hotel in Troon.

The Post wanted me to get some pictures early on in order that I could send some film back to the office on the Red Parcel Service at the nearby railway station.

Cloughie said: 'We're going to walk into Troon tomorrow morning and you're welcome to come along.'

I wasn't sure exactly what photo opportunities that might throw up, but the invitation was much appreciated.

I took a few pictures of the players, nothing particularly special, when Cloughie said to me: 'Find someone and ask them where the best place might be to have a drink and a bite to eat.'

So, I stopped this bloke in the street and asked if he knew anywhere that might be suitable and he said in a broad Scottish accent something to the effect of 'Follow me!'

He ended up taking us to a lovely private marina and we got fixed up at a nice little place. Just the job.

I thanked the man, who it turned out was football crazy, and just as he was about to go on his way, Brian said: 'Hey, bring your mate in with us!'

Well, this chap couldn't believe his luck. Cloughie set up a tab and we had a few drinks, some food and were playing pool and stuff.

I wasn't too far behind this guy in the good fortune stakes either. In the marina there was a replica of The Golden Hind. It was absolutely brilliant and Cloughie duly obliged with plenty of photo ideas, including one where he put a huge rope around Viv Anderson's neck!

Getting Brian in off-beat settings was just brilliant from a photographer's point of view. Provided he was in the mood to co-operate, you couldn't fail. Usually he was co-operative because for all his faults and cussedness at times, Brian appreciated that people like photographers and reporters had a job of work to do and were to a large extent reliant on him providing them with the right kind of material. He rarely failed to deliver.

One year, he was taking the players on a 12-day pre-season tour of Sweden and asked me if I was coming along.

'No way,' I laughed off the very thought of it. 'My paper won't pay for me to do that!'

'What if I pay for it?' Brian said.

'What?'

'I bet they'd send you if I paid for it,' he assured me.

I laughed it off really until Brian decided to ring the editor of the paper Barrie Williams. I don't think he could have got through straight away, because when he did, the conversation went something like:

'Ah, hello Mr Williams, it must be nice to have a three-hour lunch. Anyway, I've got this piss-artist photographer in my office drinking all my booze who says that if I pay the bill, you'll let him come to Sweden with us.'

'If you pay the bill, he can,' was the gist of what the editor must have said to him.

And he did . . . Sweden here I come!!!

6 You start off in the game thinking you're indispensable. It never occurred to me that I wasn't indispensable at Derby. I told them that and soon found out I was talking crap. There's always someone who can sit in your chair 9

Being a hands-on manager can take all sorts of forms, but former player MICK SOMERS is one of the few who can actually verify the legendary stories that Cloughie wasn't averse to getting behind the wheel and driving the team bus.

12

COACHING BADGE

MICK SOMERS

The days when Cloughie drove the team coach at Hartlepool have been etched in footballing folklore. Could it really be true? Did the manager actually get behind the wheel and drive the team bus? Or was it just a photo opportunity that over the years has taken on a life of its own?

Well, I can tell you for a fact that the stories are absolutely true. Brian was perfectly capable of driving the bus and did so on many occasions, though I have to say that he didn't drive up and down the motorways on match days or anything like that. We did have a regular bus driver at the club on such occasions. But if it was just a short trip here or there, it was not uncommon for Cloughie to haul himself up into the front and chauffeur us around. It probably did start as a PR stunt if the truth be known but he had a few lessons and learned how to do it and that came in useful on occasions.

It was all part of his philosophy of completely re-structuring the thinking of the club throughout. Considering he was still such a young man, it was apparent to everyone that here in front of us was someone special.

Hartlepool had been something of a laughing stock in football for years because they were always down at the bottom of the table and never did anything.

He obviously didn't have any reputation as a manager back then. All he had to fall back on was his reputation as a goalscorer out of the very top drawer.

I was at Torquay and in and out of the first team when the chairman said to me: 'We've had a bit of an enquiry about you from Brian Clough at Hartlepool. Would you like to see him?'

When I met him, you could instantly tell how ambitious he was and he gave off the aura of someone expecting to do special things.

He picked Hartlepool up by the scruff of the neck, immediately stamped his ideas and discipline on the place and laid down all the foundations for the club to rise from the gloom.

That wasn't restricted to what happened out on the pitch. Cloughie was a root and branch kind of operator who needed to know everything that was going on. And I mean everything!

In those early days at Hartlepool, there were four or five of the players who shared digs. We had a lad called Tony Parry who was a cracking player but was one of those who did like to enjoy a night out.

Tony was unashamedly a party animal who liked a drink and would stop out until all hours. It was just his way and no one thought any the less of him for it.

Most of the players were pretty dedicated but Tony was a little bit of a loose cannon in that respect and was the type who would come in at all hours waking half the house up.

One day Cloughie came around and completely out of the blue said that he was looking for a babysitter. To our surprise, he picked out Tony and on other occasions he did the same. The more sensible ones among us couldn't help wondering why he plumped for what might be considered a less reliable candidate.

'Hey, it's simple. When he's doing that for me, he's not out all hours boozing – that's why!' Typical Brian, always method in his madness.

We just missed out on promotion first time around and by the time we got it the following season, Cloughie had moved on to Derby. But make no mistake, it was all the work he had put in place that allowed that to happen.

He could be awkward and dogmatic as anyone who knew him would tell you but he also had a heart of gold.

But, going back to the bus, I recall one day he did something quite bizarre. He was driving us somewhere when the bus came to an abrupt halt. No one could work out quite what was happening.

Suddenly, Cloughie got out of the driver's seat and we were left looking on in fascination as he proceeded to escort an old lady across the zebra crossing.

Not only that, but when he eventually got her to the other side he dipped into his wallet and handed her something. I'm assuming it was a ten shilling note to help her on her way. I'll never forget that and it just showed what a kind, but totally unpredictable, person he could be.

❛ The FA Cup final is that gala occasion when thousands of people who never watch football throughout the year, suddenly turn up in the best seats and the biggest hats ❜

22

Former Forest and Manchester United striker PETER DAVENPORT
has good reason to remember a match at Ipswich but it
was a prime example of his furious boss not sitting on
the fence that ended up sticking in his mind.

13

BOOTIFUL

PETER DAVENPORT

It seemed like every single time Cloughie opened his mouth, you learned something. He was absolutely amazing in that way. Quite often when he came out with stuff or did something in particular, they were things that stuck with you for ever. How many people have that ability? And it's for that reason as much as anything that I particularly remember the afternoon of May 13, 1982 – the final day of the season. I'm guessing the fact that I scored a hat-trick as well helped, but there was a lot more going on that day in terms of the education of young footballers.

It was always going to be an unforgettable day for a young Steve Hodge who was making his debut at Ipswich's Portman Road ground. But if you wanted an absolute master class in putting down markers for young players to follow, you should have been in the Forest dressing room that day. You'd have seen Clough at his intriguing best.

Hodgy squared the ball across to me and I side-footed the ball into the net for my third goal. Because he was right near the small section of Forest supporters, he clambered up on the fence and was giving it loads right in front of them. Bad move.

Cloughie hauled him off and gave him a right rollocking for his over-exhuberant celebration.

'Do you know why I took you off, young man?'

Hodgy shook his head sheepishly.

'I'll tell you why. Because, for a start, you could have caused a riot out there and, secondly, you shouldn't be running to the supporters in the first place . . .'

The gaffer continued: 'You should be running to me because I'm the one who picks you or you should be running to your mates out on that pitch because they are the ones who give you the ball! If I ever see you do that again, I will never pick you again.'

Message received. But the thing is, I for one can vouch that Hodgy wasn't the only one who took that on board. It was only my fifth game and Cloughie's bollocking was enough to ensure that I curtailed my goal celebrations in future as well. And, as they often would, his words came back to me later when I was managing a team.

I said: 'Hey, don't get giving it the big 'I am' to the crowd. Thank your mates out there . . .' I think Cloughie would appreciate that.

But despite the rollocking for young Hodge, there was another lovely touch from the boss that day. Despite his fury over the celebration, he had been delighted with the way the youngster had played.

He got down on his knees and helped the lad take his boots off as a gesture of his appreciation at a fine display.

'You ever do that again . . .' he snarled playfully.

The other thing about that was that I had scored the hat-trick and the BBC asked if they could do an after-match interview with me. I was a newcomer to the first team after coming to the club from part-time football, so requests for television interviews was something completely new to me. And it was to remain that way for a while . . . the gaffer turned down the request.

'Thanks for asking, but he's not going to do it,' he said.

'I bought young Davenport for a bottle of scotch from Cammel Laird Football Club and if he doesn't play better than that, he will be going straight back to them.'

Point made. If there was the slightest chance of me getting carried away with myself, the boss had just stamped on it.

Then he signed the ball 'Be good Pete – Brian Clough.' Priceless.

Sometimes I wonder just what more he might have achieved had he ever been given one of the truly big jobs.

He came close to being manager of Manchester United – I'm sure of that.

He was almost approached for the job just before Alex Ferguson was brought in from Aberdeen. I know for a fact that the then chairman Martin Edwards was fascinated by Cloughie.

The gaffer absolutely intrigued Martin and when I moved to Old Trafford from Forest, if I ever got in the chairman's company there was one subject which invariably cropped up.

He was always asking about him and I'm positive he was very interested in the possibility of taking Cloughie there.

Ferguson's record now, in terms of winning things, obviously outstrips the gaffer's. But it is mind-boggling to think what might have happened if Clough had taken over at that time when he really was at the peak of his powers. What he did at Forest was little short of miraculous, but what he might have achieved at one of the world's biggest clubs, doesn't bear thinking about.

The thing with Clough is that people, quite rightly associate him with managing less fashionable clubs. But make no mistake he could have handled one of the big boys.

He was a football man through and through. Big clubs, big players . . . they were meat and drink to him. He knew what made people tick and that's something few have.

The strange twist to it all is that Ferguson's record-busting dynasty at Old Trafford might have died on the vine had it not been for a fabled turn in

24

his fortunes at Forest's City Ground on January 7, 1990. Fergie might well have become a footnote in United's history alongside the likes of Tommy Docherty, Dave Sexton and Ron Atkinson.

He has Mark Robins to thank for arguably the most crucial goal in Ferguson's long and distinguished career at the club. But for Robins' headed goal in the 1-0 FA Cup third round victory, there would not have been multiple title wins, the incredible fightback in the Nou Camp to flatten Bayern Munich and clinch European glory or the Champions League final penalty shoot-out in Moscow.

Ferguson's job was on the line. The smart money was on him being relieved of his duties had they gone out of the Cup that day. Robins' goal threw him a lifeline which he grabbed with both hands. Ferguson never looked back from that defining moment in English football history. United went on to win the FA Cup that year.

Robins recalls: "Sir Alex wrote a book and in it he was asked the question, did that goal save his job?

"He wrote that in training I would have missed it, but because I got a push in the back from Stuart Pearce it went in! Excellent! So did I save his job? Yes, I did."

❧

'Where do you go if you want a loaf of bread?'
'The baker's boss?' 'Exactly.
And where do you go if you want a leg of lamb?'
'The butcher's boss.'
'So why do you keep going to that bloody
poofs club in town?'
– Clough quizzing £1m signing Justin Fashanu
over his social habits

When legendary Forest hard man LARRY LLOYD took the law into his own hands against Southampton he was confident no one in the ground had seen his dirty deed. But he might have known there was one man who didn't miss it.

14

NUT THE DONE THING

LARRY LLOYD

Settling a few old scores with legendary Chelsea and England striker Peter Osgood came to a head, quite literally, one night at the City Ground. And guess what? Yeah, it ended up costing me money again!

Don't get me wrong – I had severely overstepped the mark – and not for the first time in my playing career - but unfortunately one of the few people in the ground to see what happened was Cloughie.

Ossie was a great player but, as quite a few people will testify, he could be very naughty at times. He was a terrific goalscorer and a player you would want in your team, but playing against him was never going to be a walk in the park. Osgood enjoys legendary status at Stamford Bridge after a career which saw him score goals for fun. He might have been playing for the Saints when I locked horns with him but he was anything but a Saint over the years we had clashed.

I'd had many a battle with him during my days at Liverpool when he was at Chelsea but on this occasion we had both moved on to pastures new. It was

a horrible, foggy night in Nottingham when our paths crossed again and by now he was playing for Southampton.

Like I said, Ossie was a naughty bastard and he was never shy of putting in tackles which could quite easily have broken my leg. I remember this particular night well because it was before the City Ground had been re-developed and the fog was steaming in up over the Trent End. It was a real old-fashioned pea-souper and the game was eventually abandoned.

But not before I'd left my mark on it – and on Ossie. I was up by the halfway line when I spotted my big chance and indicated that I wanted a quick word with him.

'Come here, I want to talk to you!' I said, catching his attention.

He came over and I gave it him there and then – I dropped the nut straight on him.

'What the fucking hell, was that for?' he snarled.

I said: 'That's for all the times you've tried to break my leg over the years.'

Ossie was going mad about it but the referee, the linesman and half the crowd hadn't seen a thing. Just a pity the same couldn't be said of Cloughie because nobody could see a thing.

He had some incredible system whereby he somehow had someone in the offices typing out fines as he saw fit and he certainly wasted no time with this one. We used to call them 'Red Trees' because the envelope had the Forest emblem on it.

Anyway, I was still in my kit having just come off the pitch when Cloughie handed me another of the dreaded envelopes – a fine of a week's wages.

'What's that for?' I said.

'You know what it's for,' he snapped.

I had no excuse did I? He didn't even like us arguing with referees, so I just had to cough for it and pay up.

' You can split footballers into two categories. There are those who can play and those who can't. You'd be surprised how many people can't tell the difference – and some of them are managers '

27

*Former Nottingham Evening Post editor BARRIE WILLIAMS
can't help smiling as he thinks back to the night when
Cloughie's transfer market activity proved to be just a
little too much for his shocked chairman to stomach.*

15

SOUP SPRAY

BARRIE WILLIAMS

I worked in the same city as Brian for more than 13 years. It was inevitable that we should get to know each other well - as well, that is, as anybody outside his family and real, close friends ever knew Brian.

I remember so fondly the night my wife and I first met Brian. There had been a high-profile bust-up between the Nottingham Evening Post and Brian over his well-publicised support for the National Union of Journalists in its bitter dispute with the paper. So, the reception I was going to get, as the new Editor, when meeting him at a fund raising event at Forest's Jubilee Club was unpredictable to say the least.

No problem. With charm and courtesy he joined our table and stayed for an hour or so – insisting that the official photographer took a picture of him with my wife Pauline. A lovely photo which we still treasure. He made it abundantly clear that he and I were starting with a clean slate.

I saw plenty of other things for which Brian was renowned, too. Like the day I was lunching in the Forest dining room with him and his chairman Geoffrey McPherson – a gentleman in both senses of the word.

Having joined us typically late, Brian announced casually: 'Oh, by the way, chairman, I've just sold Justin Fashanu.'

'For HOW much?' spluttered the chairman (Fashanu had cost the club over £1m).

'One hundred and fifty thousand,' said Brian.

'Goodness gracious. Who to?' gasped the gobsmacked chairman.

'Notts County!'

That was the first and last time I saw projectile soup.

' Kenny Burns was capable of cutting you in two and came with a bit of a reputation, yet he turned out to be as nice a lad as I've ever managed '

Clough was no stranger to battles, but when he was on the lookout for a fort, it was close friend HAROLD ROOME he turned to. Was the manager preparing for all-out war? His trusted pal reveals exactly what was going on.

16

TOY STORY

HAROLD ROOME

I've lost count of the things I made for Brian over the years. I've always been a bit handy on the practical side of things, having served my time as a coachbuilder.

'You should pack up work and make these things for a living!' he would say to me after taking delivery of yet another of my ornamental wheelbarrows. He had them in his garden full of flowers and would give them to friends and suchlike. He must have had 20 of those over the years.

Dolls houses came and went but a couple of the most memorable things I managed to sort out for Brian's daughter and grandson are perhaps the most memorable. I still recall the phone conversation going something like:

'Hi pal. How are you?' The voice was unmistakeable.

'Ok Brian. How's yourself?'

'Good, can you do me a favour, pal?'

I thought then that he was going to ask me to look after his dog for a while, which my family and I had done on a few occasions.

I shuddered at the thought because that was all I needed at that particular time. My wife June was in hospital recovering from breast surgery and I was on my own.

'Depends. What is it?'

'Can you make me a fort? He replied.

'What kind of fort Brian?'

'A bloody fort. What do you think?'

'OK, but do you want a fort, say, like Edinburgh Castle or one like The Alamo?' I replied.

'My grandson is really into cowboys and Indians and I'm looking to get him a fort?'

'The Alamo it is, then Brian.'

'Are you busy?' he asked, saying that if I was he'd get his daughter Libby to get one in London. I told him that apart from the expense, ones from shops would fall to bits in no time.

So, during the period June was in hospital, I worked on the toy fort early morning before visiting and late at night. It was any little boy's dream, even if I do say so myself and for quite some time it was kept on the floor behind a settee at Brian's house.

How time flies . . . it didn't seem that long before that I had helped Brian out of a tricky spot regarding a present for Libby when she was a small girl.

I had received a phone call from Brian at my office at the Railway Technical Centre. It was a few days before Christmas and Brian had purchased a doll for his daughter, Elizabeth.

However, he could not get a high chair to go with the doll, so he asked me if I could either get one made for him or tell him if I knew anywhere where he might obtain one.

I asked him how big the doll was and Barbara, his wife, came up with the answer. I then contacted my old mates at the Carriage and Wagon Works and asked them if there was any chance they could help Brian out. Having furnished them with all the details, their reply was basically – leave it to us!

Later that afternoon, I took a call from the lads saying that the component parts for a doll's high chair were ready for me to collect.

Before having my dinner that night, I assembled the chair then gave it a coat of primer. Before retiring to bed, I gave it a lick of undercoat.

The next morning, before going out to work, I gave it its first top coat. I repeated the procedure until the chair was finally finished on Christmas Eve. That morning, I toured Derby looking for transfers to complete the job. Eventually, I found them too.

I called at Brian's and told him the chair was ready and did he want me to bring it round? He said he would pick it up, but in the event one of his brothers came and picked it up on the way to Midnight Mass.

All my best efforts were made worthwhile a few days after Christmas when I received a lovely letter from Elizabeth which I treasure to this day.

It reads: 'Dear Harold, I want to say a big thank you for the beautiful high chair you made for me at Christmas.

"My doll looks really lovely in it. Will you please thank the men at work who helped to make it. Everyone who comes in and sees it thinks it is fabulous. I think you should open a shop and sell them. We all hope that you, June, Kevin and Julie have a very happy 1978. Love Elizabeth."

❛ The manager's office on a Sunday morning when you have lost the night before is a very lonely place ❜

30

*Former Derby Evening Telegraph football reporter
GEORGE EDWARDS enjoyed a close relationship with Clough
but admits even he was surprised the day when a couple of
bemused pensioners were treated to a trip they never expected.*

17

COUPLE IN CAR

GEORGE EDWARDS

One of my funniest recollections of Brian came about one cold and miserable winter's day when we were heading along Duffield Road in Brian's car.

He had a dark blue Triumph 2000 at the time and was extremely proud of it. It probably doesn't sound quite so grand now, but in those days if you were driving around in a Triumph 2000, you'd made it!

We both lived in Darley Abbey, not 100 yards from each other, so we would occasionally share a car into Derby.

On this particular occasion I recall vividly that Brian stopped the car having spotted an elderly couple waiting at a bus stop. He leant across in front of me and having established that they were off to do some shopping, ushered them into the back seats.

The couple were probably in their late 60s or early 70s and I do recall were not particularly well wrapped up.

Brian chatted away through the entire journey, peppering them with questions with the occasional polite 'yes' or 'no' floating through from the back.

'Shouldn't you have a scarf on? Do you like the Market Hall? What are you getting? Are you after some meat for Sunday? Do you have beef? We like beef, mind you we love lamb as well! Do you like lamb?' Brian went on.

Eventually we pulled up by the market place and the couple eased themselves out of the car onto the pavement with Brian saying warmly: 'See, you again!' as he bade them farewell.

As we pulled away, I said to him: 'Are they neighbours of yours?'

'No, idea. I've never seen them before in my life,' he said and carried on driving as if it was perfectly normal behaviour. Astonishing.

❝ Now we are allowing players to play who were once too frightened to go down the tunnel because they were going to get clattered ❞

Derby County legend ALAN HINTON reveals how he found himself on a sticky wicket when he failed to turn up for a cricket match. He thought he'd got away with it until his disgruntled boss threatened to whip his bails off.

18

STUMPED

ALAN HINTON

I once got on the wrong side of Cloughie by not turning up for a cricket match! He absolutely loved his cricket and when I failed to show for a game, he went crackers.

A match had been arranged between a Derby County representative side and Spondon Cricket Club and, unfortunately for me, my car broke down in Nottingham so I ended up not being able to play.

The funny thing about it all was that Alan Durban, who was an exceptionally good cricketer, got hammered all over the ground. He was hit out of the ground for sixes on a number of occasions and was far from amused about it.

Alan, a proud Welshman known as Taffy, didn't see the funny side of it at all and when he saw me, tore me off a strip for not turning up. He collared me about it and I told him that while I loved the game just as much as he did, my car had broken down and there was nothing I could do about it.

The next day, Cloughie has asked how the game went only to be told that the club's side had been hammered and that I hadn't shown up. Thanks a lot!

We were in the dressing room and Terry Hennessey started to take the mickey. He was holding both his hands up straight in the air to give an umpire's signal for 'six' and asking everyone: 'What does this mean?'

Taffy couldn't see the joke. I was in the toilet when Cloughie comes in and someone alerts me that the gaffer wanted to see me straight away.

I didn't realise he was actually there and shouted back: 'Tell the boss if he wants to see me, he can come in here and see me!'

Cloughie booms back: 'You'll want to go back in there when I've finished with you.'

So I came out and Cloughie roared: 'When I put a team on the board representing Derby County, be it dominoes, darts, football or cricket, I expect people to take it seriously because you are representing the club.'

As I set about explaining, he turned to me and said: 'Alan, the simple fact of the matter is that you didn't turn up last night. That's a five pound fine.'

'You've got to be fucking joking,' I replied.

32

'Right that's ten pound for swearing.'

As I protested the fine kept increasing and we'd got to £25 by the time Big Terry told me I would be better off shutting my mouth and take it on the chin.

After we had finished training I went to see the gaffer and pleaded that a £25 fine was way over the top simply for not being at a cricket game.

He said that if I signed a piece of paper agreeing to the fine, then he would give me a fiver back each week.

It was the last I saw of it – he never gave me a penny back.

❛ I'd like to think I did my bit, made my mark and gave a lot of people a lot of pleasure along the way. It was pretty good while it lasted ❜

*Cloughie didn't have to try too hard to rub Derby chairman
Sam Longson up the wrong way, but as ex-player
MICK CULLERTON reveals he pushed him to the limit the day
he decided it would be okay to 'steal' his prized luxury motor.*

19

CAR CAPERS

MICK CULLERTON

My time under Cloughie at Derby was relatively short-lived but eventful to say the least. When he came in to sign me from Port Vale, he got straight to the point.

'Are you a drinker?'

'Yeah,' I replied.

'Do you gamble?'

'A bit.'

'Do you chase women?'

'Yeah, I try to.'

'Do you catch many?'

'A few . . .'

'Good lad. Carry on,' was his reply.

But there were more bizarre encounters to come, not least the episode of the chairman's luxury motor.

I'd been playing for Derby's reserves. One morning Cloughie came into the dressing room at the Baseball Ground and looked me up and down with some alarm.

'You look dreadful,' he said.

I was actually suffering from glandular fever, but we didn't know what was wrong at that time.

'I'm waiting to see a doctor,' I informed him.

My neck was swollen and my skin had a yellowness about it – more than enough for Clough, dressed in his tracksuit - to decide urgent action was required.

'I'm taking you to hospital right now,' he said.

As we got outside, someone had blocked his car in so Clouhie took it on himself to take the keys to club chairman Sam Longson's flashy Mercedes and promptly got behind the wheel.

No more to do, he drove me to the hospital in Derby and promptly parked the chairman's Merc in the general manager of the hospital's allocated parking space.

He breezed in and managed to get the attention of a doctor who fairly quickly diagnosed that I had glandular fever.

When Cloughie got back, Longson went ballistic much to Cloughie's disgust. He was going crackers.

'Mr Longson, is your car more important than this young man's health?' he asked.

'Yes, it is actually,' the chairman countered abruptly. Cloughie threw the keys at him!

I only spent a couple of years there

in the end and never really managed to make the breakthrough I longed for. I had 17 months of my contract left, but I decided to go and see him in his office. At least he was straight with me!

'Gaffer, I hate playing in the reserves.'

'I know.'

'Is there any chance of me getting in the first team?'

'No.'

He must have seen the disappointment in my face, but explained that with the team he was assembling now, he had to aim for the top. There was only one direction for him and clearly I wasn't part of the great plan. I didn't mind that. He was straight with me – no bullshit, like some managers would have given you. At least I knew exactly where I stood.

Years later I was the commercial manager at Stoke when Clough came to the old Victoria Ground with Forest's youth team. He breezed into the boardroom and asked for me. He'd remembered!

'How long you been here now Mick?' he asked.

'Seven years,' I said.

'Hey, you must be a better commercial manager than you were a player!' he laughed.

❛ That's how much he wants to learn his trade. I'm telling you, I wouldn't go across the road to watch Notts County, never mind their reserves ❜
– on son Nigel going to watch a reserve match

*European Cup winner MARTIN O'NEILL thought it might be a
good idea to inform Cloughie that he might be thinking about
playing somewhere else. The manager agreed and made
him realise perhaps it hadn't been such a good idea.*

20

LOFTY AMBITIONS

MARTIN O'NEILL

I remember saying to him once that if Nottingham Forest didn't match my ambitions, I would be off.

He said: 'Fuck off, then.'

And I did - I fucked off to the reserves and he called me back about four months later and said: 'Are you still here?'

Brian Clough was absolutely sensational – a truly brilliant manager. I don't think Brian would disagree with that either. He would have been the first to say he was the greatest of all time.

He was England's version of Muhammad Ali, a more charismatic man you could not meet. He had everything. We were all so extremely lucky to work with someone so talented and brilliant.

While we had some talented players at Forest when he arrived in January, 1975, the club could not have dreamed of winning championships and the European Cups if Brian Clough had not been there.

He could have stepped into any given job. If someone had asked Brian to go and manage, say, the England cricket team, it would not have been a problem to him.

He felt he knew enough about any subject to go and coach it. One of the great myths about him was that he was a manager, not a coach, and seldom on the training ground. The truth is every day with Brian Clough was a coaching lesson.

People ask you to recount a Brian Clough story, but every day with him was a story with each one better than the last.

He would say something so simple, you wondered why no one else had said it. He had a great way with words, when he spoke to you, he told you straight and got the message through every time.

' You can have your chairman, your chief executives and the rest but they are nothing – nobodies – unless the manager gets it right '

*European Cup winning skipper JOHN McGOVERN went almost
everywhere with Clough but reveals how he got off on the
wrong foot with him because he liked to wear his hair just
a little longer than met with the manager's approval.*

21

SIMPLY NOT BEST

JOHN McGOVERN

I might have spent 14 years under the management of Brian Clough, but our relationship didn't get off to the most promising of starts.

If anyone had told that startled teenager at Hartlepool that he would go on to lift the European Cup twice and end up playing four of the five clubs he managed, I would have said you were off your rocker. Talking of rockers . . .

The first time I had met Clough was at a trial match at Hartlepool. I was a big Rolling Stones fan and I had long hair. Like many of the boys around that time I wanted to be the next Mick Jagger.

He barked at me. 'Stand up straight, get your shoulders back and get your hair cut. You look like a girl,' were virtually his first ever words to me. My face must have been an absolute picture. I was petrified already and not sure I ever wanted to see him again. When my mum asked me how it was going, I told her I wasn't going to go there because the Bogeyman had arrived.

I plucked up the courage to say: 'George Best has it styled like this.'

Typically, his answer was brief, to the point and delivered with the accuracy of one of Robin Hood's arrows.

'When you can play like George Best, I'll let you have it that way. Now get it cut.' Pretty soon I had it cut short – as he liked it.

The thing with him was that he was very strict and that didn't suit all players. But it wasn't a problem to me because my father had died when I was a young boy and my mother had brought me up in a strict fashion so I was used to it.

Sometimes he would say something to you in the manner of a parent talking to a small child. That wasn't to everyone's taste, but there would always be an explanation – and he would always be right.

' Coaching is for kids. If a player can't trap a ball and pass it by the time he's in the team then he shouldn't be there in the first place '

Schoolteacher TONY ROWELL taught Cloughie as a teenager and recalls how the youngster showed all the early signs of not being afraid to say exactly what he thought even if it meant jumping to the defence of the man at the front of the class.

22

EARLY SIGNS

TONY ROWELL

In forty years as a schoolmaster I must have taught thousands of boys, but Brian Clough sticks out in my memory for several reasons. He was bright and alert and seemed to have an opinion on everything. He would argue with the teachers, which was rare in a 13-year-old. But I mean argue in a pleasant way when subjects were thrown open for discussion.' *

So . . . all the early signs were there that Cloughie wasn't backwards in coming forwards even as a teenager who was the only member of his family to fail his 11-plus. Marton Grove Secondary School third form master Tony Rowell taught the young Clough English, maths, geography, history, religious instruction as well as games. And in an extract from Tony Francis' biography *'Clough'* he reveals a unique insight into the formative years that helped mould the man.

'Each term I had to produce a set of marks and put the forty or so boys in form order. Clough was invariably near the top in all subjects. He could easily have been grammar school material. Unfortunately, having failed the 11-plus, there was not much a boy could do.

He was outstanding at all games. I ran the gymnastics club after school and he was a very keen member of that – damned good too! The lads had to perform in a gym-cum-hall-cum-dining room with a hot plate at one end and a stage at the other. Clough had a lot of courage when it came to vaulting and agility work. There was so little room to manoeuvre that you took your life in your hands, hoping to pull up at the hot plate or raised area.

He was a sturdily built boy, but nimble with it. Loved his football. I can see him now in the school colours: black and white striped shirt and white shorts. Even when he got into the main school team as a third former, he would be telling the captain what to do. I refereed a lot of those games. Clough was usually right in what he said, but at times I had to tell him to shut up and get on with it.'

But Mr Rowell recalled the time when Clough's sense of fair play came to the fore after the teacher broke a window!

As PE master, I was pretty adept at throwing things. If boys didn't pay attention, I could hit them between the eyes with a piece of chalk. One day after PE we were in the classroom when Clough's mind seemed to be wandering. On the desk was a gym slipper. I threw it at him as hard as I could, but he WAS paying attention and saw the missile heading his way.

He ducked and the slipper crashed straight through the window and out into the corridor. It so happened that we had a very severe headmaster, who was walking down the corridor when the slipper landed at his feet accompanied by a shower of glass. He stormed in to find out which boy had done it. I had to confess it had been 'sir' and in front of the whole class he gave me the biggest rollicking I've ever had. When he'd gone, Clough stood up and said 'Sir, it wasn't fair of the head to do that. We want you to know the whole class is behind you.' It takes a remarkable boy to stand up and be counted in a situation like that.

I always thought he'd make it. He seemed to be successful in everything he did and you couldn't fail to get on with him. He was popular with the other boys too. There was always a laugh and a smile when Clough was around.

When I see him on television I can recollect him as a young boy with exactly the same attitude and responses.'

• *From Clough: A Biography by Tony Francis, Published by Stanley Paul.*
Reprinted by permission of the Random House Group Ltd.

❛ Success is hard to come by, but hanging on to it is harder still ❜

BBC radio commentator DARREN FLETCHER had to become mayor for the day to pacify Cloughie. But he reveals how he feared his antics at the manager's Freedom of Nottingham rehearsal might have ended up getting him the sack.

23

NIGHTMAYOR

DARREN FLETCHER

Cloughie was about to be given the keys to the city – I came close to being shown the door! I'll never forget Brian getting the Freedom of the City of Nottingham because I came within a whisker of being given the freedom to go and work somewhere else.

My boss was keen to get a piece ready for the big day. It was one of the biggest stories on our patch for a while.

His secretary Carole had been badgering him for days on my behalf and I eventually got the call to pop and see him the day before the official ceremony. It was a lovely, sunny morning and as I waited in the famous City Ground corridor, he emerged from his office and said we'd do it outside.

So there I was, waiting outside for him when suddenly a big official city council limo turns up. It was bottle green and had the city's flag fluttering on the front. This fella gets out of the driver's side wearing the full regalia and stands there.

My immediate thought was that I was going to get bombed out there and then – interview over before it had

even started.

Brian came out with a smart suit on and says that he's got to do a kind of 'rehearsal' of the next day's order of play and tells me to get in the limo with him. That was something of a problem to me because I was due to read the news on the station a little bit later on and had only planned on being with Cloughie for a few minutes. I couldn't really say no, but it was a worry because I was required back in the studio for the news bulletins.

I thought it would be a quick run through the route, a bit of an insight into this and that, a few words with Brian and back to the office. I should be so lucky.

I tried to explain that getting in the limo was not such a good idea for me, but Cloughie was having none of it.

'Get in – you're coming,' he said.

I laughed and explained that I couldn't. He wasn't taking no for an answer. The driver set off.

The two of them are chatting in the front while I am sitting in the back pondering my immediate – and long term – future.

This was pre-mobile phone days

and there was no way of letting the office know I was in a bit of a fix. The fix I was in turned out to be that I went literally everywhere with him. We went to the spot where he was going to plant a tree, then on to visit the statue of Robin Hood, the only character in Nottingham bigger than Cloughie. Then we went into the council chambers where the actual ceremony was going to take place.

Then the fun and games really started because Cloughie had me acting out or standing in for the various people, such as the mayor, who would be there on the actual day.

'Just stand there son and be the mayor will you,' he said very matter-of-factly. This went on for absolutely ages and when he eventually finished he said 'Come on then, let's work' - his way of indicating he'd do the interview.

So, we did the interview and he was fantastic. It was a really lovely piece, though I was left seriously considering if it might be my last. I am now probably around three hours late and lord knows how many bulletins I'd missed by this stage.

'Look, I've got to get back,' I insisted.

'Drop the young man off at his radio station,' Cloughie said.

My car was still at the football ground, but that was the least of my problems. Getting back to the station was the No1 priority.

'I could be in real trouble for this,' I said, all of a fluster.

No sooner had we got there, than he got out of the car insisting that he would come in and explain everything to my boss!

He clocked eyes on my gaffer and explained that he had virtually kidnapped me.

'Sorry, but I borrowed this young man today and he's been extremely helpful to me.'

Of course, as always happens with Cloughie, my boss just melted. It was no bother. I'd gone from the sack to being top man in a matter of seconds. All was well and I even managed to get over to the ground and get my car back.

Next day, I covered the whole thing with an insight and an air of authority that the listeners certainly wouldn't have expected. It must have sounded like I'd done it before. Little did they know!

The funny thing about that day was I received an official booklet marking the occasion and I asked him if he would be kind enough to sign it for me. For all the many times I had been in his company I had never asked him to sign anything before.

The slightly different thing about that was he actually put on it 'To Darren. All our love Barbara and Brian Clough.' How nice was that? And how unusual. I still treasure it to this day.

❛ Daft name Brooklyn. I wonder which one of his parents chose that? ❜

When the manager became the first man to splash £1m on a player he was eager to protect his investment. Forest star GARY MILLS recalls how Trevor Francis was left in no doubt who was boss when it came to the issue of wearing shinpads.

24

PROTECTION RACKET

GARY MILLS

Cloughie always took the view that if you were good enough, you were old enough and I have to say that it's a philosophy which has filtered through to me over the years. I'm not a great believer in the academy system.

I made my debut at 14 in the Central League with Forest and in those days it was great because you got to play at grounds like Anfield on a Saturday afternoon.

And the thing with Cloughie was that no matter who you were or where you were in the pecking order as a player, the same rules applied.

It isn't actually complicated at all – he was fair, pure and simple. Whether you were a teenager on the first rung of the ladder or the first million pound footballer, the gaffer wasn't afraid to pull you down a peg or two.

I can recall about four games in, I went on a run and hit a shot from outside the box.

We came in at half-time and he absolutely went for me and screamed: 'If you ever shoot again like that when you can pass the ball, I'll chop your balls off.' That was just him. At 14, he treated me no differently to anyone else at the club.

For me, the classic involved Trevor Francis, famously the first ever million pound player. He signed for Forest on the Friday and the following day found himself playing for the youth team against Aston Villa on a field somewhere near Nottingham.

We had been playing about 15 minutes when Cloughie stopped the game, walked straight onto the pitch towards Trevor and made a big point of asking why he hadn't got any shinpads on.

'I don't wear them,' Trevor informed him.

'You do if you're playing for me,' Cloughie assured him.

So Trevor had to run off, scramble around for a pair of shinpads and after about five minutes he came back on. Welcome to Forest!

❛ I've lost count of the number of referees who said they just loved refereeing my teams ❜

Walk on water? Well, not quite, but when a distressed man was threatening to throw himself off a bridge into the River Trent there was only one man who could persuade him that maybe it wasn't such a fantastic idea.

25

SUICIDE BID

NOTTINGHAMSHIRE POLICE

Cloughie's legendary powers of persuasion were never put to better use than one day in September, 1980, when a young man was threatening to take his own life on Trent Bridge.

The 27-year-old was clearly in an extremely distressed state sitting on a parapet and steadfastly rebuffing any police attempts to lure him back to safety.

He was on the other side of some iron railings which made any attempt to make a quick and forceful snatch far too risky.

Two police officers had been called to the world famous landmark just across the way from Forest's City Ground following reports of a man in an agitated state threatening to jump into the Trent.

Clough happened to be driving past at the time when he noticed a crowd of people and stopped to investigate the fuss.

The Forest boss sprang into action, talking to the distressed man about football. No doubt, but for the gravity of the situation, Cloughie might have informed the man that only he had the powers to walk on the water and that for lesser mortals a headlong plunge was not to be recommended. Before too long, the man moved back from the edge and clambered to safety.

Police Constable Lee Summers reveals how grateful he and his colleague were for Clough's timely intervention.

'It was a nasty situation. We couldn't pull the chap away without spearing him on the railings. Cloughie took over and helped relax him.

'He talked about the crowds who were flocking to the Forest ground and asked the chap if he was a supporter.

'It certainly did the trick. The fellow calmed down enough for us to reach him. Only Cloughie could have distracted him like that.'

Clough ended up being presented with a 'Citizen of the Month' award.

❛ Ground rules apply just as much to millionaires as they do to someone who's got nowt ❜

Clashing with strict Bulgarian officialdom isn't usually recommended, but when it was threatening to delay Forest's flight home, Cloughie decided to put his foot down as national newspaper journalist RONALD ATKIN reveals.

26

PLANE & SIMPLE

RONALD ATKIN

Brian's powers of persuasion have never been in doubt but one incident in 1980 underlined most emphatically that he could get his own way against all the odds.

It was on the way back from a trip to Bulgaria that Brian took centre stage with one of his more unusual and audacious 'charm' offensives. It was so distinctly lacking in charm that it is a real wonder he didn't find himself locked up.

I was one of the journalists returning with the Forest party from a match against CSKA Sofia. This was 1980, a time when Bulgaria was a million miles from being a holiday destination.

It was late on the Wednesday night after Forest's first defence of the European Cup and they had lost 1-0.

As Forest's charter plane prepared to depart we were already three hours late because of obstructive officialdom and red tape.

Eventually, just as we waited for take-off, a bulky Bulgar boarded the aircraft and insisted everybody got off because they wanted to re-check passports and documents.

There was a bit of a fuss because there were 55 people on the plane and they had handed out 56 boarding passes. Clearly there was a concern someone might be trying to defect.

As it became clear the official would not be happy until the entire party had got off, Clough paused from his self-appointed task of pouring champagne for the Press and made his way towards him.

'Young man, we're tired and we want to go home.'

The man looked somewhat puzzled as Clough made it clear there was only one person getting off.

'We're knackered! We want to go home,' the Forest boss continued.

'Now get off MY plane!' he roared.

This could go one of two ways and we all looked on anxiously. Guess what? The man shuffled his papers, made his way meekly to the exit, and got off the plane.

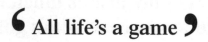

❝ All life's a game ❞

When RON ROBERTS' found himself stranded at the roadside in an horrendous storm there was a surprise tap on the car window. Now just who was that Good Samaritan standing there soaked to the skin? Surely it couldn't be . . .

27

DOWNPOUR

RON ROBERTS

The face was unmistakable even in the distorting gloom of a torrential downpour. It couldn't be. It was. The voice merely served to confirm it.

'Can I help you, young man?'

The rain was hammering down and dripping off the face of the man peering in through the driver's side window of my stricken car – Brian Clough.

As a lifelong Forest fan, Cloughie was a massive hero of mine and here he was offering me a lift or any kind of assistance even though it meant he was now absolutely soaked to the skin.

I was the landlord of a pub called the Craven Arms at the time and I'm only glad that my mother Mary was in the car at the time or else the regulars would have thought I'd had one too many recounting the tale. Mum was as gobsmacked as me when it happened.

How it happened was . . . my daughter Lorraine would have been about 12 at the time and we were driving to pick her up from school when we got caught in a really bad storm driving along the A52.

Suddenly the car came to a halt and I switched the hazard lights on. The traffic was struggling all around me, such was the ferocity of the rain. Then came the tap on the window. He was sodden. All he had on was a tee-shirt, shorts and trainers. I told him that I thought I would be okay shortly and thanked him for his offer of assistance.

With that he said 'Cheerio' got back in his Mercedes and made his way.

I just thought it was a really kind thing to do. He could have driven past without anyone knowing, but he chose to try and help – and got drenched into the bargain!

❝ The speeches, such as they were, had to be short, because I needed to be at Ayresome Park before two-o-clock to play against Leyton Orient ❞
– reflecting on his wedding day in 1959

Former Leeds and Forest star LEE CHAPMAN reveals that even though he was in his 20s, he didn't escape the manager's gaze when it came to basic hygiene. Surely he hadn't really been asked if he had washed his hands?

28

HANDS ON APPROACH

LEE CHAPMAN

As a 21-year-old with a wife, child and large mortgage, I found it very strange when walking out of the toilets to be asked, in all seriousness, if I had washed my hands!

Nevertheless, my brief 15 months under his guidance was the most eventful period of my career. I will be eternally grateful to him for enabling me to become a winner for the first time in my 11 years as a professional – two Wembley finals and two winners' medals. He may have been unorthodox but, boy, was he successful.

In business, I think the managers I played under have shaped my thinking. I have probably taken from the methodical approach of Howard Wilkinson and the flamboyance of Brian Clough most. I'd like to think I found a balance between the two whereby I plan but also have charisma and a desire to entertain.

The like of Brian Clough will never be seen again and it really is a case of thanks for the memories.

The day I departed for Leeds United turned out to be another bizarre and bewildering occasion. I was summoned into the office and sat down in the corner. To my amazement I found myself in the middle of contract negotiations with a young player who would gain full England honours.

'How much do you think you're worth son?'

'I don't know.'

'Do you like vegetables, son?' Cloughie asked the puzzled young star. He said he did.

'Which ones do you like?' was met with a stunned silence.

'Do you like cabbage?'

'It's all right,' came the rather stressed and confused reply.

'What about sprouts?'

'Yes. I like them.'

'Well, do yourself a favour and go to the greengrocer and buy yourself a bag of sprouts.'

I felt for that player. He would not be the first or last to go through that ordeal. But it was typically Cloughie, unpredictable to the last.

❛ I love retirement – I love living quietly for once ❜

29

BACON BUDDY

JOHN ROBERTSON

People have asked me over the years to sum the man up and it is so difficult to do without going on for hours. The man was a genius – I am in no doubt. It's all down to the little things he picked up on which made you think and kept you on your toes.

He used to call me a tramp and a wreck and was always making unflattering remarks about my appearance. But in a way, I loved it. If you pleased him and he let you know, you would suddenly feel ten feet tall. I think he liked me as a player and I loved the guy.

He was obsessed with my lifestyle. He would even phone me up sometimes to check what I was having for my tea.

'I hope that's not bacon sizzling in the pan I can hear!' he'd say.

My mother used to get quite upset about some of the things he said about me at times, but I can't speak highly enough of him. I looked forward to every single Saturday. I just loved playing for him.

I must admit that when our paths first crossed I wasn't looking after myself in the way that I should. Before he arrived I was on the transfer list and to be brutally honest I'd begun to feel the whole world was against me.

It was sink or swim time for me at that point and I needed a kick up the backside. Those two provided it.

I can still remember his first day so vividly. I was sat in the dressing room facing the doors when, bang, they suddenly swung open. What I really remember is the way he strode in.

He was so purposeful. He took his jacket off and in one movement flung it on a peg. I don't even know how he knew the peg was there. I remember thinking 'Jesus, he means business, this guy."

❛ I took my cheque from Leeds straight to the bank. If anyone was that shallow and stupid to sack me after 44 days, I didn't trust them ❜

What's in a name? Football's first £1m man TREVOR FRANCIS recalls how Cloughie went out of his way to put a supporter right after he was less than complimentary about his new signing. There's way's of doing things and this wasn't one of them.

30

NAME GAME

TREVOR FRANCIS

People ask me whether I found playing in the A-team demeaning and a lot was made of it at the time because it was seen as a clear example of Clough immediately putting me down and reminding everyone who was boss. After all, he had just made me the first one million pound player.

Everyone construed it as a message that however much I cost, he still had the power to stick me in the third team. I didn't take it like that and I'm convinced it wasn't meant as an insult.

The fact is it had been an extremely cold period when a lot of first team games were being called off. I'd been inactive anyway because of an injury so it was a good opportunity to get some match practice on an available pitch.

It wasn't quite two men and a dog but there were no more than 30 people there. My abiding memory is Clough giving me a lecture at half-time because I wasn't wearing shin pads. It wasn't a mandatory rule in those days and I didn't like wearing them. But he made it clear that if I wanted to last longer than one match I had to change my ways. So I had to find someone to lend me some pads for the second half.

Apart from that, there was one moment when I missed a shot and a fellow on the sideline shouted: 'You'll have to do better than that Francis!' Clough ran almost halfway around the pitch to confront him.

'His name's Trevor,' he insisted.

❝ The people who said winning the Anglo Scottish Cup with Forest meant nothing were crackers. It was something to us. It provided us with a cup and players who hadn't won anything, got a medal. They had tasted the champagne and they liked it ❞

*Peter Taylor's daughter WENDY DICKINSON recalls vividly
how a young Clough called in to see her dad at the family
home and says that whenever she does the evocative smell
of her mum's chips suddenly starts to fill the room.*

31

CHIPS A LA CARTE

WENDY DICKINSON

Whenever I think of Brian the distinctive, special aroma of my mum's chips come flooding back to me. The big thing I remember about him was how much he loved eating chips at our house.

When I look back at all the wonderful times Dad and Brian had together and the fantastic memories they created for so many people, it is such a shame that the row between them eventually overshadowed just how close their partnership was.

That's exactly what they were – a partnership. They met when they were in their 20s and stayed together for over 30 years. Yes, they fell out, but that happens in any kind of partnership – no matter how close.

People should never forget the fact that they were huge mates. If they had lived to be two old men, which sadly they didn't, I definitely think they would have made it up.

They were both taken too young and I'm sure there would have been a time when they would have made it up. I certainly think Brian wanted to do that and I'm sure dad did.

Knowing them, they would proba-

bly be shouting at us and telling us all where to get off!

The idea of the statue of the two of them together was just great and it is lovely to see them side by side again, which is where they belong, I think. They are always together in people's minds.

I was a young reporter on the Derby Telegraph when they had their major success. They won the Championship in 1972 when I was about 20, so I was old enough to appreciate just what was going on at that time.

I was only a little girl when the family were up at Middlesboro. I asked my mum when she first heard the name 'Brian Clough' and she said that she remembered it distinctly. She said dad had come home from the club one day and said 'I've seen this incredible young centre forward' but she wasn't that interested because she was making the tea.

She must have said 'Who is that then?' while she went about what she was doing and dad said: 'His name's Brian Clough.'

Mum said that was the first time she had heard the name. That would have been in the mid-50s. After that, of course, he started coming to the house and she saw more and more of him. Dad would come home from work and there would be a knock on the door and Brian would be standing there.

The funny thing is, she said he was a bit sheepish! Yes, young and innocent and rather sheepish . . . imagine! I think he kind of grew into himself.

She would say 'Come on in Brian,' and would get the chips on because, as I said, he loved her chips. She said the two of them just talked football all night – nearly every night.

That's basically how it all started and I suppose it was dad's belief in him that launched Brian. Everyone talks about my dad being the great star maker and talent scout, well Brian was his first discovery in a funny kind of way.

He spotted Brian first in a way. He was the one who thought Brian could really play when he was nowhere near the first team.

Dad had a great expression he would use to some effect. 'You're miles out!' he would say when he thought someone was way off the mark. I can see him saying it now.

Brian wasn't rated by the manager at the time and dad went up to him and said 'You're miles out! This lad should be in the first team.'

Of course, if you are a young player and you have someone shouting on your behalf and standing your corner saying how brilliant you are, you tend to gravitate together. He wasn't wrong was he?

That's how it all started and once Brian got in the team and showed what he could do, there was no stopping him. Like I said, mum insists Brian was very quiet at the outset. I can't imagine it, but that's the way it was.

The families were so close. It's not just dad and Brian – my mum and Barbara have been through an awful lot together too.

There's been an awful lot of water gone under the bridge, an awful lot of football . . . and a lot of chips!

' I'm always amazed when managers allow players to go away and think about a proposed transfer. Let them out of your sight and the chances are they'll go and sign for somebody else '

Former Notts County boss NEIL WARNOCK might only have been just across the river but says when Cloughie took a leisurely stroll past their training sessions, it became crystal clear that their two clubs were a million miles apart.

32

MY HERO

NEIL WARNOCK

I'm quite often asked who is my all-time footballing hero and it's not even close for me . . . the one and only Brian Clough. I was in charge at Notts County for a few years during his time at Forest. The two clubs are separated only by the River Trent and the joke was that Cloughie didn't need the bridge to get across.

Just being across the Trent from the great man at the same time was like winning the pools.

He took me out to lunch a couple of times and they were some of the most captivating afternoons of my life.

How could you not fail to be mesmerised by a man who achieved what he did in the game? He was fascinating to talk to and the knowledge that he could pass on was just immense. You can't help but learn from just being in the company and listening to people like Brian or Sir Alex.

I think the move to get mangers to pass coaching badges is a great thing, but it does beg the question of what would have happened to some of our greatest ever managers if those rules had been in force years ago. Cloughie, Shankly and Sir Alex don't have the required coaching badges.

I can remember as if it were yesterday, the look on Brian's face when he used to stroll past me at County training sessions.

County used to train on a ground that was the size of a postage stamp and Cloughie would walk past with his faithful golden retriever on his way to Forest's 16-acre bowling green!

So there we were the lot of us on an absolute mud heap kicking the s*** out of each other and he would stop and take a look. Then he would see me looking over because I had noticed him and he would just shake his head and move off on his way. Brilliant!

The managers I really respect are the ones who don't need a coaching manual and strings of badges. Give me the real man-managers like Clough, Sir Alex Ferguson and Martin O'Neill anytime. A few years ago there was a trend where chairmen were signing young ex-pros with famous names. It was all the rage. The whippersnappers were everywhere.

And it just didn't work. The wheel turned full circle and they went back to us old guys. But how did we get our experience? Because when we were younger, we were allowed to make mistakes and learn from them.

I don't know Martin O'Neill well, but I have huge respect for him. For sure, he was a famous ex-international who had won European Cups and titles but he did his managerial apprenticeship at Grantham, Shepshed and Wycombe.

He learned how to handle all the problems that would crop up later in his career. The first time I ever encountered him was at Wycombe, when I was boss at Huddersfield

I thought I was straight out of 'One Flew Over the Cuckoo's Nest' but he was 10 times worse, giving the ref an absolute coating in the tunnel.

I thought 'If he gets away with this, he must have friends in some really high places.'

But, come to think of it, hc is onc of Cloughie's old boys.

❝ I'd have loved to have played cricket. I love the game. I'd have loved to be opening bat. You don't need to rely on anyone, well not too many people – and that appeals to me ❞

*Former Nottingham Evening Post sports reporter NICK LUCY
was always up for an unusual story. Here he gives the
inside track on how Cloughie helped him with a cricket
bat for a man who had just had his arm torn off.*

33

HOWZAT!

NICK LUCY

I was working as a sports reporter with the Nottingham Evening Post when I embarked on one of the more unusual assignments in my career – getting a cricket bat for a one-armed man! And, you guessed, Cloughie was at the centre of it all.

By way of explanation, I knew Brian because I had been the back-up man for Duncan Hamilton, the paper's Nottingham Forest reporter. On the days when Duncan was on a day-off or not around, I would go over to the City Ground and try to get something for the local paper.

It is true, you just never knew what you would get when you were there. He could be absolutely brilliant or absolutely impossible. Some days he would be fantastic and another day, you were left wondering 'What did I do wrong?' Most of the time he was quite good with us because he recognised that the local evening newspaper served the needs of the club's supporters.

Back in 1983 there was a big story about a farm worker called Roy Tapping who chopped his arm off in a hay-bailer. The story made the head-lines everywhere because he had somehow managed to apply a tourniquet and then walk for two miles carrying his severed limb before managing to summon help.

Anyway, we got to find out that he was a big Yorkshire cricket fan and I had a brainwave. Nottinghamshire were playing Yorks at Worksop and so I came up with the idea of buying a bat and getting it signed by his favourite team. It was a good way of getting a local slant on a big story that was actually off our 'patch.'

I was covering the game that day and, purely by chance, as I was getting out of my car, Cloughie was getting out of his Mercedes just across the way. His big pal was Geoff Boycott and he had obviously taken the opportunity to pop up and see him.

We were walking through the car park when intrigue clearly got the better of him.

'What's the bat for son?'

I explained what it was for and he just sort of kindly took over things in a way that only he could.

'Hey, give it to me then . . .' and off he went.

Not only did he get the entire Yorkshire cricket team to sign the bat, but just to authenticate it, he got a photograph taken of Boycott sitting down signing it!

He just took over and did the whole thing for me, which I was extremely grateful for. Despite the fact that it was me who came up with the idea, I didn't know quite how successful my plan would be. Coming up with a good idea is fine, but carrying it through is not always so straightforward. There were some notoriously awkward buggers in that Yorkshire dressing room and we weren't sure how many would play ball. But with Boycott's mate Cloughie in charge of proceedings, it must have seemed like a doddle.

He was absolutely brilliant and delivered the bat back to me with everyone's best wishes. Mission accomplished! Well, not quite.

I went on my special mission to Stoke Mandeville Hospital to present the bat to the hero farmer only to find out that he had signed up with a national newspaper to tell his incredible story. I couldn't get to him! In the end our photographer had to settle for a snap of me handing the signed bat over to a group of nurses.

He did get the bat though and sent us a lovely letter thanking us for our kind gesture. It had all worked out in the end and I was indebted to Cloughie for the part he played in it.

' Why do people want to become directors? Because running a football club gets their photographs on the back pages of newspapers – nowt else would '

34

MYSTERY TOUR

TONY HUGHES

Obviously getting the chance to work for Brian Clough and drive his Nottingham Forest teams all around the country was something really special for me. I used to wake up on a morning and have to pinch myself pondering what a marvellous job I had.

But, as I'm sure you can imagine, there was never a dull moment with Cloughie around and on more than the odd occasion, unscheduled detours were known to happen. I recall one occasion particularly vividly when the boss took the team for an unusual visit during a trip to Middlesbrough.

We were on our way to Boro for this particular game and I had organised a police escort to take us to the match. But on the way the gaffer, completely out of the blue, told me to take a left, which was not on the route. As you did when Cloughie gave you an instruc-tion, I turned left and we ended up in this council estate.

He got me to stop the bus, the police arrived and there he was out on the pavement pointing to an upstairs window and telling everybody: 'I was born in that room!

I also remember a visit to Sunderland's old ground, Roker Park, when a large crowd of youngsters were hanging around after the match des-perately hoping to get the autographs of Cloughie and his players.

He got me to open the front door and the back door of the bus and one by one the kids streamed through get-ting his and all the players' autographs. It was like the Pied Piper. We must have been there for an hour and a half and one or two of the players weren't very happy about it.

But the kids were thrilled to bits. That was Brian all over.

❛ If we're not careful, Paul Gascoigne is going to end up like Matt Monro – dead before we appreciate his talent ❜

*Daily Express sports writer JOHN WRAGG travelled all over the
world covering Forest and so shouldn't have been that
surprised when Cloughie's request for some sandwiches
proved to be anything but a simple exercise.*

35

BROWNED OFF

JOHN WRAGG

There was one thing most newspapermen would be in agreement over – Brian Clough was always good value. When he delivered that 'Come on then, let's work' directive, you just knew you weren't going to leave empty-handed.

When Brian spoke it was pure gold. But whether he was working or not, he had such an aura about him that people just tended to go quiet and listen. In my line of work, getting up close and personal with the great man was invariably business, but occasionally it was just pleasure or a bit of a mix. I played squash with him on many occasions so probably knew him better than most but there were a few Midlands-based journalists that he 'looked after' when the mood suited him. Invariably when we were away on foreign trips covering Forest in Europe, Cloughie looked after us. He was acutely aware that we needed to justify the trip by getting plenty of copy and he was usually brilliant at seeing that we got what we needed to keep our sports desks happy back in London.

One particular memory which always makes me smile was when a group of the travelling journalists had a lunchtime appointment to see Cloughie on one of many foreign trips. There were so many in those days that, to my shame, I can't remember the exact location. What I do recall is that it was a very nice hotel set in beautiful ground and the sun was shining. The hotel had terraced gardens sitting atop massive slopes down to a river and the main part of the hotel. Cloughie had said to come around and he'd do his interviews there. When we arrived he was sitting in the sunshine in his shorts and all the players were dotted around on sun loungers around the place.

'Hey, come on shithouses. Come and sit down!' was his way of greeting us.

We started talking about this, that and the other when he asked: 'Have you eaten boys?'

'No, we've come straight here,' came the reply.

'Hey, you've got to eat, you know. Would you like a nice sandwich?' Nods of approval all round from the Press pack. Cloughie summoned Ronnie Fenton his trusty assistant, who didn't realise at this point that he was about to be asked to test his skills as a waiter.

'Ronnie – take the orders down from these lads and then go and ask the shithouse players if they would like anything.'

So, poor Ronnie started to take down the orders. 'That's one cheese, one cheese and ham, two ham salad . .' etc . . . etc.

'These young men are working. They've got to eat,' Clough assured him. It took Ron ages to take all the orders, make sure he'd got exactly what everyone had asked for and conveyed it to a rather startled waiter, who then made the long trek down to the kitchens to pass on the hefty order.

We interviewed Brian and must have been happy with what we had got from him when around three-quarters of an hour later, a crocodile of waiters appeared trundling up a huge amount of steps. Above their shoulders on huge silver salvers they were carrying the most fantastic array of sandwiches and clearly knew who the head honcho was as they brought them up to near where Cloughie was holding court. Imagine the looks on their faces when he roared mischievously:

'Hey, hang on a minute you lot . . . I said brown bread!'

The waiters froze temporarily, looking slightly dumbstruck, when Cloughie's mischievous giggles assured them everything was just fine.

' Sinatra said the written word comes first and the music comes later. In football the one who picks the player comes first and all the bullshit comes later '

From picking up Billy Bremner to picking up cups, there was no one better than the legendary DAVE MACKAY. The former Tottenham star was used to getting his hands on trophies and few realised he wasn't about to stop just yet.

36

BEST IS YET TO COME

DAVE MACKAY

Dave Mackay was already a legend at Hearts and Spurs before Cloughie audaciously persuaded him to see out the twilight of his playing career at the Baseball Ground.

In typical Mackay fashion he became a legend there too. George Best said the gritty Scot with the silky skills was the best player he'd ever played against. Clough described him as the greatest player in Tottenham's history. The signing of Mackay was arguably Clough's greatest ever capture. A lion on the field and off it, Clough chanced his arm that he could get him and pulled off an absolute coup.

You can't help wondering if Clough came back from his successful mission to tempt Mackay by humming one of his favourite Sinatra tunes 'The Best is Yet to Come.'

'Out of the tree of life I just picked me a plum. ~You came along and everything started to hum. Ain't it a real good bet the best is yet to come!'

Dave Mackay, leader of men, was on his way to Derby and things would never quite be the same again. Even the great Sir Alex Ferguson has the famous picture of Mackay and Billy Bremner hanging on the wall of his office. For those unfamiliar with it, and there can't be many, the picture shows Mackay hoisting the fellow Scot and Leeds captain off the ground with an expression on his face which is raw anger personified. Mackay reveals that he is not a fan of one of football's most iconic shots and then why he should have perhaps asked Cloughie for a box of matches!

* * *

I get asked to autograph that picture all the time. But I don't like it because it portrays me as a bully. He's smaller than me and I'm picking him up. I'm not a bully and I don't like bullies. He was a brilliant player but a dirty little bastard. He kicked me on the leg I'd just come back from breaking twice. If he'd kicked the other one, I could have accepted that. But he kicked the broken one and that really annoyed me. I could have killed him that day. I'm a good pal of Alex and he does have that picture hanging in his office.

* * *

I must be one of the few people to render Brian Clough speechless. When I told him that I thought I would like to join him at Derby, you could have heard a pin drop for a good five seconds.

I had never come across anyone quite like him. He was a one-off. His enthusiasm was infectious and his confidence quite shocking. He looked a bit more like a trainee bank manager than a football manager.

Because of the broken legs, I wasn't the same player. Brian fancied me as a captain and as a sweeper which did appeal to me. A role like that would open up the prospect of playing for a few more years.

I was amazed when he asked me because I was going to Hearts. After the '67 FA Cup final I went to Bill Nicholson and told him I didn't think I could do the job anymore. Hearts were going to make me player manager.

That weekend when I was up in Edinburgh, Brian phoned my wife Isobel and asked for a contact number for me but he wouldn't say who he was so she didn't tell him.

When I got back thinking we were going back up to Scotland, there at Tottenham waiting on the Monday was Brian. By lunchtime I had signed for him.

Working under him was brilliant – he picked on everyone else but me. If it was a bad game on a Saturday, there would be a meeting on the Monday. But I always had Mondays off anyway!

The other players never gave me problems. I think I was quite popular with the guys. Roy McFarland, Colin Todd, John McGovern were all brilliant players – and Archie Gemmill later too.

One thing I do remember is after I took over as manager from Brian. He had gone to Leeds and burned Don Revie's desk. He came to see me in my office to sign John McGovern and John O'Hare and said:

'Why haven't you burnt my desk?'

❛Signing Shilton was like buying a great painting, like a Constable or a Turner. You just know in a year or two's time it is going to be worth twice what it cost you ❜

When referee JOHN WORTHINGTON sent-off two Forest players, he didn't know what sort of response to expect when the manager came in to see him afterwards. But, as he recalls, you could always expect the unexpected with Cloughie.

37

REFFIN' HELL

JOHN WORTHINGTON

Back in the early nineties I was reffing Port Vale v Forest in the Midland Intermediate League at Keele University. During the first half, one of my linesmen signalled for a foul against a Forest forward, whereupon the player bellowed 'f*** off 'in his face.

Given that there were no more than a couple of hundred people at the game, it goes without saying that virtually everything that was said on the pitch could be heard by spectators. After I sent him off, another of their players said the same thing to me after I gave a free kick against him. I simply had no choice but to administer exactly the same punishment.

Forest lost the game and when we were back in our room there was a knock on the door and in walked Archie Gemmill, closely followed by Cloughie who stood there but didn't utter a word.

As you would, I immediately thought 'here we go' expecting a load of protests. But the great man's response absolutely staggered me. He shook me by the hand and said if I hadn't sent his two players off he was going to take them off anyway and play the rest of the game with nine men rather than make any substitutions!

He was quite clearly incensed by their behaviour and was quite happy to let me know that he wouldn't tolerate it.

We heard Archie go next door and ordered them all onto the bus without showering and told them that they would not be stopping for their usual post match fish and chips on the way home.

As if that wasn't punishment enough, he finished off by saying that they were all to report to the City Ground at 8am the next day which was a Sunday where Cloughie would be speaking to them. There wasn't a peep out of them.

A couple of months later and I had Forest again and this time they were under the charge of John Perkins. I asked John what had happened following the match I'd been in charge of. He said Cloughie walked in and suspended the two players from the club for 28 days and upon their return they were to turn up with their parents whereupon he would tell them whether or not they were going to be sacked.

I won't mention the names of the players but suffice to say they were kept on - one of whom went on to be a full Scottish International and the other represented England at U-21 level. After all the examples I witness of tolerance and justification of abusive behaviour, I can't help thinking this was a marvellous example of the discipline he instilled in his players.

It makes the actions of some of today's so called superstars all the more reprehensible and one thing is for sure – referees everywhere would have a far easier and more enjoyable job if Clough's principles still prevailed.

Back in 1993, when Cloughie announced his retirement from the game prior to Forest's last home game against Sheffield United following relegation from the Premier League, things were understandably very emotional in and around the City Ground. However, there was one final involvement with the club - the Midland Youth Cup Final at Forest's ground the following Wednesday night. To add spice to the occasion it was against Derby County and yours truly refereed it.

There was one slight problem. I was away on a break in Keswick that necessitated a 180 mile journey back home before setting off on a 60 mile journey to Nottingham on the day of the game.

When I arrived, I asked Forest's secretary how many they were expecting and he said at least 15,000. When I led my three assistants out, the sight was just amazing. The ground was full on all four sides (the attendance was 24,687) all wishing to bid farewell to the great man. I must admit with all that driving I was absolutely knackered but the adrenalin was coursing through my veins and despite the game going into extra-time, I felt like I could have gone on until midnight. I found raw emotion to be a wonderful drug. I had never experienced anything like it – and probably never will.

Forest won and after the presentations to both sets of players and the officials, we were making our way up the tunnel where Cloughie was conducting a live interview on Radio Nottingham. He immediately stopped and shook me warmly by the hand.

'Young man, you had a great game,' he said generously, before resuming his interview. A few minutes later there was a knock on the door and in he marched in wearing that famous green jumper and proceeded to hold all four of us in awe for about an hour about his life in the game.

Everyone was really choked. He recalled his times playing for Middlesborough and Sunderland and gave a graphic account of the injury that finished him as a player.

The sight of Cloughie crying started us all off. There were tears from all of us when he said how sad he was to be bowing out but he had enjoyed every minute of it. You couldn't help but feel you were witnessing a little piece of history. He had us spellbound with his stories and fascinating recollections. You didn't need to see his tears to know that he was leaving a big part of him in that ground where he had created so many magical memories. A little piece of footballing history was soon to be fading into the background. Cloughie had straddled several decades in the game and made an impression on so many lives.

Then there was a polite knock on the door and this time it was Nigel who had come to take him home. Brian got up and kissed us all warmly on the cheek before departing. A great man indeed and a moment I will cherish forever.

‘ Once the hurt of being out of work had gone, I wanted to kiss the Leeds board, not strangle them. I was the luckiest man alive, because I had won the pools without filling in the coupon. I was the richest bloke in the dole queue. I could have drunk champagne, not Tizer and eaten caviar rather than fish and chips. It was all thanks to Leeds ’

Forest star GARY MILLS was just 18 when he starred in the European Cup final but he reveals how he had his bottle tested four years earlier when Cloughie put him in a very awkward situation with one of his star players.

38

GETTING SHIRTY

GARY MILLS

I was only 14 when I signed for Cloughie at Nottingham Forest, but although I might only have been a boy, it was an instant transition into a man's world.

In my hours at home and school I was just a normal teenager, but when I reported for 'work' at Forest, I was treated no differently from the others.

The day I signed there was a game later that evening and the boss took me into the dressing room. The boss stood me smack in front of Terry Curran, who was a bit of a star player at the club at the time.

Cloughie said: 'Terry, do you know who this is?'

Terry, understandably, looked a little surprised gave me the once over and said 'no.' Big surprise!

'This is the lad who is going to take your shirt off you in a couple of years,' Cloughie warned him. I bet he was really worried.

After the game, the boss took me into the dressing room again and addressed Terry again.

'Hey, you did okay tonight' he said before turning to ask me a question.

'Are you better than him son?'

I shrugged my shoulders. It was one of those awkward situations where showing a lack of confidence might be seen as some form of weakness.

'Yeah, I think so,' I replied.

Cloughie laughed out loud, pointed at Terry and said: 'See, there you go Terry. I told you he'll take your place.'

❝ On occasions Elton John has been known to dress like a Christmas tree. But he doesn't only sing better than the other 91 chairmen, he also talks a lot more sense than 95 per cent of them ❞

City Ground legend GARRY BIRTLES starred in so many of Nottingham Forest's big European nights it's hard to remember everything, but he admits he's still puzzled by exactly why Liverpool godfather Bill Shankly was on their team bus.

39

SHANKS' PONY

GARRY BIRTLES

I always thought the gaffer was inde-structible and when I heard that he had died I was in bits. Later it dawned on me that I would never now know the answer to something that has puzzled me for years – what was the great Bill Shankly doing on the Forest team bus that night we humbled Liverpool in Europe?

One of the stand-out things I remember about one of the great European nights in British football is that the legendary former Liverpool boss hitched a lift from our team hotel to Anfield for the second leg of that first round match.

Don't ask me how that came about. It didn't seem normal but not much ever did under Brian Clough. I'm guessing Shankly must have come to our hotel and we took him to the game. I never asked why. You just didn't!

And what was about to happen was certainly not normal. Liverpool, the defending champions, were set to crash out as the next two European Cups embarked on an unbelievable journey to Nottingham.

By the time of Shanks' unexplained appearance on the Forest team coach, the damage had been done because we were 2-0 up from the first leg.

Drawing Liverpool in the first round just hadn't seemed right. Partly because it wasn't much of a trip and partly because they were such a fantastic team and we thought we were bound to lose. We had never played in the European Cup before and it looked like we might be going out without even leaving the country.

Deep down we were a bit scared but the gaffer told us we didn't need to worry about the opposition. He said we were better than them and we had nothing to be afraid of as long as we played our own game. He always said things like that – he wasn't one for filling your heads with tactics or warning you what opponents might do. He'd just say, go out and play.

What was about to happen was little short of incredible. After I scored the first at the City Ground, Phil Thompson assured me that a single goal wouldn't be enough to take to Anfield. So, when Colin Barrett got us a second, cocky young thing that I was, I went up to Thommo and said 'Will two be enough then?' He was speechless. I shouldn't have done that to a respected England international but I was just high on what was happening. There was still the second leg . . .

Masterstrokes were the stock in trade of Cloughie. He was a psychologist of the highest order and never missed the opportunity to drop an ace on the table if he felt there was an opportunity.

He sent us out as a team to walk in front of the Kop an hour before kick off in our blue blazers and grey flannels. He just told us to go out there and stroll in the goalmouth if front of a seething mass of Liverpool fans.

A vast array of stuff was thrown our way and I remember dodging apples, oranges and all manner of food. But for Brian Clough it was simple. He sent us out there to make it clear we respected them and that we knew all about their fabled powers, but we did not give a shit. The sight of us strolling around laughing and joking just riled them all the more.

We held them to a 0-0 draw, went on to win the trophy and retain it. Unbelievable isn't it? It's like Barnsley doing it. Every time I watch Liverpool now, I look for the flags on the Kop, because there's a two-year gap in the dates. They go from '77 and '78 to '81 and I always think: that's us that is. That gap – we did it!

❛ They apply themselves off the field with their big houses, fast cars, agents and fat wage packets – but some seem to have forgotten that they can only do all that because of football ❜

When Cloughie got the sack at Leeds he hadn't got too much to celebrate but as Elland Road legend NORMAN HUNTER reveals he still took time to give him a champagne moment before walking out of the door for the last time.

40

BUBBLY EXIT

NORMAN HUNTER

I find myself strangely protective towards the memory of Brian Clough despite the fact that it took him until the 44th day of his reign at Leeds to say anything nice about me. Not bad considering he was famously only in charge for . . . 44 days!

I didn't have any relationship with Clough whatsoever. But, oddly, on the famous day he was sacked, he walked into a meeting of my testimonial committee.

He was carrying a bottle of champagne and I think he'd had a few. 'Raise all the money you can for this man because he deserves it,' he told them.

Later I discovered that he had tried to sign me for Nottingham Forest, so he can't have thought I was all bad. But, he genuinely never said anything nice to me in all his time at the club.

For most of his days at Leeds he was trying to buy Colin Todd to replace me!

Even though Clough turned out to be a disastrous appointment at Elland Road, only a fool would fail to acknowledge his greatness as a manager.

What happened at Leeds was one heck of a tale. Don Revie, The gaffer was leaving to take over England and had recommended Johnny Giles as his successor. Promote from within, the Liverpool way, seemed like a solid idea. Maybe the club wanted to mark a change of direction but we were all very surprised at the Clough appointment.

It was no secret he had a problem with us and the way we played. Every time we came up against him he would be jumping up and down shouting from the touchline. There was hostility right from the start because we knew he never liked Leeds or what we stood for.

He had been appointed at the start of the week, but Monday, Tuesday, Wednesday passed and we kept asking 'When's he coming? What's going on?' Then when he finally turns up it is to tell us to throw our caps and medals in the bin along with the infamous comment about Eddie Gray, how if he was a racehorse he'd have been shot. A bit harsh.

I'm not sure he was ever going to have much of a chance after that. The players didn't down tools on him because we were professionals. But the atmosphere was awful and in those circumstances, you are never going to play your best.

The Boss does not get the credit he deserves for creating the best side in Europe. He also created a family atmosphere which didn't last under Clough.

I remember getting on the team bus with our keeper Dave Harvey and on the news they were saying that Leeds were trying to sign Todd and Peter Shilton. That was the first we'd heard about it and was the sort of thing that wouldn't have happened under Don Revie.

Watching the film The Damned United brought back a few memories and the basic truth is in there. Clough didn't give himself a chance at Leeds, which was a shame. If he had come in softly, softly, making changes as he went along, perhaps it could have worked . . .

> 6 It never ceases to amaze me that so many people have so much difficulty in assembling a good football team. How can they make such a simple job so complex? 9

Former Arsenal star BOB WILSON once put his head on the block by predicting Forest's bubble would burst. Clough's men went on to win the league and the manager decided there was only one way to make him eat his words.

41

BURSTING BUBBLES

BOB WILSON

As a manager, his success almost defies belief. Cloughie rightly takes his place as one of the best of all time. My contact with him was memorable. Through our TV work, I spent many hours in his company and most of them could be described as eventful to say the least.

Always, his initial look towards me was one of scorn. Basically he thought I was a bit soft, an educated grammar school boy who played for a 'posh' club in what essentially was a working man's game. Brian just didn't do 'posh.'

I suppose in his mind I wasn't the prototype footballer in his mind because I went to university on the prompting of my dad who urged me to get a 'proper job' rather than rely on such a precarious business trying to carve out a career in professional football.

I treasure a photo in which Brian is thrusting the league championship trophy in my face. Early in that brilliant campaign for Forest, I had reported for Grandstand on their away win at QPR. Boldly I declared that 'Nottingham Forest were lucky to get all the points and although they are the new favourites to win the title, I think their bubble will burst.'

Brian was the master at courting publicity and made sure this was plastered all over the papers.

Brian's response to my prediction made banner headlines in the local Nottingham evening paper. He castigated me – even suggesting I should lose my job.

I wasn't fired by the BBC, but at the end of the season I was invited to interview him at the City Ground just so long as the local paper could also take the gloating photo with the championship trophy being thrust in my face accompanied by the words: 'Now, young man, what was it you said about our bubble bursting?'

❝ Football only becomes a grey game when there are grey people in charge ❞

When DAVE BREWSTER walked into a newsagents with his son to get a paper he couldn't have realised just what was in store. Cloughie was serving behind the counter and the young boy was to get a surprise he couldn't have bargained for.

42

UP FOR THE CUP

DAVE BREWSTER

Having watched Forest for years and having regularly attended reserve matches as well, I shouldn't really have been surprised at anything Cloughie would do. But seeing my young son holding the League Cup aloft was something quite extraordinary . . . and we had only popped in for a paper!

Like I said, I've seen some of the great man's eccentricities first hand, so I knew you could never second-guess what he might do next.

I recall being at a reserve game on one occasion when a small group of lads started banging their seats up near the back of the stand. The next thing you know, guess who is right behind them? Yep.

'You little lot are destroying my ground!' Cloughie barked.

He went absolutely berserk. The youths didn't know where to put themselves and immediately shrank back in their seats. There wasn't another word out of them. The look on their faces was a picture – probably about the same as mine in that little newsagents shop in Bramcote back in 1978. I was passing the shop and had my young son Gary with me. Forest had just won the League Cup, beating Liverpool 1-0 in a replay held at Old Trafford.

When we walked into the shop that Sunday morning, little could we have known the surprise in store for us. There was Cloughie behind the counter sorting out newspapers!

Suddenly he produced the League Cup trophy and summoned my lad over towards him. Gary was just gobsmacked.

'Here you are young man. Do me a favour will you? Pop this in the window - right where everyone can see it!"

6 People wonder what kind of an England manager I would have turned out to be. There's only one answer – a bloody good one 9

England's World Cup winning skipper BOBBY MOORE hadn't banked on the persuasive powers of Cloughie when the Derby boss came calling. He wanted to sign the West Ham star and wasn't prepared to take no for an answer.

43

MOORE OR LESS

BOBBY MOORE

Even by Clough's outrageous standards, his ambitious attempt to lure World Cup winning skipper Bobby Moore and Trevor Brooking to Derby is right up there with the very best. In terms of where it ranks for sheer audacity, few of Clough's moves for players would even come close. The fact that Derby chairman Sam Longson knew nothing of a staggering £400,000 bid to try and prise the two away from their beloved West Ham, merely adds to the tale.

This was the start of the 1973-74 season and you would have thought anyone hoping to raise a cheque for such a staggering amount would have sounded out the man whose signature was going to be on it. Not Clough. He managed to get hold of Moore's home phone number and used every ounce of his persuasive powers to fix up a secret meeting with the player at the luxurious Churchill Hotel in London.

Peter Taylor had played a key part in setting things up and was as shocked as Clough when Moore chose to divulge details of the hush-hush liaison in his autobiography, *Bobby Moore,*

Everest Books, 1976.

Clough teased Moore by saying: 'I hear you're interested in winning a league championship medal.'

'Well, who wouldn't be?' came Moore's reply.

Clough: 'Would you play for Derby County?'

'Why not?'

'That'll do for me.'

The two of them went off for lunch in the hotel's restaurant only to be turned back by the manager because – can you imagine this? - Moore was dressed in a casual sweater and shirt.

A furious Clough vented his wrath and made it clear that his team would never stay at the hotel again if 'MY' player was treated so shabbily.

Moore protested that he wasn't a Derby player yet, but it was a request that fell on deaf ears.

Clough insisted he was going to ring Ron Greenwood up that very minute but in his excitement decided to go one better than a mere phone call. He felt the best way to move on any potential transfer was to actually pop in and see the West Ham boss personally. And verification of that encounter was confirmed by Greenwood, *Yours Sincerely, Collins Willow, 1984.*

Greenwood said Clough walked into my office with one of his directors and said he wanted a chat.

'I want to sign Bobby Moore and Trevor Brooking,' said Clough.

'You can't be serious,' Greenwood replied.

'Every man's got his price,' he insisted.

The West Ham boss told him there was no point continuing the conversation because neither was for sale.

'Well, if I can't have Moore, can I have Brooking? And if I can't have Brooking, can I have Moore? Clough continued.

Greenwood couldn't make Clough understand that he wasn't interested in even talking about a deal but promised to pass the offer on to the West Ham board.

An exasperated Greenwood revealed that he felt he might as well have been talking to himself.

'Clough carried on talking about money as if he hadn't heard me. The figures were rising by the minute,' he gasped.

❛ Bill Shankly talked more sense about football than the rest of the Football League put together. Mind you, I'm excluding myself from that assessment ❜

Former Forest and England international VIV ANDERSON recalls how his manager took the sting out of racial abuse and came up with a typically off-beat solution to helping the full-back deal with a potentially tricky situation.

44

NOTHING FOR A PEAR

VIV ANDERSON

Only Cloughie could come up with the answer when I found myself having to deal with racist abuse as an inexperienced 19-year-old.

I was substitute for a game at Carlisle and the gaffer had told me to go and warm-up. Bear in mind this was the mid-70s and black footballers were still something of a rarity.

As I ran up the touchline, they were giving me dog's abuse and hurling fruit in my direction – bananas, apples, pears, the lot.

I decided it might be wiser to get myself back up the touchline and re-take my place alongside the boss in the dugout.

'I thought I'd told you to warm up,' he said, looking at me quizzically.

'I have done boss, but they are throwing fruit at me.'

'Well get your f****** arse back out there then and fetch me two pears and a banana!'

There's nothing funny about racism, but I still smile when I consider Cloughie's response. It was his way of having fun with what was a racist act. But what he was saying was that there was no point me sitting next to him cowering, that would mean the idiots had won.

He pulled me over afterwards and said to me: 'If you let people like that dictate to you, I'm going to pick somebody else because you are going to be worrying about what fans are going to say rather than concentrate on playing football.'

I was just 19 and finding my feet. But after that I made sure there was nothing, whatever it was that people shouted, that would have a bearing on what I did.'

Not that Anderson was exempt from Cloughie's withering humour when it suited him. He had long since become England's first black footballer when on March 7, 1981 he had an absolute shocker in a game widely rated at the time as a classic. The Observer headline summed it up succinctly: 'MATCH OF THE SEASON.'

It was an FA Cup quarter-final match at the City Ground between European champions Forest and the treble-chasing league leaders Ipswich. It unfolded like something from the pen of a scriptwriter – except poor Anderson hadn't been holding the pen.

Ipswich went 2-0 up, Forest roared back to take a 3-2 lead before the visitors grabbed a late equaliser. Thrilling enough, but within that 90 minutes, fate had conspired to give Anderson a shocker. His dreadful backpass handed Paul Mariner the opening goal. Minutes later he conceded a free kick and then headed it past his own keeper Peter Shilton and just when it seemed things couldn't get worse . . . they did. Anderson dislocated his shoulder just before half-time and was taken off.

As if that didn't give the enthralled Press lads enough to write about, Cloughie was at his acidic best afterwards.

'Castration would have been a kindness after that 45 minutes,' was the gaffer's blunt appraisal of his fullback's non-appearance for the second half.

When pressed on if Anderson would now be unfit for the replay three days later, Clough said with a deadpan expression: 'All being well, yes!'

‘ You have to convince players that you are the greatest thing they have ever come into contact with. If you say Father Christmas exists, they have to believe it ’

Former Manchester City chairman PETER SWALES was on the panel of FA representatives that interviewed Clough for the England job in 1977 and gives a candid and illuminating account of just what went on behind closed doors.

45

ENGLAND SNUB

PETER SWALES

December 5, 1977 – the date that might well have changed the face of English football forever. On a crisp, sunny morning, Brian Howard Clough swept into Lancaster Gate on a tide of public backing for the blue riband job in English football. That he was the people's choice to become England manager was beyond any doubt whatsoever. But the cobwebs at the FA weren't ready to be blown away that easily. Within the confines of the corridors of the soccer establishment there was more than a distinct reluctance to even consider such an outspoken braggart as Clough. The suspicion and distrust went far further than that. But for one man – Sir Matt Busby – Clough wouldn't have even been granted an interview.

The legendary former Manchester United boss intervened when it became clear that Clough was to be dismissed so readily that he wouldn't even be granted an audience. The influential Sir Matt could see the sense in at least being seen to be interviewing the man held in such high regard by the public at large.

This was coming-up-to-Christmas 1977 – Mull of Kintyre topped the charts with the Brighouse and Rastrick Brass Band at No 2 with Floral Dance. This was what remained of Jubilee Year – and if the Establishment wasn't ready for the Sex Pistols, football's hierarchy were equally less enamoured with inviting this soccer punk into its cosy set-up. FA chairman Sir Harold Thompson shuddered at the very mention of Clough's name. With that background in mind, the most intimate and revealing version of what happened that day comes from the late Peter Swales, interviewed by Tony Francis for his book *'Clough – a biography, Stanley Paul 1977.'* Tony, who the author got to know pretty well after hours spent together on the car park outside Clough's office, put in meticulous research for his book. Having gone down the same route myself, I have to say that his account by Swales is far and away the best and most revealing I've seen on one of the defining days of Clough's career. To this day, well over 30 years later, when his name crops up in conversation you will often get the: 'He should have been the manager of England' response. 'The greatest manager England never had' has almost become a sub-title to his life story. For that reason alone, it would be wrong to pass up on an eye-witness account of what happened that morning. Particularly as it reveals a fascinating insight into how Clough's engaging charm wrong-footed his fiercest opponents and came close to winning them over.

Swales, who died in 1994, revealed: "We were ninety per cent against him before he walked in. It would have been a miracle if he had got it.

"Sir Harold was paranoid about Clough. He didn't want to grant him an interview in the first place and promised to 'sort him out' once he got him into the interview room."

Fat chance. Clough came in on the blind side and totally transfixed the lot of 'em.

'Good morning, gentlemen,' he began. 'It's a bit early for this, isn't it?' Before anyone could reply. Clough addressed each of them in turn: 'Good morning, Sir Harold, nice to see you looking so well; good morning, Sir Matt . . .' and so on.

Swales continues: "He was magnificent. I'd been used to seeing him wearing shorts and carrying a squash racket, but he was dressed in a very smart suit and behaved impeccably. He gave by far the best interview of all the candidates – full of common sense and above all, patriotic. He came as near as dammit to winning us all round and getting the job. If Ron Greenwood hadn't been around, he'd have clinched it."

But the establishment went for the safest bet and appointed Greenwood, passing up the chance to perhaps change the course of English football.

• *From Clough: A Biography by Tony Francis, Published by Stanley Paul. Reprinted by permission of the Random House Group Ltd.*

❛ Taylor began telling the board that Derby team was so good that even chairman Sam Longson could manage it. And Longson began to believe it ❜

When former Luton and Tottenham boss DAVID PLEAT popped in to see his old pal Cloughie at the half-time interval he ended up not seeing the rest of the match. The Forest boss was ready to hand out a private tutorial which has lived with him to this day.

46

A GAME OF ONE HALF!

DAVID PLEAT

When I was a very young manager at Luton I went up to watch our reserves play at Forest. At half-time, Brian motioned for me to join him in his office and I followed him in.

In those days, the half-time interval was just 10 minutes and so I had time for a nice cup of tea and was then just about ready to go back out and watch the game.

When the 10 minutes was up, the referee sounded the bell which could be clearly heard in the dressing rooms, boardroom and offices and I glanced at Brian to indicate that it was time I was making my way back.

'Where are you going?' he enquired, seemingly mystified that I might just want to leave his company and watch the second half of the game.

'I'm just going to . . .'

'Sit down. You will learn more listening to me for 45 minutes than watching that crap.'

Well, like I said, I was very young and Brian was such a forceful personality that when he made observations like that, it could have the effect of knocking you back on your heels a bit. I wondered what I should do.

Brian said that his journalist friend Vince Wilson was on his way and they would be doing their newspaper column for the Sunday Mirror. Well, I just sat there. And, as you would expect, it was a fascinating 45 minutes. Brian could talk about anything. He was amazing in that respect. It could be politics, the Middle East, the environment, you name it – he had a view on it.

I drove back to Luton and I remember thinking to myself 'Bugger me, I came all that way and only saw 45 minutes of the match.'

Mind you, I learnt something many years ago that Brian himself was a great advocate of – you don't need to watch players too long in a game waiting for them to show you something. If you haven't seen what you were looking for in 45 minutes or an hour, chances are you won't.

Brian was quite an astonishing person whether he was playing to an audience or just being part of one. My wife and I went to see Tony Bennett at The Barbican Theatre in London and after the show the guy who fixed up the tickets for us asked if we would like to go backstage to meet him.

Well, as you can imagine, we jumped at the chance. It's not every day you can get up close to see a legendary singer like the great Tony Bennett.

We were taken down to the parts of the theatre mere mortals never see and as we were ushered in to see the singer, we bumped into Brian and his wife Barbara. There he was chatting away to Tony Bennett as if he had known him years. It was just the way he was. I couldn't believe it. Upstaged again.

❝ If Leeds had stayed loyal and shown a bit of courage, I would have given them the one thing Don Revie didn't get his hands on – the European Cup ❞

When tough nut Forest defender KENNY BURNS joined the club he came with a wildman image. But the European Cup hero explains how Cloughie took him straight out of his comfort zone by dragging him off to a sweet pea show.

47

TAKING THE PEA?

KENNY BURNS

The great Brian Clough made sure my introduction to life at Nottingham Forest was one I would never forget – he dragged me off to a sweet pea exhibition!

I'm serious . . . there was me, a rough and ready kid from Glasgow, walking around a garden centre with my girlfriend, admiring the flowers.

It's hard to believe now, but like so many things with Cloughie, it is a memory I will take with me to the grave.

To be perfectly honest, I thought peas were things you had with sausages and chips. The floral variety was a new one on me.

Some people seem to think he was a bully and a dictator and yes, he could be at times, but when you are dealing with footballers it is like dealing with kids and so often that's the only way to really make them get the message.

Players will take liberties if they are allowed to but that didn't happen with the gaffer. Many people thought that the likes of me and him would be oil and water, but nothing could be farther from the truth.

I came with a troublesome reputa-tion, but I had a great rapport with him. He turned out to be the best manager I ever worked with. He was a dream.

I never had a dad and he became like a father figure to me. He made me a better player – but he made me a bet-ter man as well. While there might have been some who predicted our relationship was destined for disaster, they were not only wrong – they were miles off mark.

Brian Clough was probably exactly what I needed at that time. He said some very kind things about me over the years and I think it is fair to say we both held each other in such high regard.

It was an ominous start though, because the very day he signed me, he said: 'Hey, I might want to sell you again!'

Birmingham boss Willie Bell thought I had been tapped up, but the truth was I had never spoken to Brian Clough in my life. I was in Spain when I got a call from Bell saying Birmingham had agreed a fee of £140,000 with Forest.

A couple of days later Cloughie called me and we arranged to meet at a pub.

'Get your hair cut,' was his barbed parting shot as he left and we arranged another meeting.

And that's when I was introduced to the wonderful world of sweet peas! This was something completely new to me because up to that point the only pea I was familiar with was the mushy variety.

It turned out that there was a sweet pea exhibition and the gaffer was having a new variety named after him.

I didn't have a clue what was going on. But that memory has stayed with me – as things so often did where the boss was concerned.

He gave it to you straight. If you were shit, you were shit; and if you were great, you were great. Simple. It worked.

He didn't let bullshit baffle brains.

❛ I don't decide things like that. I decide where The Queen lives and how much money we give her, mundane things like that, but not titles ❜
– on suggestions he should be knighted

Former Forest winger ALAN HINTON knew the boss was trying to get the psychological edge when the two of them battled it out on the tennis court. But just what was it that had Cloughie on his knees and close to crying with laughter?

48

PLAYING FOR LAUGHS

ALAN HINTON

For all of Clough's legendary dicta-torial ways, don't let anyone kid you he hadn't got a terrific sense of humour. Far from it. I've seen him lit-erally crying with laughter. While his sidekick Peter Taylor was the really funny guy of the two, Cloughie wasn't averse to having a real good laugh. Infact, I quite often had him on his knees begging me for mercy.

Let me explain. I regularly played tennis with him and he was absolutely wicked in his criticism of my second serve, which was so damn slow. I've lost count of the number of times I would look across the net and he would be there on his knees laughing.

'What are you doing?' I would ask.

And he would be spluttering, hardly able to get his words out as he ridiculed me for what was undoubted-ly the real achilles heel of my game.

'What am I doing?' he'd reply.

'That second serve of yours – I could knock it back even if I was on my knees,' he'd say.

Yes, he liked a joke as much as the next man and that's why I always think the split with Peter was such a tragedy really. Pete made him laugh and I

know that he acknowledged that on many occasions.

Taylor was funny, not so much what you would call a straightforward joker relying on the strength or not of a gag, but a man with a natural comic's tim-ing. It was just his ways more than anything.

Peter was naturally funny. He would pull a funny face or come out with an expression that could dissolve tension in an instant. That break-up should have had a happy ending and I for one am sorry it never did. That rift should have been repaired.

I always remember one day when four or five of us at Derby went to the races with Peter. Cloughie loved his sports – particularly cricket. He played squash – and tennis, of course – but he was never into horse racing like his mate.

Peter made out that he knew every-thing Lester Piggott was up to. He claimed to have an 'insider' who knew anything worth knowing about Piggott's mounts. So, sure enough, in the first race, he let us in on a piece of privileged information from his 'insid-er.'

'Lester won't be trying in this one,' Peter assured us, eager that none of us wasted our money by putting a single penny on the great jockey's mount.

Well, as the last furlong approaches, Piggott comes storming down the far side of the track. He's jumping in the saddle and beating the shit out of his horse as he puts in the ride of his life approaching the line. He's gone past the post absolutely neck-and-neck with the other horse.

'Bloody good information that Pete!' one of us must have observed.

The first announcement came over the public address stating that the race had, as expected, gone to a photo finish. Eventually, after much deliberation in the stewards' room it was decided that Piggott's horse had actually been pipped to the post by the width of a cat's whisker.

'Told you he wasn't trying!' Peter exclaimed with a mischievous grin.

❛ Laughter is so important. Show me a club where there's laughter in the dressing room as well as talent in the team and I'll show you a club that wins things ❜

49

RAKING IT IN

HAROLD ROOME

I once found myself in a slightly embarrassing position thanks to Brian and a new rake!

Brian's love of gardening is well documented and he didn't need any persuading to take a trip to a garden centre. My late wife and I were with him on one occasion when he expressed an interest in buying a rake.

He spotted a very good one which should have been around £28 but was marked down at a sale price of £18. Now, no one could ever accuse Brian of being a mean man. Over the years I lose track of the number of gestures of astonishing generosity I have witnessed. But sometimes, it was like he just wanted to chance his arm and see if he could get away with something.

On this occasion, he said that he fancied buying the rake but said: 'I think I'll offer them £15.'

I started to move away from him. I knew he had plenty of cash on him and was merely trying it on. Also mix into the equation that everyone at, and around, the till knew exactly who he was and it wasn't hard to see why I was pretending I wasn't with him.

Sensing that he was putting me on the spot, but unable to resist the challenge of testing his legendary persuasive powers, Brian moved to the front of the queue and said:

'Young man, I'd quite like this rake, but I'm not lying when I say I only have £15 on me.'

Big surprise . . . he got away with it, much to the amusement of all the people watching on who went home with an amusing tale of Brian Clough raking in some extra cash.

❝ Some observers manage to convince even themselves that some complicated, technical things are happening when they're not. Some so-called experts come out with a right load of bullshit ❞

Respected national newspaper journalist DAVID MILLER became a regular squash partner of Clough's. Here he reveals that the Forest boss was just as competitive on the court as he was in everything else he tackled.

50

SQUASH SPICE

DAVID MILLER

I may not have had as close an association with Brian Clough as his biographer John Sadler, but over many years, having witnessed his entire career as player and manager, he and I enjoyed a relationship sometimes intimate, sometimes controversial in my role as journalist, often humorous and almost always compatible. Here was a man who was never less than frank, often emotional, regularly cantankerous, intent on being sincere but too often his own worst enemy.

We occasionally played squash together. I warned him, unavailingly, several weeks in advance that forces aligned against him at Elland Road spelt doom for his appointment as Leeds' manager.

To his discomfort I revealed in the Daily Express an occasion when he would be obliged to apologise to the Nottingham Forest committee. To his amusement I once upstaged him when arriving to collect him and Peter Taylor from their hotel in Athens, prior to a friendly match against Olympiakos, driving the Mercedes of shipping millionaire Nico Goulandris, the club president.

Our squash confrontations were tense, occasionally hilarious when I won a few points, an illustration of his compulsive competitiveness whatever he was doing. Should I gain momentary advantage, I would immediately be met with that laconic drawl – "Hey, young man, where do you think you're going?" And he would raise his game a level or two to halt my presumption. When it was all over and he had thanked me, and duly congratulated himself, we would retire to his office, still in a sweat, and he would rapidly produce a couple of wine glasses to dilute any health benefit that might have been gained from the previous hour. I detected even in those early days at the City Ground the root of the malaise that would ultimately lead to undermining his reputation and indeed his life.

There has been no-one, not even Malcolm Allison or Alex Ferguson, who possessed the nerve of Clough. None but he could have asserted on arrival with Leeds, so dominant under Don Revie: "By next April, whether or not we win anything, I will have proved even to Billy Bremner, that I'm as good a manager as Revie – or better. I'll convince this club, and the city, that my way is right. I know at the moment almost everyone doubts me, I know the knives may be out, but half the battle is being aware of this."

Such was his overriding confidence that not for one moment could he contemplate failure. When I suggested to him that the sands were already shifting beneath his feet, he retorted: "They cannot afford to get rid of me."

He was on a four-year contract worth reputedly more than £20,000 a year, a huge sum in the Seventies: for instance substantially in excess of what Frank O'Farrell had been receiving before sacked by Manchester United. Yet the man who had risen to fame as manager of Derby, had become intoxicated with his own celebrity as commentator during the World Cup of 1974, would discover that national acclaim can swiftly perish – in this instance within a matter of forty-four days at Elland Road.

In a way, he never stood a chance. The ego which he misguidedly thought was his insulation in fact proved to be his flaw. He had thought he could intimidate the Leeds' array of accomplished international players, but in collaboration with directors who lost their nerve when early results were poor, the players conspired to pull the rug from beneath him. He put on a brave front, when withdrawing to regather his ambitions in the sanctuary of the family home.

"I could have managed. I could have straightened things out on the pitch without too much trouble if it had been just a matter of handling the players, or just the directors. I was finally, totally, compromised when the opposition of both merged."

I'm no psychologist, but it seemed to me that Brian Clough was an example of a naturally talented child possessing untold self-confidence derived from a devoted mother. He learned eagerly and energetically when young, yet throughout his life was profound in his inconsistencies. From manager Alan Brown at Sunderland, he learned as a young player the virtues of self-discipline, yet while he exerted the same control over players when he became a manager, his own self-discipline often disintegrated. He had no hesitation in telling Garry Birtles, his Forest centre-forward, to get off the bus on the way to the airport and "find you own way", when Birtles moaned about an early start. Yet the manager thought nothing of publicly referring to Professor Sir Harold Thompson, chairman of the FA, as "that mad Professor", or lampooning Italians as "cheating bastards". Such indiscretions compromised what chance he might have had of succeeding Revie as England manager in 1977. When that job was in the offing, he magnified his reputation for instability by threatening to quit Forest and return to Derby, guilelessly asserting "all I've ever wanted is to manage players such as Roy McFarland and Archie Gemmill". The question was not so much whether he was fit to manage England as whether he was capable of managing himself? Three traditionalists on the FA, Thompson, Bert Millichip of West

Bromwich (later FA chairman) and Tagge Webster, former amateur international of Corinthian-Casuals, ensured that Ron Greenwood and not Clough was appointed, never mind some support for him from Sir Matt Busby. When given the chance to establish a future claim, when appointed manager with Peter Taylor of the England Youth XI, the pair of them lacked patience to master the potential.

Moreover, Clough would always fall foul of his commercial ambitions. Even among the family, he had been known when young as "Moneybags", yet contradictorily would publicly condemn Stuart Pearce for attempting to double his salary when full-back for Forest. Criticism mounted when the TV programme "World in Action" raised the issue of improper selling of Cup Final tickets, which Clough described as "garbage". Accusations of increasing alcoholism could not be dispelled. "Sure, I drink a bit too much", he would concede. Yet he was the Samaritan who had once stopped impromptu when driving across Trent Bridge to help talk a suicide case from jumping into the river.

Clough's humanity was at the forefront of almost everything he did, was the backbone of a personality which miraculously persuaded a host of often unexceptional players to produce exceptional football. After 44 days with Leeds he would be 18 years with Forest, and when the candle burned low, with no trophy between 1980 and 1988, his conviction was undimmed. "We're playing exactly the same – good football". Capable of assaulting his own supporters if they invaded the pitch, he was recalcitrant. "Some people think me a bully, but I've never meant to be – maybe it's the way I talk."

Though we recall his many eccentricities, what we remember most is the star-studded football he generated, so wonderfully disciplined and devoid of foul play.

‘ Sir Matt Busby was a great manager, but he made one mistake in the boardroom. When Manchester United were looking for a manager, he didn't pick the phone up and call the one man who would have walked the job – me ’

Nottingham Forest keeper STEVE SUTTON got more than he bargained for when he turned in a forgettable first half display. Angry Clough dished out his own unique brand of 'coaching' that he wouldn't forget in a long time.

51

EAR-BASHING

STEVE SUTTON

Getting an ear-bashing from Cloughie took on a whole new meaning for me on one occasion out in Spain. He could leave you with your ears ringing at the best of times, just with his sharp tongue. But, take it from me, his hand came a lot sharper.

We were playing our first game on a pre-season tour of Spain, immediately after the departure of legendary Forest keeper Peter Shilton. We could see Gibraltar from where we were but little did I know that pretty soon I would be seeing stars.

We were 2-0 down at half-time. The first had gone through my hands because I was really quite nervous and, to be perfectly honest, I hadn't done brilliantly with the second either.

We were sat in the dressing room when the door smashed open and the gaffer stormed in. Before I could even move, he whacked me around the side of the head.

'If you're expecting to take over from Shilton playing like that, you've got another think coming young man.'

Hardly the introduction I was hoping for. I knew he was like that – able to praise you or slap you down with equal force and I also knew I'd just have to take it.

We ended up losing 2-1 but I played a lot better in the second half and was hoping that I had least gone part-way to redeeming myself. Best bet was to just sit quietly and consider it a result if he totally ignored you!

I am not exaggerating when I say, I think my ear must have still been red even if it was 45 minutes later. Cloughie came over to me.

'Steven, now that's coaching for you. Well done, second half, son.'

❝ Gary Mills was just 18 when I played him in the European Cup final. Management is about judgement, not the ability to read birth certificates ❞

Cloughie had a real problem with people being late - unless it was him! Sunday Mirror journalist STEVE MILLAR found that out to his cost but still ended up with the exclusive story that no English football fan really wanted to read.

52

NO TO ENGLAND

STEVE MILLAR

I was with Brian Clough the night he finally slammed the door on being England manager.

It was to me that Clough confided the book was now closed on whether he'd ever take on the job he had coveted the most.

Mind you, I have to say I only got there after a stressful M6 panic attack and the most almighty of bollockings from the great man. Let's take it up from the very beginning.

I didn't exactly get off to the best of starts with Cloughie, though that was my mistake because the path had been smoothed by his big pal Vince Wilson. Vince was my colleague on the Sunday Mirror and he had been mates with the Forest boss since his early days back playing up in the North East. Vince was really close with Brian. But on this particular occasion Vince was on holiday and so I was handed the responsibility of doing Clough's weekly column for the paper.

Forest were playing a UEFA Cup game against Vorwarts Frankfurt-Oder at the City Ground on this particular Wednesday night. Brian's secretary Carole had told me he would see me at 6pm on the night of the game but not to be late!! Sod's Law I got stuck in traffic on the way down from Manchester and eventually arrived at around 6.30pm in a right lather.

My understandably agitated demeanour was hardly helped when Carole said: 'The gaffer won't see you now. You're late and he is very annoyed.'

What was I going to do? Ringing in to the London office the next morning to tell them I hadn't got the stuff for the Clough column and the reason I hadn't was because I had turned up late, hardly bore thinking about. I was in a right panic.

I hung around in the corridor in the hope of just catching him to explain what had happened and maybe arrange to come back. At around 7.25, he appeared.

'Young man, are you Steve Millar?'

'Yes, I am Brian,' I said rather meekly.

'You're late and I don't like people who are late.'

'I'm very sorry, but I got stuck in traffic.'

'That's no excuse. Come in my

office,' he said.

'But you're kicking off in five minutes!' I exclaimed.

I went in to his office where I was handed a large Scotch along with the biggest bollocking of my life about being late. How ironic that it was just a week later when the unpredictable Clough showed it was often a case of 'Do as I say, not, do as I do.'

He explained that the following Wednesday he was doing TV summarising for England's crucial European Championship qualifier against Denmark at Wembley. I could see him down there to do next week's column and he offered a meeting place – and a time!

'I'll see you at the Aberdeen Angus Steakhouse after the game. Make it 10pm because I'm travelling home with a party of the directors from Forest.'

How was I, or anyone else, to know that England's hopes of qualifying for the Euros in France was about to completely unravel and Clough's opinions would be sought so voraciously?

England lost 1-0 to the Danes and went tumbling out with Bobby Robson cutting a forlorn figure as he faced the wrath of an incredulous nation. This was the most humiliating defeat since Poland knocked us out of the World Cup at Wembley in 1973 – the night Clough famously dubbed Polish keeper Jan Tomaszewski a 'clown.'

This might have been 10 years later, but Clough's take on it all was something shell-shocked armchair punters would lap up. After all, just six years earlier Clough had been snubbed for the England job despite being the unanimous choice of the people.

Little surprise then that when I arrived at the arranged meeting place, there was no sign of Clough at the steakhouse. A party of the Forest directors were there, so I was assured that I was in the right place but when he would arrive was anybody's guess.

As midnight approached, I was yet again starting to panic a bit. Time was running out if he didn't spare me ten minutes. Tomorrow would be out of the question for doing the column because no one would get back until late and Clough was hardly likely to go into the ground on a Thursday.

Friday was a busy day for me doing other things for a national Sunday newspaper without having to arrange a trip down to Nottingham and hang around waiting for Clough. Suddenly I started to wish I'd never been handed the column in the first place. It was causing my nothing but grief and much more of this I might end up in the A&E department at Wembley Hospital.

At around ten minutes to midnight he breezed in through the door as if nothing had happened. The Forest party had eaten; everyone was waiting to go and, yet again, I was nursing an empty notebook and an extremely heavy heart. Brian asked if I had eaten to which I quickly replied that all I was really interested in was getting stuff for the column. Brian's sense of urgency didn't seem quite so acute as he quizzed the chairman as to whether he'd dipped his hands in his pocket and bought everyone a drink. Anxiety forced me to get a little bolder.

'Brian, it's a quarter-past-twelve and I haven't got a word down. I'm getting a bit desperate here.'

'Hey, it's too late to do it now,' he said, which was just about the last thing I wanted to hear. Apparently, the word had now filtered through that the coach taking them back to Nottingham was leaving at 12.30.

'Honestly Brian, I'm in a right panic here,' I said.

The thought of a long journey back to Manchester stressed out by the fact that I had nothing in my book and nothing to tell the office when I rang in early next morning filled me with dread. I think even Brian realised that he didn't want to put me through that. He called me to him and wagged that famous finger in my direction, as if to assure me everything would be alright.

'Young man. Go away from here with your intro in your head and this is it . . .'

I waited with baited breath. It needed to be good. He agreed to call me in the morning and give me the rest of the stuff to go around it. It was a start . . .

Brian continued: *'This was the night I finally knew I didn't ever want to be England manager.'*

What a tale. The people's champion was finally publicly declaring he wouldn't go near the job everyone had wanted him to take. I drove home happy, Brian phoned me the next day to put the meat to the bones and my bosses were delighted. I'd got there – in the end!

❛ I was just too risky for the England job. The FA wanted Ron Greenwood – good guy, safe, but boring. They wanted the whole thing kept cosy. They wanted to take their wives on overseas trips, travelling first class and staying in nice hotels. They wanted to wear the England badge on their blazer. Bugger the World Cup ❜

Legendary Nottingham Forest defender LARRY LLOYD was up near the top of the list of people who could get Cloughie's back up. But even by his own standards his row with the manager just a few minutes into one game beats the lot.

53

TAMPA TANTRUM

LARRY LLOYD

I've always been known for my down-to-earth approach to life – and my footballing principles are no different either. Showy, fancy stuff I give a wide berth to and while that may be applauded by many, it went down like a lead balloon the day Tampa Bay Rowdies came to play Forest in a friendly game.

I'm just not the type of character who can raise any enthusiasm for friendly matches at the best of times, but this was the kind of showpiece that was definitely not my style. There were dancing girls with pompons on the pitch, god knows who else sailing down onto the pitch on parachutes – all American razzamatazz. What a right load of old bollocks.

Anyway, about four minutes into the game, the ball was played to me and, given my couldn't-give-a-toss disposition at that particular moment, I decided it might be a nice idea to back-heel it. As the ball came to me, I attempted to deal with it in a manner perhaps not normally accustomed with a brick shithouse central defender and ended up tripping and falling over!

Up went the board – Number Five – and I suffered the slightly unusual fate of being substituted after just FOUR minutes.

As I trudged off the pitch towards Cloughie I just couldn't help letting him know what I thought about that particular decision.

'You're a fucking loony you are!' I shouted in the direction of my perplexed boss.

To my surprise he yelled back: 'And so are you – fuck off!'

Not a problem. I did just as he said and went home.

❛ Women run everything you know. The only decision I've taken in my house in the last 20 years is recognise Angola as an independent state ❜

Baffled JOHN MOTSON found himself being pilloried by Clough
for a commentary he had done. Shocked onlookers witnessed
the outburst, but it was a case of forgive and forget when
the manager offered an unusual olive branch to Motty.

54

SHITHOUSE

JOHN MOTSON

'Shithouse!' yelled Brian Clough, and his jabbing forefinger was pointing in only one direction. Mine.

It was early 1987. Nottingham Forest were in London to play Arsenal in a League Cup quarter-final. Clough had been walking through the main entrance at Highbury into Arsenal's marble foyer, when he spotted me near the bust of Herbert Chapman.

'Shithouse,' he repeated, storming towards me now.

I backed off even farther, fearing that the statue of Arsenal's famous pre-war manager would take a battering at any moment.

'I pay my licence fee because I expect the BBC to be fair,' he snarled. 'Not biased like you were at Tottenham on Sunday.'

I should point out straight away that the match he was referring to was a North London derby at White Hart Lane. It was Arsenal whom Clough believed I had favoured in my commentary.

'Bloody disgrace,' he boomed.

All this time, his embarrassed Nottingham Forest players were trying to get past him into the dressing room corridor. Just as shocked were a handful of people standing near the ticket window on the far side of the hall.

The mascots and their parents couldn't help hearing his outburst either.

Eventually Clough's coaching staff coaxed him away and I moved sheepishly through the door to the players' tunnel, where the teams for that night's League Cup quarter-final between Forest and Arsenal would be announced.

The previous Sunday, Arsenal had beaten Tottenham 2-1 to extend their lead at the top of the First Division. George Graham was in his first season as Arsenal manager and was assembling a vibrant young team including David Rocastle, Michael Thomas, Tony Adams and Niall Quinn.

It was a performance in which I detected a spirit and a character that were going to take Arsenal places.

I was shaking slightly at the unexpected tirade from Clough, but was determined not to let it affect my commentary. As Duncan Hamilton revealed in his award-winning book *Provided You Don't Kiss Me*, 'Brian

Clough used the word shithouse like other people said please and thank you.'

Nottingham Forest lost that night to goals from Charlie Nicholas and Martin Hayes, but that didn't stop *Sportsnight* wanting an interview with Clough. As one of my early editors said: 'Get him to read the telephone directory and people will listen.' The man was pure box office.

I made my way gingerly round the frozen track at Highbury that January night. The temperature had dropped considerably during the game and by the time I spotted Clough waiting by the interview camera I was frozen. I was probably shivering over the reception I expected to get.

'Are yer cawld, John?'

The familiar Middlesbrough accent cut deep into the night. As I got closer to Clough I could see he was holding a flimsy paper cup. Rather like the jabbing finger earlier, it was for me.

'Ere, get this down yer, young man,' he shouted.

I was over 40 at the time, but compared with his earlier fury, 'young man' was almost a term of endearment. I took the cup of kindness from Clough, expecting it to be either tea or coffee. I should have known better. It was full to the brim of whisky.

And there, on one cold evening in North London, you had the contradiction that was Brian Howard Clough. Chairmen, players, supporters, newspapermen, commentators – none of us ever knew which side of his unpredictable nature we were going to encounter next.

‘ I'm a Socialist who's been lucky. I've got a few bob, a nice house and nice things around me. I see no reason why everyone shouldn't have what I've got ’

Former Republic of Ireland skipper ROY KEANE tells the story of when he was really given the chance to shine by his unpredictable boss. As if he needed reminding, the midfielder was being told to keep his feet firmly on the ground.

55

CHANCE TO SHINE

ROY KEANE

There was never any danger that I would get carried away by making my debut at Liverpool, but just in case . . .

When I met Brian Clough in the dressing room at the City Ground the following morning, he asked me my name!

'Roy.' I replied.

The gaffer took off his shoes, which were very muddy, as he had been walking his dog, Del, round the pitch.

'Give those a clean for me will you Roy?'

I knew he was keeping my feet on the ground to stop me getting carried away. I'm sure that if I brought my shoes in for one of the players to clean these days, they'd throw them back. Things have changed.

I'm certain he wouldn't like what is going on in the game now with fitness coaches taking over and ProZones, weights, dieticians, pasta and bananas, but he would survive today, definitely.

He would stand up to the challenges although he might have been reluctant to move with the times on the scientific side. But I can bet Sir Alex Ferguson would tell you it took him a while to change his ways without forgetting what you are all about.

Brian Clough would have adapted and made his mark at whatever club he was at because he knew his football and I think the modern-day player would be able to put up with him. Players of any generation would love to play for him because he was different.

Brian Clough was a one-off, so let's not kid ourselves that we'd copy him. He did things off the cuff, but he knew his football. Make no mistake about that.

You don't win European Cups and English titles unless you know your stuff.

❛ Barbara says to me repeatedly: "I don't care what you do at the ground, but when you come into the house, try and smile" ❜

93

When top referee CLIVE THOMAS found himself in a spot of bother he found a trusted ally in Clough. The Forest manager even fixed up secret meetings with the out-of-favour international official and advised him on how he should handle things.

56

SECRET MEETINGS

CLIVE THOMAS

I had meetings with Brian Clough which have remained a secret until now. We met up in all sorts of places – Nottinghamshire's Trent Bridge ground or hotels around the place. I was in trouble with the Football League hierarchy and even though I was the top marked referee, I was suddenly dumped into the lower reaches to officiate at Fourth Division games. Brian proved a strong ally and friend during those dark times.

One thing he always said to me was 'Be strong. Take on the players, take on the managers, but be yourself.' I will never forget that."

I rang him once and said: 'Brian, I'm having a problem with the Football League.'

My high profile and controversial ways didn't always go down well with everyone. The problem was that despite being the top marked referee and always doing top flight games, I had suddenly been dropped to covering the likes of Aldershot and Doncaster in the Fourth Division.

'We'd better meet,' Brian said and we arranged to liaise at a hotel in Birmingham city centre, by New Street station. It was one of several times we met up for a chat.

We had about two hours together and his answers were just so typically blunt and simple that they just made total sense.

'The only way to beat them is to go to Aldershot and give exactly the same performance as you would at Manchester United. You go to Aldershot and as you arrive at the ground, treat it just like it is Old Trafford. Think the same way as you would if you were going there or to Highbury. Rise above it.'

It made such good, sound sense and I think it shows Brian to be beyond generous with his time when he could quite easily have not wanted to be bothered about my problem.

' I kicked the cat twice – at least he got two more kicks than England did! '

Former West Ham defender TONY GALE reveals just why he was forced to smile when he first bumped into Cloughie as a youth player with England. But it would all end in tears when fate dictated the two would meet years later.

57

WE MEET AGAIN

TONY GALE

When referee Keith Hackett implemented the 'new' professional foul rule and showed Gale the red card he virtually handed Clough his first ever crack at an FA Cup final. Gale was sent off after just 22 minutes of West Ham's semi-final clash against Forest at Villa Park in 1991.

Up to that point Second Division West Ham had looked the better side, but Forest, driven on by Roy Keane, suddenly took the upper hand and ended up scoring four goals without reply after Gale's untimely exit.

Referee Hackett doesn't need telling his decision drastically affected the outcome of the game and admits: "Gale was sent off for a foul that would not have been a yellow card the week before."

It was little consolation to the big defender or The Hammers, but it helped send Clough to Wembley in search of the one trophy that had eluded him.

But here, Gale reveals that he had met Clough before – and couldn't raise a smile that day either!

* * *

My most famous meeting with Cloughie came when I was sent-off in the FA Cup semi-final . . . but not many people know about a meeting I had with him some 14 years earlier.

To this day I still can't believe the sending-off. There were only 22 minutes gone in our big match at Villa Park when ref Keith Hackett sent me off for a professional foul on Gary Crosby.

We were up against it after that. It was the only time I was sent off in a career which took in over 700 games.

I've never forgiven Hackett for that. I still think he was trying to prove a point with the new rule.

Cloughie didn't say anything to me that day. He was probably celebrating the 4-0 win that had taken him to the final for the first time in his career.

He might not have said anything then, but he wasn't short on words the very first time I met him – I was though!

Very few people know this, or make the connection, but I was actually Cloughie's skipper for a very short period of time.

I was a youngster at Fulham at the

time when he was given the job as England Youth manager after he had famously missed out on getting the senior England job to Ron Greenwood.

A chap called Ken Burton was running the team when the bombshell was dropped that the infamous Clough and Taylor were about to be put in overall charge.

We all knew of him because of his high-profile on the telly and stuff but two of the lads in the team – Chris Woods and Steve Burke – were at Forest and so we were certainly pre-warned that here was a guy who you wouldn't take liberties with. We were all shaking in our boots by the time we eventually got to meet him. It was at Lancaster Gate and Cloughie breezed in.

'Who's captain?' he asked. I sheepishly put my hand up.

'Smile son,' he said. I couldn't – I was too scared.

'Football's a game for people who smile son,' he said.

I found it difficult that day and how was I to know that when our paths crossed on that fateful day 14 years later, I would have nothing to smile about again.

' When you have had a couple of steel girders dropped on your big toe at 12 o'clock and you have to go and play football at 7.30 it can be hard work '
- on playing part-time

The gamblers in the Derby dressing room were in for a shock when Clough took swift and decisive action to curb their ways. Former Derby Evening Telegraph sports reporter GEORGE EDWARDS reveals what happened.

58

ALL BETS OFF

GEORGE EDWARDS

Peter Taylor was a natural comic and the one man who could always bring a smile to Brian's face. He wasn't a joke-teller as some would have you believe. His humour doesn't actually translate well into the written word at all, but he was an incredibly funny man. He was more a corner-of-the-mouth delivery man, a bit like Tommy Cooper, Spike Milligan and Les Dawson all rolled into one.

Peter could make Brian snort with laughter and I have lost count of the times that some silly gesture or remark from Taylor snapped his pal out of a bad mood.

Nothing was guaranteed a laugh more than Taylor's inability to master names of either people or places. Len Cantello, the West Bromwich Albion player, became Galento, Lentello or even Canaletto; Mike Summerbee at Manchester City was merged with team mate Colin Bell to become Mike Summerbell and so on. Peter turned mangling the English language into an art form, but when he was in full flow, he could have everyone in his company splitting their sides with laughter.

Peter loved a bet. Football was his obsession but betting was definitely in his DNA. He was rarely away from a racing paper and from time to time passed on strong tips to the dressing room gamblers among the Derby team.

There was a betting shop quite close to the ground frequented by the players who liked a wager, but Clough made a point of always getting to know his players and their habits.

One afternoon a small group of players had slipped out to place a bet and came back celebrating after the horse had romped home.

Their jocularity was soon curbed on their return to the ground when they found a notice pinned on the dressing room door.

'Any player visiting a betting shop wearing training gear will be fined one week's pay. Brian Clough.'

❛When you get to know me, what you see is what you get – and it's not bad❜

97

Could it be true that Cloughie was seen about in Marks & Spencer seconds jumpers? Former Derby and Forest star ALAN HINTON is the man who knows the full facts behind the story and was happy to let the cat out of the bag.

59

FAMOUS WHITE BOOTS

ALAN HINTON

Everyone remembers me for the famous white boots. There was only myself and the great Alan Ball wearing them back then and they really were quite revolutionary. Nowadays they are the norm. In fact, given the fluorescent greens, yellows and pinks that the players wear today, white pales into insignificance.

But you have to remember that these were the days when you could have boots in any colour of your choice – as long as it was black!

The one thing that people, quite understandably, want to know is what Cloughie's reaction was the first time he clapped eyes on them. The funny thing is, he never once made a fuss about them.

I thought he would give me some right stick over them but, surprisingly, he never did. He didn't have a problem with them and I was staggered. Perhaps it was because I was his supplier of Marks & Spencers' quality seconds pullovers, that he kept quiet about them, but more of that in a minute.

The background to it all, quite simply, was that a company called

Hummel approached me through a representative of theirs and asked me if I would wear the revolutionary new boot. I suppose I was something of a pioneer. The fact that they offered to pay me £1,000 for my troubles certainly was a deciding factor. Anyway, one or two of the lads might have made the odd comment, but Brian kept his thoughts to himself on that particular subject.

Like I said, perhaps he feared I would spill the beans about his line in fashion. I doubt it – he wore my jumpers all the time. Dave Mackay had a tie company and lots of us would wear his ties. It was all going on at Derby in those days!

It's hard to imagine the likes of Jose Mourinho and Arsene Wenger going on TV wearing M&S seconds, but it never bothered Brian. It certainly didn't do his image any problem.

In fact, my business sideline was something which led Cloughie to bend his rules for me. He was a stickler for saying: 'You lot know the rules – no drinking after Wednesday.'

I went to see him and told him that Thursday was a busy day for me in my business. I used to have to go and get all my stuff, bring it back and unpack my vehicle and by the time I'd finished it would be eight o'clock. I told him that what I liked to do was nip to the pub after I'd finished, have just a couple of pints which allowed me to relax and I'd be asleep by 10.30 pm.

'Okay, you can do that,' he said, realising it was a routine that worked for me.

Sometimes the rules were ignored – but only at his say-so. We'd go to the Midland Hotel the Friday night before a game and Brian would bring a crate of beer in.

'Have what you want but be careful,' was all that he would say. You could have a couple of bottles of beer and he wouldn't bother. Can you imagine that happening the night before a game these days?

' In Yorkshire we like using proper first names as Anthony Adams, Robert Moore and Terence Butcher would have found out if ever they had played for me '

Even when a streaker ran on the pitch, it couldn't throw the former Forest boss off track. But as BBC radio commentator DARREN FLETCHER explains, it was a less than orthodox remark which had the listeners in stitches.

60

NAKED TRUTH

DARREN FLETCHER

To the day I die, I will never forget one game I had the pleasure of covering with Cloughie providing the match analysis. Manchester United were in town and Cloughie, Garry Birtles and myself were on hand to let the listeners know how John Gregory's Derby were doing.

But the thing that springs to mind was the emergence of a streaker. Cloughie loved that. The fella, wearing little more than a smile, raced down to the one end of the pitch and was actually swinging on the crossbar.

We were live on air, but that didn't stop Cloughie having his say on the matter.

'I hope the Derby players have a close look at that lad's balls because they've seen none of the ball so far,' he said with a chuckle.

So that went out live on air for a start. Only he could get away with it!

I remember doing an England match with him when they were playing Serbia during Sven Goran Eriksson's reign and it was that famous day when, because of all the substitutions being made, players were passing the captain's armband around.

They were literally tossing the armband among themselves as they were being replaced. Well . . . Cloughie was beside himself about it.

He was so annoyed. It just absolutely irritated him that the England captain's armband was being treated so lightly. He felt it was a real lack of respect and wasn't having it one bit. In one particular exchange, the armband fell to the floor and for Brian that was the ultimate insult. He went barmy. Cloughie was fiercely patriotic, but I think there was a bit more to it than just that. He carried a bit of a grievance that he was picked only twice to play for England before his career was cruelly cut short by injury.

He was proud of those two caps and didn't like to see something like the England captaincy being treated so shabbily. Add to that the fact that he also missed out on being England manager when everyone in the country wanted him to be appointed apart from the FA and he had a bit of a thing about it all.

Of all the people who I've had analysing with me over the years, no one could compare. He was in a league of his own. No one came within a million miles. Listeners hung on his every word. There was an unconditional love with Cloughie. You could feel that whenever you were in his company. I have been lucky enough to be with him on numerous occasions and the warmth that he generates from people is astonishing. He didn't have to try and win anyone over. He had them eating out of the palm of his hand from the first minute he opened his mouth.

I recall one day he was absolutely top of his knock and I said to him: 'You know what Brian? I could quite happily shut up, just listen to you and not commentate.'

Quick as a flash came the reply: 'Son, the listeners might appreciate it if you did!'

‘ I absolutely adored that red-brick house, with its lovely wooden gate and the garden round the side where Dad grew his rhubarb and his sprouts ’

*How could GARY MEGSON have ever seen himself sitting in the
Nottingham Forest manager's chair after a torrid time there
as a player when Cloughie signed him and very quickly
decided that it had all been a big mistake?*

61

BEYOND THE GRAVE

GARY MEGSON

In one of the truly bizarre twists of Clough's career, Megson ended up taking over as Forest manager after a less than harmonious spell at the City Ground as a player. Clough signed Megson in the summer of 1984 then infamously froze him out saying he hadn't realised the midfielder 'couldn't trap a bag of cement.'

That cutting phrase became national headlines and Megson, one of life's more intelligent players, quickly realised that his future under Clough was going to be tricky – and brief. Five uncomfortable months later, he was sold to Newcastle without having made a single appearance for Forest's first team. Megson's spell at the City Ground as a player was a rare blip in an 18-year playing career which took in the likes of Everton, Newcastle, Sheffield Wednesday, Manchester City and Norwich. The midfielder had a reputation for always putting in a shift – a quality which should have gone a long way with Cloughie.

But, for whatever reasons, the Forest boss decided that the £450,000 he'd paid Sheffield Wednesday would have been better spent elsewhere and

Megson found himself out in the cold. Virtually from day one, it seemed he was fighting a losing battle to win over the boss and quickly came to the same conclusion as Clough – that a quickie 'divorce' was the only natural conclusion to such an unhappy marriage.

For him to return years later as the manager, was a turn of events so seemingly far-fetched it could have come from a scriptwriter's imagination. But it wasn't all gloom and his miserable spell at the City Ground was punctuated with the odd laugh and glimpse of the Clough magic. He reveals:

* * *

You talk about how football has changed. Well, he took us to Majorca once and the players went to a bar about 50 yards from the hotel. Anyway, we've all had too much to drink, so instead of going back the 50 yards we came, we have walked about three miles around the other way because the senior players said that Brian would be between the bar and the hotel waiting for us.

We eventually get back about three in the morning, it's pitch black . . . and suddenly we hear 'G'night lads!' He knew what we would do, because he just knew people.

He didn't treat me particularly well, in fact I was suicidal sometimes at Forest. But when I left, he was terrific!

I found what he said about me really strange, particularly given that he had signed me only a month before. That might say something about Brian Clough as a scout. I was a bag of nerves after that.

But when I became Forest manager, Carole Washington who was my secretary and had also been Brian's, gave me a message from Brian's widow.

What it said has to stay private, but it was about my abilities as a manager and I can tell you it meant the world to me. Apparently he had been going to give me a ring but then passed away.

Typical of the man – he slaughters me to the whole world and then I get a private message from beyond the grave!

❛ I was always taught the importance of clean shoes. Mind you, I had to polish them hard because I wore the toes out of most of them kicking a ball around ❜

62

I'D DRINK TO THAT

PHILLIP TAYLOR

I know for a fact that the one big regret my dad had – and I'm sure Brian had too – was that they never picked up the phone and said 'Let's go and have a beer!'

They should have done that. Too many people concentrate on the 10 per cent of the time when things went a bit wrong between them. Ninety per cent of the time, which spans about 30 years, they were absolutely brilliant together and, for me, I think that's how they should be remembered.

In a way, it was dad who discovered Brian. He was the one who stuck up for him at Middlesbro when the other players thought he was cocky. I can't think why!

It was dad who threw an arm around him and protected him. They were friends for life after that. Brian was a cracking player and good company and that's what dad liked.

A lot of people try to dissect their partnership and go on about who did what but, to me, that's a load of rubbish. They were a proper partnership where they both kind of did everything and it's hard to differentiate between the two roles.

I just think that together they were brilliant. There was certainly a chemistry there. That's what I like about the idea of the statue of them together. That's how they should be remembered.

My main memory of Brian being around was when I was about six or seven, I suppose. We used to live just over the road. I remember a lot more about the Derby days because I was a lot older then. I used to 'babysit' Nigel and Simon. I'd be 13 or 14 and they were nippers. I used to have to keep an eye on them. They were a handful at times – especially Nigel, surprisingly enough.

They were exciting times. We were immersed in football 24 hours a day and it was unbelievable really – like having your own roller-coaster ride.

I might be biased, but I know I'm certainly not alone, when I say that I honestly don't think dad had the recognition he deserved for the part he played in the phenomenal success they enjoyed. Take nothing away from Brian, he was the iconic manager who deserved all the recognition he received.

People I have spoken to, some of their former players, have said the relationship worked well because it was a kind of good cop-bad cop set-up. Dad was, naturally, the good cop. The one who would put a friendly arm around someone or offer a word of encouragement after Brian had ripped into them.

I guess that's why it worked. People can forget that two men working together running a football club was a revolutionary thing at the time. But both had qualities which complemented each other and it proved to be a stunning success.

But that's why the statue idea was one that went down so well because it was an idea of the supporters. It was their wishes to pay tribute to them together – and that's what I like about it.

❛ Winning the title with Derby was one of the miracles of the century. Our triumph proves there is hope for all the little people of the world ❜

When the Derby team bus was pulled up by the police for breaking the speed limit it called for a bit of fast thinking. But Derby star ALAN DURBAN explains that Cloughie's defence had one rather big, call that gaping, hole in it.

63

FAST THINKING

ALAN DURBAN

I always remember us Derby lads setting off for Newcastle one Friday morning and the police stopping the team bus on the A1 because we were breaking the speed limit.

They flagged us down and we pulled over onto the side of the road while discussions went on between Eric our driver and the police officers.

Anyway, the one policeman decides to make his way down the bus and says mischievously: 'Which one is Mr Clough?'

Well, he was from the North East, so he knew which one he was all right. Anyway, Cloughie didn't take too much finding and the officer proceeded to address him.

'The bus driver has just told me that you are the one who is telling him that you have got to get there early for this football match!'

'Did he now?' Cloughie's eyebrows suddenly hit the skylight as the officer continued.

'You are putting him under too much pressure. Next time, we won't book him, we'll be booking you.'

Once everything had calmed down and the police had gone on their way, Cloughie laid into Eric.

'Hey, not only will we be getting a new bus driver, we'll be getting a new bus company, if you carry on . . .'

But the funniest thing about the whole comical episode which puts an entirely different slant on it, was that it was only Friday. We weren't even playing until the next day so quite what the rush was, I don't know.

' Beckham's Mohican haircut is grotesque. It's not a hairstyle – it's a mess and it is also a downright insult to the England captaincy which is one of the most prestigious posts in sport '

When young local radio reporter PAUL MACE managed to get the Forest boss to break his silence, it was pats on the back all round at the office. Perhaps, at long last, Cloughie was ready to strike up a relationship with the station.

64

SHOCK TREATMENT

PAUL MACE

I was working for the local radio station – Radio Trent – and Brian, in his infinite wisdom, hadn't done a single interview with them for two years.

I was a freelance and had been working for the station for only a month when I was handed the poisoned chalice.

Basically, what it entailed was going down to Nottingham Forest on a Friday lunchtime, wait there and ask for an interview with Mr Clough and hang around before coming back with nothing.

It was a standing joke that he hadn't done an interview of any description for an eternity but the feeling was that the station should at least go and ask if only to be turned away. That may all sound a bit pointless, but it at least gave the station an answer if any fans came on grumbling that he was never on. They had legitimately made the effort and the fact that Brian Clough interviews on Radio Trent were as rare as duck's teeth was not for the want of trying. Tomorrow was the last day of the season and Forest were playing Sheffield Wednesday.

So, I didn't so much pick the short straw than had it handed to me as the rookie who clearly had nothing better to do than hang around on the car park outside the Jubilee Club at Forest's ground.

'Make sure you ask him – and make sure he says he won't do it,' were my rather worrying pre-snub instructions from those who had all been sent out on 'Mission:Impossible' at one time or another. It was with something of a heavy heart that I set off in pursuit of the one and only Brian Clough.

I had never met him before, was 27 years old and not afraid to admit to being a little bit scared of him. I've since discovered he had an equally intimidating effect on almost everyone who met him.

The players came in from training and about 15 minutes later, the manager came into view. Our eyes met and I sensed there would never be a better time to ask the fateful question.

'Hello Mr Clough. I'm Paul Mace from Radio Trent. Is there any chance of an interview?'

'Not today, I think, young man,' he said crisply but very politely.

'Okay,' I replied somewhat dejectedly. If Radio Trent's recent history was to be re-written, then it was not going to be by me.

I decided to wait and try again and about half-an-hour later when he went by, I chanced my arm.

'Mr Clough. I know you said before that you wouldn't do anything but it is the last game of the season. Any chance of an interview just to round the season off?'

'I don't think so young man,' came the reply.

This was pre mobile phone days, so I made my way towards the pay phone just inside the door of the Jubilee Club to ring the office and pass on the widely predicted course of events.

'He was very polite about it but I'm afraid that it was still no . . .' I said, when I was suddenly interrupted by an instantly recognisable voice booming over at me.

'Young man. Follow me.'

'Fuck me,' I thought as I quickly put the phone down. This can't be. Surely not?

'Follow me. It's the last game. You said it. I've not done your station for a long time. Yes, right. Fire away.'

He offered me a cup of tea before assuring me: 'You can ask me anything you want. You've got 10 minutes!'

Ten minutes? My God. I could absolutely fill my boots in 10 minutes.

I played local football and he asked me what position I played and took a real interest. This was heaven!

I started the interview and Del Boy his golden retriever barked.

'Be quiet!' he barked back.

It was one of the best interviews you could have hoped for. He spoke not just about the game against Sheffield Wednesday, but the game in general. He was at his inimitable best and I knew I had just put a big dollop of radio gold onto my tape machine. Going into the office with this was just more than anyone could have dreamed off. I'd done it.

'Thanks very much,' I cooed.

'Not a problem, young man. Any time.'

I rushed back to the office where the flags were out. Pats on the back all round. I was THE man of the moment. The stuff on tape was electric and got syndicated all over the place. Did it get any better than this?

First game of the following season, not surprisingly, I was sent down to the scene of my, thus far, finest hour.

'Mr Clough. Any chance?'

'Not today, young man and don't you get hanging around because I won't be doing one either!'

Ah well . . . it had been bloody good while it lasted.

❝ I don't rely on footballers. If I relied on them I'd have been out of a job 20 years ago ❞

THE ONLY WAY IS UP: Clough and Taylor pictured in Derby in 1968.

SMART YOUNG MAN: *Derby hairdresser John Borrington makes sure Clough keeps well groomed.*

Picture: Derby Telegraph

SHOPPING FOR SIGNATURES: Clough signs autographs for fans as he opens a supermarket in Ripley, in October 1973.

QUICK GETAWAY: A slick-looking Clough gets ready to hit the road in 1977.

ON YER BIKE: Cloughie decides two wheels are best in August, 1975.

BINNED: A passport for Wales? Discover the real background to this famous Cloughie pic (Chapter 85).

HAPPY DAYS: Clough and Taylor have plenty to grin about after landing the league title at Coventry in 1978.

NOW THEN, YOUNG MAN: Cloughie makes a point to a local police officer before a match between Forest and Leeds in March, 1993.

Picture: Nottingham Post

DOG SQUAD: So just who is that playing wide left?

It's Cloughie's retriever Del Boy who takes his place in the line-up with the Forest team of 1988-89.
Back row(left to right): Brian Laws, Gary Fleming, Garry Parker, Steve Chettle, Darren Wassall, Brian Rice, Steve Hodge. Centre:
Liam O'Kane(coach), Tommy Gaynor, Terry Wilson, Steve Sutton, Hans Segers, Colin Foster, Neil Webb, Brian Clough (manager).
Front: Nigel Clough, Lee Glover, Des Walker, Stuart Pearce, Franz Carr, Gary Crosby and . . . Del Boy.

PLEASE KEEP OFF
THE GRASS AREA

SUBTLE REQUEST: Clough makes his point before an FA Cup tie with Halifax in January, 1988.

SHOCKER:
Ooh, I say young man . . .
Cloughie sees a streaker
from the commentary box
(See Chapter 60).

HELPING HAND:
Clough gives his backing to
Geoff Hoon's parliamentary
campaign in May 1992
(See Chapter 92).

BURNS NIGHT:
Kenny Burns and Clough with
the League Cup trophy after
Forest beat Liverpool 1-0
in a replay at Old Trafford.
March 22, 1978.

ON A PLATE: Cloughie picks up yet another Manager of the Month award as a boyish Roy Keane gets a taste for picking up trophies.

SHAKE ON IT: Two Derby County greats get together as Arthur Cox and Clough launch an Evening Telegraph appeal in 1993.

BUBBLY TIMES: Taylor and Clough celebrate a champagne moment with some of their silverware.

NOT FUNNY: A somewhat bemused Ian Bowyer looks on as Clough tackles a very big clown (see Chapter 113).

SHIP AHOY: Nottingham Post photographer Trevor Bartlett couldn't believe his luck when Cloughie started fooling around with Viv Anderson and Colin Walsh prior to the UEFA Cup clash with Celtic in December 83 (see Chapter 11).

Picture: Nottingham Post

PAPILLON:
Trevor Bartlett's special
relationship with Clough
allowed him to get this
most unusual shot
(see Chapter 85).

RIGHT: Clough allows
star snapper Trevor to
give the European Cup
a cuddle - after all
he's taken enough
shots of it!

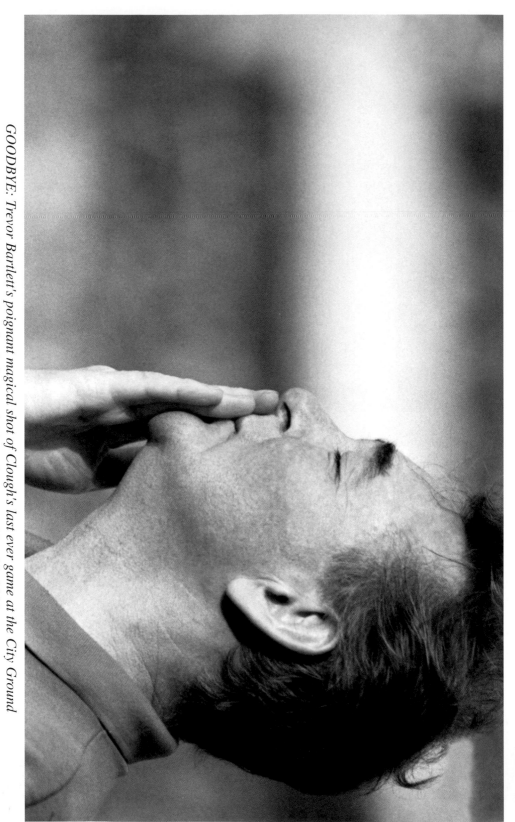

GOODBYE: Trevor Bartlett's poignant magical shot of Clough's last ever game at the City Ground - the County Cup final clash with Notts County on May 11, 1993.

*Derby fan DENNIS YATES and his mate were making their way
back from an away match at Middlesborough when they
unexpectedly found themselves providing a hasty taxi service
for Cloughie who was in something of a hurry.*

65

TAILOR-MADE

DENNIS YATES

I used to travel all over the country to watch Derby but a bizarre, chance meeting in Middlesborough, back in 1969, has stuck with me to this day.

I'd always had a strong bond with Derby County Football Club because I'd lived near their ground in the 1950s. You could hear the roar from where I lived and it always fascinated me.

I have a confession to make as well – sometimes, as naughty boys do, we would sneak on the buses and nick the odd sandwich or two.

Anyway, my pal Ivor Webster who was a passionate follower of the club, resurrected my interest and got me into watching them home and away.

We followed them all over the country and on this particular occasion in early 1969 we had watched them play at Boro's old Ayresome Park ground and were patiently waiting in the queue of cars trying to leave the car park.

The next thing we knew, we spotted Brian standing there looking anxiously at his watch as if he was waiting for a taxi or someone to pick him up.

My pal wound the window down,

leaned across me to congratulate him on the result and to our astonishment he asked Ivor if there was any chance we could drop him off at his tailor's as he had a fitting appointment for a new suit at 5pm!

I can only presume that as he was born in the area and was a legendary player at Boro, he had a particular tailor that he had used for years and was taking the opportunity to kill two birds with one stone.

He jumped in the back and didn't even wait for one of us to say 'yes.'

Not that we were worried about that. The main concern was that the queue of traffic was bumper to bumper from the ground right down to the main road.

Brian was visibly getting more agitated that he was going to be late for the appointment and told Ivor in no uncertain terms to by-pass the queueing cars by simply driving straight past them.

'Lad, get down the outside lane of this traffic,' he said. My pal Ivor seemed to love that. He went hurtling down the outside lane, past all the cars until the raised arm of a policeman brought him to an abrupt halt.

The policeman had a stern look on his face as he approached the car and asked Ivor what the hell he thought he was doing.

That was Brian's prompt to lean forward in his own inimitable fashion and say: 'It's all right young man, I have an urgent appointment.'

The officer instantly recognised our VIP passenger, apologised profusely and then held up the oncoming traffic as he waved us on our way!

Strangely enough it wasn't the first time our paths had crossed with Brian, but the previous time a year earlier, so nearly ended up in changing the course of football history!

It was the summer of 1968 and we were out in Ivor's car and happened to be driving along Ferrers Way, in Allestree, where Brian lived at the time.

Ivor didn't know the exact address of Brian's house but had a good idea where it was so when we got in the general vicinity, we decided to slow down to take a peep.

Moments later, a small boy of about two came running into the road after a football, closely followed by a man.

Ivor managed to stop just before hitting the lad and the man grabbed hold of the boy and gave him an almighty ticking off, telling him never to do such a stupid thing again.

It turned out to be Brian and young son Nigel, who might not have gone on to play for Forest and England had we not been dawdling along that day.

' I think young Paul Gascoigne has a lot of talent. I've asked our coach driver if he sees him in the Wembley tunnel, to try and knock him down '

66

FOREST FIRST

SEAN HASLEGRAVE

You wouldn't have thought that having a right go at my manager would have been the right way to impress Cloughie – but that's how it turned out.

I ended up becoming his first ever signing for Nottingham Forest as Clough embarked on carving out his own incredible piece of footballing history.

It was September, 1974, and I was playing for a Stoke City side gracing the European stage. The previous season an Alan Hudson-inspired team had helped the club clinch a UEFA Cup spot and we were drawn against the mighty Dutch side Ajax – at that time rated one of the best club sides in the world.

We played the first leg at home and drew 1-1 courtesy of a Denis Smith far post equaliser then had our work cut out to try and progress in the second leg.

Brian had just been sacked by Leeds and had been invited out to the second leg tie by our manager Tony Waddington. Anyway, during the second half of the game I was subbed and wasn't very happy about it.

As the manager took me off, I let him know exactly what I thought about the decision. It was one of those heat of the moment things when your thought processes are blurred by the intensity of the occasion but I ended up pushing him and giving him a mouthful.

So, after the game, it was fair to say the gaffer wasn't very happy with me and I ended up speaking to our skipper Jimmy Greenhoff for a bit of advice on how best to try and repair the damage.

'I was a bit out of order there,' I admitted to Jimmy seeking advice on how best to handle the situation. Jimmy said that there was a big reception on and I would be best advised to seek the gaffer out, be a man about it and offer my apologies.

So I went into the reception and managed to spy the gaffer. I got up close to him and said 'Boss, can I have a word please?' As he came towards me, a figure stepped into centre stage from, seemingly, out of nowhere.

'Hey, young man, don't you fucking dare say sorry!'

'What? I'm just going to apologise to the gaffer . . .'

'Don't you get saying sorry,' Clough went on.

I must have looked totally perplexed and I dare say the gaffer might have been struggling for words too.

'I loved it when you did that. Listen, in a very short space of time I will get another club and you will be my first signing.'

The rest is history. Cloughie got the Nottingham Forest job and guess what? I became his first signing!

Things didn't actually work out for me at Forest. I badly twisted my ankle early on against Bristol City. Cloughie started screaming at me to get up. I wasn't used to that at all. He didn't like injured players. Considering he had his career cut short by injury, I found that surprising, but maybe it was the reason. Who knows? Anyway, the injury turned out to be a bad one and signalled the beginning of the end of my time at Forest.

I joined Preston feeling Cloughie had washed his hands of me but got on with kick-starting my career again. We got promoted in my first season there and in the summer I went to Majorca with some of the lads. Ricky Thomson came running out of a bar saying excitedly that he'd bumped into the Forest team with Cloughie and some of the directors in a restaurant just down the road. Apparently he had asked where I was and told them to come and get me.

I thought if he slaughters me, I will have a go back. So I walked in.

'Sean, how are you mate? Here come and sit next to me. Lovely to see you. What would you like to drink?' he said

'Champagne please,' I replied.

'Waiter! A bottle of your best champagne for my mate Sean please.'

‘ He's had enough rest through suspensions. He's had more holidays than Judith Chalmers ’
— *on Roy Keane's disciplinary record*

Former Aston Villa golden boy GARY SHAW was a striker to be feared but he reveals that the Forest manager knew exactly how to make him anxious with a timely warning about the two bruisers he was about to come up against.

67

GENTLE REMINDER

GARY SHAW

I once discovered Brian Clough's psychological tricks weren't restricted to just battle-hardened old pros. I was a kid of about 19 and had just broken into the Aston Villa side when Cloughie gave me a gentle nudge – well, a full blooded slap actually!

Villa were playing at Forest and I was in the reception area at the City Ground about an hour before the kick-off sorting out a couple of complimentary tickets for my dad and his mate.

I was on Cloughie's territory and boy was I about to find out! I was sorting through the tickets so my old man and his pal wouldn't have any problems getting in, when suddenly someone gave me a really massive slap on the backside. I turned around thinking it was one of our lads, only to see none other than Cloughie with a huge grin on his face.

I must have looked shocked even though I had met him before when I was involved in the England Youth set-up that he was briefly in charge of.

'Hey, blondie. Now don't you go taking the piss out of my two centre halves today!'

It was quite a compliment really, but I couldn't help thinking that if I had temporarily put to the back of my mind today's opponents, he was giving me a sharp nudge.

Forest's two centre halves were none other than Larry Lloyd and Kenny Burns. Big Larry was a man mountain, built like the proverbial brick outhouse. He wasn't the quickest but he left the odd one he missed for the ferocious Burns to deal with. Kenny had no teeth and a menacing stare which could send a chill down your back.

I wasn't short on confidence but I couldn't imagine for one minute taking the pee out of that pair. It had scared me to death just turning around and seeing Cloughie without being reminded that those two were waiting for me. I'm sure he was well aware of that . . .

‘ If the directors don't like what I do, they can sack me and get someone else ’

113

Former Southampton and England star MICK CHANNON rubbed Cloughie up the wrong way when they appeared as TV analysts together. Clough decided that a favourite Frank Sinatra song best summed up his feelings.

68

HORSEPLAY

MICK CHANNON

Brian Clough! What a nice man he was. I remember being so impressed when I first met him away from football. We spent a summer together at ITV doing the Mexico World Cup. He was a lovely man until they turned the cameras on and then BANG! He became a completely altered character. He would look down his nose at me and call me 'Young Man' and tell me I knew nothing about football!

* * *

The Southampton and Manchester City striker with the famous 'windmill' goal celebration, turned his back on football to pursue a career on the turf where he became a hugely successful racehorse trainer. You can't help wondering if the defining moment in that career switch came when he was a World Cup panelist alongside Cloughie back in 1986.

At half-time of France's opening game of the tournament, the French had failed to break down Canada's resolute defence. Channon launched into Michel Platini.' He's hardly broken sweat,' thundered Channon. 'He hasn't run a yard!'

'The great ones don't need to,' Clough said with a characteristic jab of the finger.

Now Channon is in a business where the great ones definitely need to turn in a burst of speed. Enter the words of Cole Porter . . .

England were struggling against Morocco and when Channon began ranting about how England lacked any players who could 'get by' people, Clough decided to call on a few lines from one of his favourite Sinatra songs 'Let's Do It' to stop the irritation. Channon blazed: "The Italians do it, the French do it, the West Germans do it . . .'

Just off camera and with piercing delivery, the unmistakeable Clough voice could be heard.

"Even educated fleas do it . . .'

' Fear of relegation can dominate your life. In my case at Forest, it consumed me '

Cleaning players' boots was all part of the apprenticeship when you were a youngster at Forest. CHRIS REID reveals how a bit of spit 'n' polish plus gardening duties at the manager's house was all part of the learning process.

69

BOOT CAMP

CHRIS REID

I cleaned the boots of one of Forest's greatest ever players – some would say the greatest – and even he never knew which way Cloughie would blow. So as a humble apprentice, what chance had I got?

John Robertson's boots were my responsibility and even if the boss did slaughter him for virtually everything else he wore, I always made sure his boots were immaculate. That was my job and I made sure they were spotless. In fairness to Robbo, I must say he was a great tipper.

Brian Clough would slaughter Robbo, even though everyone knew he loved him. He was a fantastic player who was instrumental in the two European Cup wins but had a reputation for not being the snappiest dresser. Cloughie would rib him at any given opportunity, calling him a tramp or having a go because he was puffing away on a cigarette.

He would deliberately tear into Robbo and make an example of him, then the next thing he was telling everyone he was the best. That was one of the beauties of Cloughie – you just never knew what was coming.

Apprentices these days don't even clean the first team players' boots and I think that's a terrible thing. It instills discipline and gives you a target to aim for – the day when YOUR boots are cleaned by one of the kids.

It sounds really old-fashioned now in these politically correct times, but if Cloughie had clipped me around the ear I wouldn't have gone home squealing to my dad about it. Mainly because the first thing my dad would have asked was: 'Well, what did you do?'

I remember one day turning up to train and in his unmistakeable manner, he pointed to me and a couple of the other lads and said 'You little lot are coming with me.'

We ended up at his house and he dished out tools – hedge trimmers, rakes and things like that.

'We are cutting this hedge and tidying up the garden today,' he'd say matter-of-factly. And he could do that, because what he said went.

Come lunchtime he marched us down the road to his local pub the Joiners Arms and would bark at the landlord, tongue-in-cheek:

'Don't get serving them beer!'

The whole thing about doing mundane duties was a double-edged thing for him. One, it made sure no one became a prima donna or got carried away with himself. And, two . . . it ensured he always had a gang of 'unpaid' helpers to keep his lovely garden maintained.

I think in a way as well, he wanted you to see the kind of spoils that were there to be had if you had a successful career. He wasn't showing off, just illustrating that if you buckled down you might end up with a nice house and lovely family that he clearly derived so much pleasure from.

It was always mind games with him. I recall once losing 8-1 against Manchester City in the FA Youth Cup. He came into the dressing room and absolutely laid into us.

The next day we were expecting a heavy training session but instead he just took us all on a stroll along the banks of the Trent and every so often stopped to tell us what a shower of s*** we were!

❛ I'm not sure who Fergie regards as his best ever signing at Old Trafford but there can't have been one better than Roy Keane ❜

In his darkest hours after getting the chop at Leeds, Clough still had time to seek out showman DUNCAN McKENZIE and issue him with a piece of advice which came straight from the heart.

70

DON'T CHANGE

DUNCAN McKENZIE

Even when he had just got the sack, Cloughie took time to implore me to carry on doing the things I did best. Getting the boot at Leeds after just 44 days was massive news back in 1974 and the passage of time has only seemed to make it a focal point of that whole period.

There's been a book, a film and endless hours of discussions in bars all across the land about that fascinating moment in time.

My slight problem back then was not only that I was living right in the middle of it, but the man controversially being shunted through the Elland Road exit door was the man who had just signed me!

But, for me, it speaks volumes of the man that even in what was at the time his darkest hour, he took time to have a word with me on one side.

I was only at Leeds under Cloughie for a few weeks before he got the bullet. But when the end came, he came up to me and said: 'Young man, keep up those flicks, nutmegs and back-heels. Never change!'

To hear someone like him say what he did make me feel great. Here was this guy who was a born winner and one of the best managers this country has ever produced saying such complimentary things.

Not that I escaped the sharp end of his tongue on occasions – but for the right reasons.

I always remember he used to shout at me: 'What are you doing in our half? You're no good to me there. You're a liability. Get back up there where you can score goals.'

❛ Benfica had no chance at our place, absolutely no chance – especially after I arranged for half the River Derwent to be piped onto the pitch the night before! ❜

Former Manchester United, Leeds and Scotland star GORDON STRACHAN recounts how he was in for a surprise visit and a shock request when Cloughie came into the away side's dressing room to celebrate his birthday.

71

SNAP HAPPY

GORDON STRACHAN

I watched all the stuff on Brian Clough that came out at the same time as the film The Damned United. Now, that man was a character.

Leeds were playing Forest at the end of one season – second last game of the year I think - and Howard Wilkinson was in the middle of his team talk.

Suddenly 'BOOM!' the door breaks open and Clough is there with a photographer saying 'It's my birthday and I want my picture taken with you young man!' He was pointing at me. I looked across at Howard and he nodded so I said 'Aye, no bother.'

We got the picture taken, he gave me a big kiss and that was it – he walked out again and said 'Boys, enjoy the game.'

Why did he do it? Because it was his birthday. Why me? No idea, I was the only one of his age, maybe.

Cloughie had some straightforward advice for Strachan during his time in the managerial hotseat at Coventry City. 'Gordon should calm down and take no notice of the TV boys. He should trust his own judgement and, most importantly, keep playing golf with his chairman. That might be his shrewdest move of all!'

Strachan admits to being an unashamed admirer of Clough's abrasive style and the flame-haired Scot's often prickly relationship with reporters who asked what he considered to be stupid questions, often met with a response that could have been straight from the great man himself. One exchange went thus:

'This might sound like a daft question Gordon, but you will be happy to get your first win under your belt won't you?'

'You're right – it is a daft question. You are spot on. So much so that I'm not even going to bother answering it."

> **❛ I'm sure people used to wonder: How on earth does his wife live with that? I can tell you how she did it – brilliantly ❜**

Former Scotland star ALAN McINALLY reveals how he was given some well-intentioned injury advice from the concerned Forest boss - the only slight problem was he was on the opposite side playing for Aston Villa at the time.

72

A BIT OF ADV-ICE

ALAN McINALLY

Cloughie once helped me out with an injury. There's nothing too unusual about that you would think, except for the fact that I happened to be playing for the opposition at the time.

I was playing for Aston Villa in a home match against the great man's Nottingham Forest team. Graham Taylor was the Villa manager at that time.

I remember it well. I had just gone off on a really long run and finished it off with a left foot shot which flew just wide of the post. But I felt a sharp pain in my groin. I thought I would be okay and be able to run it off, so I carried on playing. But it quickly became apparent that I wasn't going to be able to shake it off so easily and that I was going to have to be subbed or risk causing much worse damage.

The dug-outs at Villa Park were the old type where they are kind of dug into the ground, making it tricky to get in and out of. Because they are so tight, people have to move out to make space for you and then move back in.

I motioned over to the Villa bench that I was struggling and needed to come off. I was literally coming off the pitch to carefully make my way into the dug-out. Suddenly I heard a distinctive voice from the other side where the opposition dug-outs were.

'Hey, don't you sit in there young man. Get yourself into the dressing room and go and get some ice on that!

I genuinely didn't know what to say. I looked at my gaffer who was looking at me as if to say 'get in here.'

Cloughie caught my attention again and seemed determined to give me the benefit of his advice. Let me make one thing clear - he certainly wasn't being smart with Graham who he had a lot of time for. For whatever reason he had my best interests at heart and decided he knew precisely the right course of treatment.

He repeated himself. 'Don't be sitting in the cold in that dug-out when you are injured. Get yourself into that dressing room and get some ice on it.'

So, I looked at Cloughie, looked at the gaffer and then glanced at our physio Jim Walker, who knew Cloughie very well, seeking any kind of pointer.

But Cloughie was such a legend, I

decided to take his advice and made my way back to the dressing room to get some ice on it.

I thought it was nice that although I wasn't his player, he was genuinely concerned that I got it looked after properly. If he'd told me to go and run around the car park, I would probably have done it. That's just the way you were in his presence.

I might have been a big, bustling striker, but I was like a little schoolboy the day he gave me his own special bit of advice.

❛ When I'm gone I want to be remembered as somebody who contributed good things to that great English game of ours ❜

Former News of the World journalist DAVE HARRISON was close to Clough in the later years and was ghost-writer for his columns. Here he reveals how he had to step in when the manager bestowed the OBE on his young son.

73

GONG CRAZY

DAVE HARRISON

Cloughie loved kids and would always make a fuss. Invariably when I met him he'd ask how my missus was, ask about my son Daniel and chastise me for never bringing them to see him. One day I took them along and Cloughie turned on the charm as only he could.

My son Daniel was around seven or eight at the time and Brian was talking away to him like he'd known him for years.

'Do you know what an OBE is?' he asked. Daniel shook his head.

'It's something The Queen gives you when you are particularly good at anything. She gave me one for being a football manager – which I was quite good at you know!'

Daniel looked intrigued and Cloughie told him to hang on – he was going to go and get it. Brian returned with his gong and handed it to my son.

'It stands for Old Big 'Ead,' he continued. 'You can take this if you like and show it to all your friends at school.'

'He can't do that,' I interjected, worried that my scatter-brained youngster would accidentally leave Clough's prized OBE somewhere and it would be lost for ever.

'Hey, it's okay,' Cloughie insisted.

'No, honestly. It's very good of you to show it him and I'm sure he'll never forget it, but you keep it safe here,' I insisted.

It was just typical of the man. I've never met anyone quite like him, before or since.

He thought like a journalist and never, ever failed to come up with something of interest. I've spent hours in some people's company and gone away puzzled as to what the line to the story might be.

With Cloughie, you had the opposite problem. You might only have been lucky enough to have a few minutes with him, but invariably you went away wondering what the BEST line was. There was so much . . .

❛ **The secret of management is character – and I've got it** ❜

121

Award-winning sports writer JAMES LAWTON admits he's still baffled to this day on just what prompted Cloughie to start dishing out an unusual offering as he prepared to go in for a meeting with the Football Association.

74

APRICOT FOOL

JAMES LAWTON

I collided with Clough on relatively few occasions. I use that word deliberately because rarely did you simply just meet him. Bizarre, unpredictable behaviour was never far away when you were anywhere remotely near the man.

I recall covering a disciplinary hearing at the Football Association headquarters. Clough had been hauled up to answer some charge or other and I was among a group of reporters hanging around outside to cover the story. Waiting outside, no matter what the weather is an occupational hazard to a sports writer. But I remember this particular day because it was freezing cold with a biting wind that chilled you to the marrow.

Clough appeared briefly and we rushed forward to ask him if there was any chance of a quick word.

'Hey, you'll all have to wait, like me!' came the reply.

We were all shivering, fed-up and eager to get the required ingredients for the story and retire to somewhere less inhospitable.

Eventually he went into the boot of his Mercedes and emerged with a tray of apricots which he duly started to hand around to the pack of hacks. I declined if only because I couldn't think of anything less which would satisfy me on a bitingly cold day than an apricot!

I just couldn't help thinking what an eccentric show of behaviour it was. I was surprised how players played for him. That they did – and astonishingly well – was a mystery to me. Perhaps it shouldn't have been. It struck me that he dominated people mentally.

I once asked Archie Gemmill what it was about playing for Clough and he said he didn't know but it wasn't affection. Archie said he just seemed to have some God-given knack for bringing the best out of you. It took a tray of apricots to make me see just how that might be the case.

❛ Shilton was a class act – and class acts don't come cheap ❜

122

Former Coventry and Wimbledon boss BOBBY GOULD was desperately seeking advice when he took up his first managerial job, but here he reveals how getting hold of Cloughie wasn't quite as easy as he had imagined.

75

85th TIME LUCKY

BOBBY GOULD

So much of what Brian said might have sounded so simple but when you took a closer look, it just smacked of good old-fashioned common sense. He was vociferous in his criticism of those who tried to over-complicate things with what he considered mumbo-jumbo. He had no time for the men with clipboards who concentrated more on tactics than what he considered to be the most important thing – the players.

When I took my first management job at Bristol Rovers, I decided to seek out his advice and see if he would be kind enough to pass on some advice of how to go about things.

Desperate to learn everything I could about my new profession, I decided to ring five top mangers and ask them if they would be kind enough to each give me the benefit of one piece of advice.

It made perfect sense to me. I might have enjoyed a long playing career, but here I was in my mid-30s about to dip my toes in the shark-infested waters of football management. It was time to learn – and learn fast.

I decided to ring Ron Saunders, Bob Paisley, John Lyall, Lawrie McMenemy and Cloughie.

In actual fact, things so nearly didn't get that far. My reign at Rovers was so nearly one of the shortest in football history when I found myself in a situation that wise old owl Cloughie wouldn't have found himself in.

I threatened to quit within 48 hours when I discovered most of the players were on more money than me. Previous boss Terry Cooper had persuaded the directors to push the boat out and had been able to offer his signings decent money. Some of the lads were on £400 a week and I had shaken on £250!

I didn't think the club had given me the full picture and I wasn't going to settle for less than what I considered was fair. I rang the financial director Martin Flook at midnight and told him the board would have my resignation letter the following morning. It was soon sorted with a pay-rise for me in double-quick time and from that point on our working relationship was good.

I was so thrilled to be in control and puffed my chest out each time I sat at my desk at the start of the day. As well as my office at Eastville, I had one at the training ground at Hambrook three miles away and soon put the telephones in both of them to good use.

Ron Saunders told me discipline in the camp was important and said not to be soft on anyone. Bob Paisley urged me to choose a system, hang my hat on it and not let anyone talk me into anything else.

John Lyall insisted it was vital the players enjoyed their training and always looked forward to going back in the next day, but my brain still had the capacity for another couple of nuggets of information . . . dial M for McMenemy and M for Master.

Lawrie reckoned I should keep the Press room cabinet well stocked with Scotch – five bottles before the game, five at half-time and ten at the end – 'so the bastards won't know what they are writing!'

Then I took a deep breath and flicked through my book for a number for Nottingham Forest. I asked the girl on the switchboard if she could put me through to Brian Clough.

Eighty-four calls later – I know exactly how many I made because our telephonist had to log them all – success!

'Brian,' I stammered somewhat nervously.

'It's Bobby Gould at Bristol Rovers. I'm a young manager and wondered whether there was one piece of advice you could offer me, please, as I start my career.

'Young man, I'll give you two tips. The first is to call me Mr Clough. The second is to make sure you get your backroom staff right.' Then the phone went down. But what he said proved to be right. It took me seven years to build my coaching team to my satisfaction – and I won the FA Cup to prove it.

If I was somewhat taken aback by Brian's abruptness – and I was – there was more to come. I rang the same number at the City Ground on behalf of Martin Flook who was looking for help with one of his charities.

The conversation quickly swung to the possibility of a lucrative friendly at Eastville and Cloughie's demands were the most bizarre I've ever heard! And they were nothing to do with money.

'I'll bring a full first team down to play your lot as long as your physio will massage my feet,' he said.

Roy Dolling, a diamond of a bloke, was a bit nervous about his task and on the night of the match we kept sticking our heads around the door to make sure his toe-tweaking was just right by the master.

> # 6 Stan Bowles liked flying even less than I did and was even known to disappear at the prospect 9

Former Derby defender RON WEBSTER was in the dressing room when Clough served up his very first team meeting at the Baseball Ground. Even then the young manager showed that if there was one thing he was short of it wasn't confidence.

76

SOMBRERO TIME

RON WEBSTER

Brian Clough's very first team talk at Derby was quite incredible and I can remember it to this day.

What you have to bear in mind is that standing there in front of some pretty seasoned pros was a fresh-faced young man whose only managerial experience was with Hartlepool.

His self-assured confidence of what he wanted to do really could have backfired spectacularly.

He was quite blunt, saying something to the effect of 'If any single one of you doesn't want promotion then come and see me and you can go.'

He said a few things along those lines setting out what he intended to do – and looking back, everything he said seemed to come true. It was quite amazing really.

Even at half-time in matches he would say things that just seemed to come off. It's no wonder we started to believe he had the Midas touch.

He certainly got everyone's attention and it just snowballed. Everyone started to go out and think they were world-beaters.

I have never met a more charismatic man and never will. From the first minute I set eyes on him it was clear that here was someone completely different. I suppose it could have all gone wrong and he'd have been dismissed as someone with a big mouth who couldn't back it all up. But he was far more than that.

The thing was, he didn't speak tactics as such. He was just direct on what he wanted you to do. If you didn't do something, he would just keep on at you until you did. And if you didn't pick it up then he'd go out and get someone else who would do it.

Where he excelled was that he could spot a player he thought could do a specific job for him. Signings he made, came off and suddenly a club that was doing nothing rose to the top.

He managed to get us playing entertaining football on a Baseball Ground pitch that was an absolute mud heap for most of the season. He had even been known to water it! The pitch wasn't fit half the time – only the wings where Alan Hinton played. The rest was like a swamp. But people shouldn't be kidded by that because you only have to look at how many games we won away from home to see that we could play.

Brian pulled off some extraordinary feats and made them look simple. It was like he invented some of the things that are now just taken as part and parcel of the modern game.

But who could have known when he flung the dressing room door open for the first time that we would go on to become champions.

It was May, 1972 when I enjoyed my finest hour under Brian and, typically, he wasn't even there! He had gone with his family to the Scilly Isles while Peter Taylor had taken the Derby team out to Spain. We had just completed a fiercely competitive season which had seen us in the title shake-up. When we flew out to the sunshine we didn't know that we would be crowned champions there. We'd finished our season and needed results to go for us to become champions. But Liverpool drew 0-0 with Arsenal and Don Revie's Leeds United side had gone down 2-1 at Wolves against all the odds to leave us as champs.

At the risk of making it sound like the dark ages, this was very much pre-Sky TV, mobile phones or personal computers so, if I remember correctly, a phone call was made to the hotel to tell us we were champions!

The Press were out there in anticipation and the photographers had obviously gone to the nearest available shop and chipped in together for a load of massive sombreros for us all to wear. We were jumping in and out of the swimming pool at the hotel and generally having a good time.

It was incredible to think we were champions – and the man who had masterminded it all wasn't there with us as we took in exactly what we had done. I don't know why we were so surprised with such an incredible manager in charge.

When I look back on it, it was like he saw a massive jigsaw jigsaw in front of him and he was on a mission to get all the parts to fit.

❛ I fined John Robertson just hours after winning the European Cup. You don't bend the rules – not even for heroes ❜

Former Liverpool and England legend JOHN BARNES recounts the tale of when a rogue headline in a tabloid newspaper proved to be the last thing Cloughie needed as he prepared his Forest youngsters for a crucial FA Cup clash.

77

BARNES ON TOAST

JOHN BARNES

I remember once being caught up in a bit of a fuss with Brian Clough who had, quite rightly, got upset over a rather unfortunate headline which appeared in a national newspaper.

In fairness, I must say that he was always very respectful to me whenever our paths crossed.

To get things straight – the offending headline which caused all the aggravation was not of his making or of the player who found himself caught up in it all. It was a very young and inexperienced Steve Chettle who probably found himself on the sharp end of Cloughie's tongue just prior to their meeting with Liverpool in the FA Cup semi-final.

It was a shame for the lad really because the newspaper story that appeared that day put undue pressure on him and Forest through no fault of his own.

What happened basically was that prior to the game, the paper had done an interview with Chettle in which he'd been asked what his favourite pre-match meal was. He'd said that he usually had beans on toast.

A headline writer clearly saw an opportunity not to be missed and landed the poor kid in hot water.

On the morning of the game, the interview appeared with a big headline on it 'I'll have Barnes on toast!'

Imagine Cloughie's face! I was in the form of my life at the time and he probably blew a gasket knowing that if I hadn't seen the article myself, someone was sure to point it out to me!

Anyway, I had a really good game that day and we ended up beating Forest 2-1 to book our place in the final.

At the end, Cloughie hid his obvious disappointment and congratulated me on my performance.

He smiled and said 'well played,' but he had that kind of knowing look on his face. He didn't need to say any more. We both knew what had happened, but it was still nice of him to acknowledge me that way when he obviously would have been bitterly disappointed.

* * *

Chettle reveals all these years later that, infact, he wasn't torn off a strip by Clough but that he still gets frequent reminders about the article.

'He didn't say a thing – I don't think he had to. The thing about it all was that I actually hadn't said anything derogatory, nor would I have done. I read the piece in the paper and the actual words were fine. It was just that I didn't realise at the time that sometimes papers can take journalistic licence to the very extreme and I ended up copping it.

The article itself was fine and was a fair reflection on everything I had said. It was just the 'I'll have Barnes on toast' headline that didn't do anyone any favours.

The squad all went for a walk around Sheffield on the morning of the match and there loads of Liverpool supporters' coaches going past us with their fans holding up the paper to the windows. I wasn't going to be allowed to forget it that easily and. Like I said, sometimes it still crops up now.

6 When I was admitted to the heart unit somebody sent me a get well message that said they didn't even know that I had one 9

So just what could it have been that upset BOB WILSON so much?
The former Arsenal keeper reveals the reason why he lost
his temper so badly that he had to be held back from
throwing a punch at the mischievous Forest boss.

78

ARGY BARGY

BOB WILSON

Brian was the master of the wind-up and on one such occasion it led to me wanting to thump him. Some people might find it hard to believe that someone as seemingly mild-mannered as me could suddenly lose it, but I was ready to clock Cloughie and had to be held back.

When I go, I really go. If what he did in front of 63,000 people at Highbury was intended to get under my skin, then it certainly worked. The red mist came down and I had to be physically restrained by my Arsenal team mates from getting to Cloughie and whacking him.

It was 1972 and we were playing Clough's Derby side in an FA Cup Fifth Round replay. We had drawn 2-2 at the Baseball Ground and things were proving equally as tight in the second game with the score at 0-0 after 90 minutes. The extra-time team talks took place on the pitch and then the referee signalled for the coaches to leave the playing area as the team prepared to kick-off.

I knew Brian reasonably well by this time because we had been working together at the BBC for a couple of years. But I couldn't have anticipated what was about to come next. Brian walked straight into our Arsenal team group and deliberately barged me over. I went flying and as I clambered to my feet, our lads had all on to hold me back from showing him exactly what I thought of that.

It was his way of rattling me, trying to get me to lose my temper and focus. I expect he walked away with a little grin on his face.

But I have to say that for all the times I have clashed with him – and there have been a number – I look back on our relationship with much fondness. Brian was compulsive. You get people who the minute they walk into a room, just light it up. There is a real presence there and he certainly had that. His presence came via his mouth. When he opened it, you just listened. Even if he was wrong, you felt he was right purely because of the manner in which he spoke.

I sometimes rubbed him up the wrong way because I dared to argue with him. He didn't like it when an upstart like me, particularly a 'posh' one as he perceived it, challenged his views.

You took your life in your hands if you challenged Brian's beliefs too strongly. You certainly jeopardised your chances of getting an interview with him that was for sure. It could be dangerous to argue with him because all thoughts of an interview would go flying out of the window until he thought you could see his point of view.

I had gone up to do a piece with him and when I caught up with him he remarked: 'Bet you couldn't get around the roundabout because of the striking miners?'

I dared to point out to him that an equal amount of them making their feelings known that they wanted to work.

Brian went absolutely ballistic. What a bad move! Fifteen minutes later I was still getting it both barrels as he launched into scathing attacks on Prime Minister Margaret Thatcher and her government.

But for all his prickliness and rudeness at times, I have found him warm, generous and captivating too.

I was once at a Frank Sinatra concert in London when I bumped into him and he couldn't resist putting one over me again.

'Young man. I saw you earlier standing up at the back there – I'm on the front row!'

Well, he would be wouldn't he? And I think I'm probably right in saying that his hero Sinatra was quite possibly the only person he was in awe of.

❛ My Barbara made it crystal clear that she wanted no part of some of the antics that put my name in the headlines ❜

National newspaper journalist RONALD ATKIN became a friend of the man who called himself Old Big 'Ead. But where did that name actually originate? Here, for the first time, it can be revealed the exact origins of one of the most famous nicknames in sport.

79

HEAD START

RONALD ATKIN

Everyone knows the 'Big 'Ead' nickname that Brian cherished so much, but very few know its exact origins. All is about to be revealed and the credit, somewhat strangely, goes to former QPR chairman Jim Gregory.

It was December 1979, and I had been sent to Nottingham to interview Forest's latest, rather unusual, signing Stan Bowles from Queen's Park Rangers. I was working for The Observer at the time and certainly didn't need prompting to ask the colourful Bowles the intriguing reasoning behind linking up with Clough.

'So, Stan, why Forest?'

'Well, I got this call from Gregory telling me a top club had come in for me,' Bowles said.

'Who is it, Tottenham?' he continued.

'No. it's Big 'Ead and his mate,' Gregory revealed.

Bowles and his betting shop ways did not last the distance at Forest, but the nickname endured, right up to the last days of Clough's life.

Brian thought it was a magnificent moniker and was so chuffed that next time the team went out to Majorca, he

and Peter Taylor were photographed wearing huge, outrageous sombreros. Clough's was labelled 'Big 'Ead' while Taylor's had 'His Mate' around the hatband.

How sad that such a strong friendship should break down so badly. The early signs that all was not well can definitely be traced back to a book launch I attended.

Taylor had written a book called 'With Clough, by Taylor' and the rumours circulating were that his partner was far from happy about it. Clough, whose face and name featured prominently on the jacket, did not turn up for the launch.

The word, according to the Sunday newspaper which serialised the book, was that the two of them were at each other's throats – a possibility which naturally intrigued all the journalists present at the reception.

Taylor, a large, affable silver haired ex-goalkeeper, was forced to admit when pressed that his pal was annoyed because he had not known in advance about the book, but briskly denied any talk of a feud.

When in Clough's company, he was

very sarcastic about the Taylor book. He felt it traded on his name too much and that its major selling feature was the fact that it was about HIM, not Taylor. He was also annoyed about the apparent secrecy of it all.

Two hours later, they flew off side by side in their usual front seats for a European Cup match in Sofia soon.

Over dinner that night Taylor reiterated the firmness of the partnership but pointed out that their winning ways could well end up being the reason why such a star could only shine brightly for so long.

'There is no way we will go our separate ways, ever. But if our success continues at the same rate, our careers as managers will be shorter than if we were just middle of the road.'

Taylor's assurances were well meant and, no doubt, from the heart, but to those present, we couldn't help wondering whether we had just seen the first cracks appearing in football's most famous double act.

❛ When he sat in his office and told me he wanted to get out of the game, I cried ❜
– on Peter Taylor's decision to quit

How can you go into contract talks and come out having been ordered to strip off? Forest's STEVE CHETTLE remembers the day he went in asking for a rise and came out wondering exactly where it had all gone so badly wrong.

80

TORN OFF A STRIP

STEVE CHETTLE

Signing for Forest was a dream come true for me, a local lad who had watched them starry-eyed from the Trent End perched on my dad's shoulders.

I actually started out as a 12-year-old on the other side of the river at Notts County and was thrilled when Alan Hill took me over to Forest to meet the great Brian Clough. I owe him so much in every respect even though he did scare me to death at times and gave me one or two sharp lessons along the way.

Things that he instilled in me as a young boy have stuck with me to this very day. He drilled respect and manners into me. He made me stand up to shake hands with him and that's something that has remained with me. When I meet anybody, I always stand up and shake their hand – it's a habit.

But the one thing that is still so vivid in my mind is the day I went in for my first contract negotiations with him and ended up coming out of his office in virtually just my socks and pants!

I was just 17 and just coming out of my apprenticeship when my contract talks took an unusual and somewhat unexpected twist. Myself and Phil Starbuck, a young lad who was scoring goals for fun in the youth team, were due to go away on a pre-season tour of Holland when the gaffer called us in individually to lay out exactly what was on offer.

'I'm going to offer you a contract. I'm going to offer you this much etc, etc and you've got two minutes to think about it,' he said.

Phil and myself had a brief chat outside and he said that seeing as how the money wasn't a big step up from what we were on already, we should perhaps go in and ask for a bit more. Fair enough. I went in first . . .

'With respect gaffer, we were really looking for a few pounds more,' I said boldly.

'Oh, really?' he said, clearly taken aback.

'Right, take your tracksuit top off then,' he said.

'What?'

'Your tracksuit. Give it here. And the bottoms. You won't be going anywhere,' he informed me.

I left his office unrecognisable from

how I'd gone in, The sight of me in my socks, pants and a t-shirt clearly indicated to Phil that my talks had not gone according to plan. No rise and no trip to Holland, just for good measure.

Phil went in and signed his. He went away with the lads, while I stayed at home!

It was a shattering blow but one which seemed to stand me in good stead eventually. I came back after pre-season and was told the gaffer wanted to see me. He offered me improved terms and I think I was also the first player he ever offered a five-year deal.

Whether he had been testing me or not, I'm not sure, but he seemed to kind of respect that I had stood up to him a bit. It took a dressing down, quite literally, to get it, but it was the start of a fantastic career at the club.

' Have you put it through the bomb squad? I'm not that popular you know '
– on being presented with a crystal rose bowl

No one liked getting the Spanish sun on his back more than Cloughie but as former Derby and Forest star ALAN HINTON can vouch, the threat of being told that a trip to Majorca was in danger of being cancelled was never too far away.

81

MAJORCA THREAT

ALAN HINTON

It's fair to say Cloughie subjected us all to the Spanish inquisition if our form showed signs of dipping. When it came to getting plenty of rest into players, the gaffer was something of an innovator.

Afternoons off were plentiful and he would say 'You boys will appreciate all this time off around March when we will be the freshest team in the country by a mile!'

He would whisk us off to Majorca mid-season to get some sun on our backs and dip our toes in the water. Cloughie felt a few days in Cala Millor, his favourite haunt, was just the tonic for tired legs and minds.

But he used the Majorcan sunshine as a stick to beat us with too. If we were having a bad time about February or March time he'd warn: 'Hey lads, that trip to Majorca is in danger.'

He knew how to play the game and knew that kind of warning was favourite to get the desired reaction.

'How can I go to the board of directors and ask them for all that money to take you boys away for a good time, if you aren't winning?' he'd say.

All of a sudden we'd go on a run. The senior players would see to that, making sure we all pulled our fingers out and got our minds back on the job in hand. And there it was, for all to see - Cloughie's man-management at its best again.

❛ **The good thing about the rule changes is that players who were once scared to death, go out like King Kong, running about all over the place thinking no bugger can kick them now and that's no bad thing** ❜

Close friend HAROLD ROOME will always remember the look on the faces of the customers at his local pub when he waltzed in proudly carring the league championship trophy that had just been won by Clough's Derby side.

82

TROPHY TALE

HAROLD ROOME

When my late wife June, my son Kevin and I lived at Darley Abbey we used to frequent The Talbot pub at Belper, where the landlord was a chap called Dan Rogers.

Anyway, the three of us set out one Saturday night to go to the pub but first off, had to call in at our dear friend Brian Clough's house.

Brian took us into the kitchen and when we got in there the table was absolutely covered with all the trophies won by Derby County. And there in pride of place was the First Division Championship Trophy with the winning ribbons still on it. What happened next is like something out of a film.

'Where are you off to did you say?' Brian enquired.

'We're just going up for a drink at The Talbot,' I replied.

'Do you get any of our supporters in there?' he asked.

'Yes, plenty.'

'Season ticket holders?'

'Yes, quite a few,' I replied.

'Would you like to take this cup up to show them?' he asked.

'You're kidding aren't you?'

'No.'

'You've got to be having us on.'

'Absolutely not,' he said, turning to my son Kevin.

'Son, you take the cup and your dad can take the base. But hey, I want it back here safe and sound by 10.30 or you'll be for the high jump.'

And so, no more to do, we got into the car and made our way to the pub proud custodians of one of the most famous pieces of footballing silverware around.

The pub was absolutely packed and no one could quite believe it when we just walked in with the trophy. You should have seen their faces. Only Brian could have thought of that one.

Just to convince ourselves as much as anything that it hadn't all been a dream, we had a picture taken of the family with the trophy.

Since that day we have been brief guardians of every single trophy won during Brian's glory years at Nottingham Forest too – and that includes the European Cup which we had for three days.

I took that one to show my workmates at the Railway Centre at Derby.

By mid-afternoon, word had got around that the European Cup was about and people were coming from all over the place to see it. That night we took it to my mate's pub at Melbourne and when we got home at midnight, my children Kevin and Julie were waiting to take it to bed for safe-keeping.

How many people get such an opportunity to get so close to a cup that has been held aloft by some of the greatest players the world has ever seen?

We realised just how fortunate we had been when the wife of one of Kevin's workmates treated her Manchester United-mad husband to a surprise visit to Old Trafford. When Kevin asked him what his day had been like, he replied excitedly:

'It was fantastic. I even saw the European Cup.'

It's very hard not to make it sound like one-upmanship but, what can you say when it's the truth, hard to believe as it may be.

Kevin replied: 'I've slept with it!'

❝ Would I have been a good England manager? I happen to think I would have been brilliant ❞

Ex-Nottingham Evening Post editor BARRIE WILLIAMS had more than his fair share of run-ins with Cloughie but, as he reveals here, the Forest boss showed the caring side of his nature when he gave a disabled boy the star treatment.

83

BEAUTIFUL BOY

BARRIE WILLIAMS

Brian was the guest of honour at an event to celebrate the achievements of Nottinghamshire's disabled athletes.

As he stood in the County Hall with the assembled company of disabled sportsmen and women, their families, friends and supporters and the good and the great of the county, the door opened and a mother pushed through a wheelchair carrying her terribly disabled teenage son.

So awful and visually repulsive were this poor shrunken boy's afflictions that people, as they do in such circumstances, averted their gaze, looking down at the floor, ahead at the walls, up at the ceiling – anywhere rather than towards the wheelchair.

Not Brian Clough.

He strode with deliberately exaggerated gait over to the boy and his mother, lifted him gently out of his wheelchair and gave him a huge kiss. Then, with one arm around mum and the other holding the boy he marched them into the middle of the VIPs and ordered: 'This is a star . . . look after him.'

That night, as the editor of the Nottingham Evening Post, which organised the event, I was standing next to the great man when he presented all the awards and as one brave disabled competitor after another came forward to meet him, Brian cried – openly, unashamedly and without a hint of self-consciousness. Halfway through the ceremony he turned to me and with tears streaming down that famous face he told me: 'I get emotional when I see REAL talent.'

Then, in more accustomed Brian Clough style, he barked: 'Hey Barrie, just you bloody make sure I'm doing this again next year."

That was a side of Brian Clough, soccer legend and hard man, few people ever got to see and I'm glad I was one of the lucky ones.

❛ I've always felt that if you are going to be a manager – or anything else for that matter – you might as well be the best one there is ❜

None of the Nottingham Forest players ever doubted that the manager could wield the big stick. But as PETER DAVENPORT recalls, even they were surprised when they were summoned to a meeting where Cloughie walked in swinging the branch of a tree.

84

STICK OR CARROT

PETER DAVENPORT

Cloughie wasn't averse to the big stick treatment if he felt his players were coming up short. And when I say big stick, I mean BIG stick. We hadn't started the season particularly well and I remember it was around the time Neil Webb had just signed for the club.

The gaffer called a meeting in the club's Trophy Room and we all waited there at the specified time, knowing full well that we hadn't been summoned there to be congratulated. I think we'd been told to be there for 11am prompt which, it goes without saying, we were. But by midday, there was still no sign of the gaffer. We were just kept there waiting and waiting and if anyone did feel like abandoning the whole thing, I think they soon thought better of it.

Eventually the doors flew open and Cloughie stormed in with Ronnie Fenton his assistant and head of coaching Alan Hill. He was carrying a huge branch off a tree. This wasn't a stick – it was fully 10 feet long and quite thick.

God only knows where he'd got it from and just what he planned to do with it, but he proceeded to rip into the lot of us while pointing with the branch.

'You haven't been doing it!' he barked at one player, pointing his stick, before rounding on another.

'If you don't buck your f****** ideas up, you'll be on your way,' he went on.

'As for you, well you've been absolutely useless,' he continued, eventually going around every single player and giving them what for.

All players are different but I think it's fair to say most of us were a bit upset at this astonishing blast from the gaffer. It certainly got to me and when I got back to my digs in town, I decided to give my parents a call.

I really was quite taken aback by the whole episode and couldn't wait to unload on my parents by telling them what a horrible so-and-so Clough was.

Bear in mind that I was one of the gaffer's favourites. Normally it wouldn't be for me to say that, but I was. He would often give me extra days off so that I could spend a bit more time back at home in Merseyside. Some of the lads felt I got

139

a bit more leeway than most – and they were right.

The stick episode though had got to me. But, I was thrown completely out of my stride when the first thing my mum said was 'Oh, isn't your manager a lovely man?'

Lovely man? I could hardly believe what I was hearing. Then, all became clear.

Cloughie had sent my mum the biggest box of chocolates and a bunch of flowers and basically a message saying it was all his fault. He'd done that with every player – wives, girlfriends etc all receiving a Cloughie gift to get them onside.

All these years later, I still marvel at the psychology of all that stuff. Oh, and by the way, just in case anyone wondered . . . we ended up finishing third that year.

6 Some people liked to think it was a flash in the pan. It lasted 20 years – some flash in the pan 9

Clough built up a great relationship with Nottingham Post photographer TREVOR BARTLETT who recalls the day he was treated to a special photo opportunity when the manager voluntarily put himself behind bars to pose for a quick snap.

85

PAPILLON

TREVOR BARTLETT

Talk to any reporter who has dealt with Brian and they will tell you, to the man, that he knew exactly what they required in terms of headline-making copy. Ask any of the radio or TV lads and they will also tell you that Brian knew exactly what they required and inevitably provided them with an 'out' to finish their piece with.

Well, let me tell you, Brian was a dream to photographers as well and I should know because I've taken more pictures of him than probably anyone.

He'd just get ideas and say: 'Hey, take a picture of me doing this . . .' He was absolutely brilliant at thinking ideas up and, I've got to say, seemed to enjoy it as well.

Ill-informed people try to tell me that he had no time for the press and suchlike, but when he was in the mood he was spot-on. A lot of his good friends and people he really liked were in the business.

There were a lot he despised and many he wouldn't give the time of day, but if you got on with him he'd be great – most of the time.

Don't get me wrong, he had his moments and if he wasn't up for it, wild horses wouldn't make him do it. Could he be awkward? Just a bit! Could he be rude? Absolutely. Brian was Brian and he'd made a name for his forthright opinions and stand-points. No one would make him do anything. You had to just hope he would go along with things some-times.

He was quite mischievous really. At times he would have an almost naughty-schoolboy kind of humour. Brian was up for some daft stuff if it made a nice shot. Countless times he's come up with an idea and the office must have thought I'd done brilliantly to get him to do something, but as I said, he'd often be the instigator.

I recall him stage-managing a picture where Ron Fenton dropped a snowball on Stuart Pearce's head - one of my best ever front page pictures was entirely his idea.

Something had been going off at the club that he wasn't very happy about and one day up at the training ground, he shouted to me: 'Trev, come and take a picture of me behind this fence!'

'Why?' I said, somewhat bemused. He crouched down and got his head behind the bars of the fence.

Did you see that film Papillon on the telly last night? Well, I feel just like him,' he said.

It made an absolutely cracking picture of the one and only Brian Clough peering through metal bars as if he were a prisoner.

Another time, on a similar theme, Brian was having a mega-row with the Forest chairman Maurice Roworth over Des Walker. The chairman wanted me out of the room, but Brian typically took no notice of that whatsoever.

'Go and get yer cameras, Trev,' he insisted.

The lift in reception was one of those old-fashioned ones with a kind of criss-cross trellis door on it. Brian got behind it and got me to snap away and I still remember to this day the picture I got from that.

Some of his ideas were so bad they were brilliant! The story at the time was that he supposedly wanted to be manager of Wales and the Forest board weren't happy about it, even if it was on a part-time basis.

Brian, typically, made a right fuss of it all and the story was in every national newspaper for days as the story rumbled on as to whether he would do it or not.

Eventually, the story was breaking that the Forest board had told him to forget any notion of taking the Wales job. As the ultimate act of defiance, Brian rang me and said:

'Hey, Trev, come down to the office. We'll do a picture.'

I got down to the ground and made my way in to find Brian had already got an idea of what the shot should be.

He had this idea of a picture – him tossing his passport in the bin to show that it had been against his will. It was great and it was a fabulous snap which appeared everywhere.

The fact that you don't need a passport to get in or out of Wales just wasn't the point really . . .

❛ Football is like a golfer's swing. The more complicated you make it, the more likely it is to go wrong ❜

When rock superstar Elton John knocked Forest's dressing room door even he couldn't have bargained for the the response he got. Former Forest keeper STEVE SUTTON reveals Cloughie's classic welcome for the former Watford chairman.

86

COME IN ELTON!

STEVE SUTTON

Even genuine 24-carat rock superstars weren't spared the sharp end of Cloughie's mischievous sense of humour. The story of when Elton John came into our dressing room down at Watford one day enjoys legendary status among the players.

Elton's love of Watford Football Club is well documented and somewhere along the line the gaffer must have been told to expect a visit.

We were quite used to having celebrity visitors dropping in – the gaffer's mate Geoff Boycott popped in from time to time. But Elton John!!! I don't think any of the players would mind admitting that we were all pretty much in awe of someone as famous as that.

Not that meeting up face to face with the legendary star with millions of record sales and one of the most instantly recognisable faces on the planet was going to faze Cloughie.

The thing with the gaffer was that he had such a strong personality himself. His views and the way he delivered them had the unnerving effect of kind of overpowering you. That goes for whether he was being affectionate or scathing to someone. I have seen people totally overawed in his company. He had this thing about him. He could silence a room.

I'm sure Elton John, who seems to be a pretty good laugh himself, knows what it likes to reduce people to jelly just by his sheer presence. He had us players in his pocket but not the boss. I think the players were dumbstruck just on hearing the reply to the knock on the door.

'Who is it?'

'Elton . . . Elton John.'

'Come in young man,' urged Cloughie. The door half-opened as the Rocket Man himself popped his head around to make sure it was okay to enter.

'Come on in you fat poof!' said Cloughie welcoming Elton with a beaming grin. Pure class.

❛ My advice to other managers? Say nowt. Win something. And then talk your head off ❜

Landlord of the Joiners Arms pub, just down the road from where Cloughie lived, TREVOR MARTIN recounts a lovely story of how the manager helped come to the rescue when rain threatened to make a complete washout of a charity event.

87

RAINING CHAMP

TREVOR MARTIN

I'd known Brian for some time before I took over at the pub because I ran one of the Allestree Juniors teams and he would come and present the prizes. In actual fact, when I took over here, Brian rang me and wished me all the best but he rarely if ever came in. By that time he used to go down the Darley Abbey British Legion. I think he got more peace and quiet there and I fully understood.

But I once saw Brian come into his own and really show his magic when I organised a big fund raising event after we lost our three-year-old son Christopher to a rare illness. He suffered from a condition called Reye's Syndrome and so little was known about this at the time that we decided to try and raise some money to make people aware of exactly what it was.

So, we arranged a big fun day, gala events etc and I wrote to Brian asking him if he would open it for us. He said he would, of course, because apart from anything else he did have a wonderful affinity with children.

As it happened, we couldn't have picked a worse day. It absolutely threw it down and we had to borrow tents from the local scout troupe to make the best of things.

The rain was relentless and people were getting soaked to the skin. But the thing that sticks in my mind about that day was that Brian came down as he said he would and spent about an hour-and-a-half entertaining the kids and also went around all the stalls wishing everyone all the best and then disappeared.

About 5.30pm, completely out of the blue, he arrived back and had brought with him a commemorative plate marking Forest winning the European Cup.

He said: 'I know you have all had a horrible day, but please put this in the raffle for tonight and maybe it will earn you a few bob!'

I thought that was fantastic and spoke volumes for the man. It was a terrific gesture. He needn't have bothered to take the time and effort to do that. It just showed what a thoughtful man he could be.

Another thing I remember was that he went into the chip shop one night and the kids were playing on the fruit machine. Brian went across and said

'If you lot stop wasting your money on that thing, I'll buy you all some chips!'

That's just the kind of guy he was. He did an awful lot of good in little ways and didn't seek any credit for them. I've been in the Co-op store down the road from us when there has been an elderly lady waiting to pay for her bit of shopping and he's gently waved to the girl on the till to tell her to go on her way and that he'd pay for it. That's fantastic and I know for a fact that I'm not alone in seeing him do that type of thing.

❛ I'd love us all to play football the way Sinatra sings . . . all that richness in the sound and every word perfect ❜

Forest legend KENNY BURNS could tackle anything or anyone in his days as Forest's rugged enforcer at the back. But the Scot openly admits that when it came to trying to outfox Cloughie, he was always left thinking he'd come out second best.

88

A RISE, SIR KENNY?

KENNY BURNS

You never got one over the gaffer, but he certainly didn't mind letting you think you had! If you walked out of his office, thinking you had stolen a march on him, chances were that you had been eating out of the palm of his hand all the time.

Twice I went in to ask for a pay rise and thought I had done okay – or so I thought for at least two minutes.

The first time was after we had won the League Cup and the league championship. I had also been voted Footballer of the Year just for good measure and I thought I deserved a reward.

Knowing that BC would knock me back, I decided to ask for a higher figure of £350 a week and take it from there. I went into his office, put my slightly inflated figure to him, waited with baited breath and almost fell off the chair in surprise when he said 'OK.' I walked out of the door punching the air, until I realised that I could easily have asked for more. Shit.

The following year we won the league and the European Cup so I thought I would try my luck again. My plan was to ask for £850 and settle for £750.

I put it to him and he just said 'OK' again. No argument, nothing. I walked out very much the elated wheeler-dealer just like the first time until I realised that there was absolutely no doubt he must have just done me again!

6 **When I had to go for interviews for jobs, I was asked questions by directors who had no idea of the answers. How can you ascertain the correct answer to something when you know bugger all yourself?** 9

Legendary football commentator JOHN MOTSON reveals that when the Forest boss used to pass on his team news he wasn't averse to giving some extremely candid opinions about the players he was planning to include in his team.

89

TEAM NEWS

JOHN MOTSON

Unpredictability was his trademark. When I used to phone Clough for his team on a Friday, he would put players down like no other manager.

'Nice lad. Pity he can't play,' he once said of Viv Anderson, who went on to become the first black player to win a full England cap.

'If we're lucky we might get a performance out of him,' he said of Martin O'Neill, whose own style of management owes much to what he gleaned from working under Clough.

It was the same with the media. One day you would be invited into his office for a bottle of champagne; on another he would be uncontactable. Sometimes I would hang around in the corridor for hours having arranged to interview him. Then he would bound in waving his squash racket. 'I'm fat and forty,' he said as he challenged me to a game.

More often than not I got my information from Peter Taylor. Peter had a conspirational air on the telephone. 'I'll mark your card,' he would say at the beginning of the conversation. And he always ended it the same way.

'Don't tell Brian I told you.'

This, of course, was part of their act. It was good cop, bad cop. But it certainly worked in the dressing room and the Press room. Following Forest in Europe was now an eagerly sought-after assignment by those of us who, up to now, assumed that Liverpool would be our representatives in the European Cup.

As there was no seeding then, the two clubs met in the first round in the 1978/79 competition – Forest as league champions and Liverpool as holders. Clough's team won the first leg 2-0 at the City Ground, and I was at Anfield when the teams drew 0-0 in the return. By now Clough and Taylor had the goalkeeper they had always wanted. Peter Shilton was outstanding in the second leg and Clough was in typically bombastic mood when I interviewed him after the game.

'Perhaps now, John, people like you will realise we are a good side,' he barked.

Those of us in the media were never privileged to see quite how the partnership worked behind the scenes. Both men were stubborn and could be volatile. And there were stories of blazing rows and slammed doors. But as a professional partnership, it worked perfectly. Put simply, Clough was the motivator, Taylor the talent spotter.

Whether it was Garry Birtles, whom they picked up for next to nothing from Long Eaton, or Trevor Francis, whom they made the first million pound player, Taylor could tell at first glance if they would fit the bill. Only a few months after joining Forest from Birmingham, Francis scored the winning goal in the European Cup final against Malmo.

When they defended the trophy the following season, Forest were drawn against the East German champions. Dinamo Berlin, in the quarter-finals. Forest lost the first leg at the City Ground 1-0, and things looked ominous when we arrived in Berlin for the return. The Cold War was at its height and the hotel in the eastern sector was grim to say the least.

Taylor gave me the team and said Francis would line-up wide on the right. But, to my surprise, as soon as they kicked off he was playing up front. He scored twice; Forest won 3-1 and went through 3-2 on aggregate. On the final whistle, Sportsnight wanted an interview with Clough. John Shrewsbury, my producer, left the commentary box five minutes from the end and persuaded Brian to wait for me to get round the pitch before he went in the dressing room.

This he did, and when I had finished the interview Taylor came out of the tunnel and grabbed me. 'Sorry about that,' he whispered.

'We saw how frightened the East Germans looked when we came out of their dressing room and changed our tactics. Trevor was only told then to play up front!'

❛ My wife said to me in bed, 'God your feet are cold.' I said, 'You can call me Brian in bed dear! ❜

Wing wizard ALAN HINTON recounts the hilarious tale of when Liverpool legend Bill Shankly came into the dressing room and found himself on the receiving end of Clough's wit after missing out on a star signing.

90

SHANKS LAUGHS

ALAN HINTON

Not too many people know that Cloughie and Bill Shankly had an awful lot of time for each other. The gaffer absolutely adored the Liverpool legend and, let me tell you, Bill really liked Cloughie too. Whenever we played Liverpool, Shanks would usually make an appearance in our dressing room. But there was one occasion when I do remember Shanks getting wound up by the boss.

The background to the story was that Liverpool had just lost out to Manchester United in a race to sign midfielder Lou Macari in a £200,000 deal from Celtic. Macari was going to sign for Liverpool and it all looked done and dusted but for the intervention of United legend Paddy Crerand.

He spotted Macari in the stands watching Liverpool and reported back to Matt Busby. Macari ended up at Old Trafford much to the annoyance of Shanks. He was furious and famously declared: 'The lad couldn't play anyway. I only wanted him for the reserves!'

Anyway, this particular afternoon around that time, Cloughie called Shankly into the dressing room and then proceeded to catch him on the hop.

'Hey Bill, so tell us what you make of Man United stealing the lad Macari from right under your noses.'

'Bandits' Shanks spluttered. 'Bandits!'

I remember that as if it were yesterday because I thought bandits was such an odd word. But that was what he said.

I think the two of them were quite similar in some respects. They were both very charismatic with a great way with words.

Either of them could light up a room just by entering it. When they were anywhere, the focus of attention was on them. It is certain that we will never see their like again and feel fortunate to have seen the pair of them first hand.

❛ It becomes difficult to remain normal after the kind of life I have led ❜

Former Coventry boss DON MACKAY had close dealings with Cloughie when he sold him two of his star players. Stuart Pearce went on to become captain of England but that didn't stop the Forest manager claiming he had been sold a couple of duds.

91

PAPER TALK

DON MACKAY

I once put in a bid for one of Cloughie's players, typed out on a piece of toilet paper!

How it all started off was that Brian came to one of our reserve games at Coventry. I was in my office at half-time when he informed me that he'd really like to sign my left back.

'Micky Adams?' I said

'No, I want to buy your left back,' he said.

'But Micky . . .' I continued.

'Stuart Pearce – the one that will play for England one day,' he said.

'If he plays for you he might well do that,' I replied.

It turned out that he was really keen on getting Pearcey, but we were still in the throes of a relegation fight so to be fair to Brian, he left it alone for a while.

Eventually, he got in touch with our chairman John Poynton and said he would be interested in taking both Pearce and our central defender Ian Butterworth.

The fee was sorted between Brian and our chairman and was the best part of a million pounds. I drove them both to go and meet Cloughie and Mr Poynton instructed me to bring the cheque back with me because the club badly needed the cash.

I had tried to negotiate a deal that meant I might get a player back as part of it and asked Brian if he would throw his son Nigel in, but it came to nothing because Coventry were insisting that it was a straight cash transaction.

Anyway, the rest is history. Butterworth became an established first team player at Forest while Pearce went on to become an absolute cult figure and England star into the bargain. Brian can't have made many better signings than Pearce.

He was exactly the right man at the right time to take Stuart on. Pearcey could be a bit of a loose cannon at times and needed someone to get to grips with him. Having said that, Stuart must take an awful lot of credit himself for becoming the fantastic player he was.

But whenever our paths crossed, Brian would always grumble about the two 'shit' players I'd palmed off on him!

One day, I wanted to sign his Scottish full back Jim McInally so I got my secretary to type out a note on some toilet paper saying something to the effect of that if he ever wanted to return the two shit players I had sold him, I would be prepared to talk business.

Unbeknown to me, he kept that note in his desk and occasionally got it out to show people. I know that because his old assistant Alan Hill told me the story.

I had great admiration for Brian and can recall one day when I did get a bit of praise off him that meant quite a lot to me.

We had played Forest on Boxing Day, absolutely ran all over them and got well beaten! We must have had 18 corners to their three and yet we still ended up losing 4-0.

I studied Forest until I was sick of the sight of them and spotted just how and why they caught teams on the break so well. We played them at home about a month later and managed to hold them to a creditable 0-0 draw.

Walking in after the match, came some welcome acknowledgement from the master himself.

'I see you are learning, young man!'
Thanks Brian.

❛ It's imperative that you get players to relax because in any profession you do better when you are not afraid ❜

BBC radio commentator DARREN FLETCHER could hardly have known what he was in for when Clough insisted they should make a trip to the Derby boardroom. Defence Secretary Geoff Hoon was left thinking it wasn't such a good idea.

92

ATTACK ON DEFENCE

DARREN FLETCHER

When Brian had a point he wanted to make, there wasn't much that could stop him. His missus knew how to put him in his place but she was in a pretty exclusive club.

Reputations or titles mattered not a jot to Cloughie as I found out one day when he decided he was going to have a go at an Honourable Member of Parliament.

It was like a scene from a Western when the saloon doors swing open and in steps the man in black. The only good thing – or bad – for me was that I was standing directly next to the 'baddie.'

It was a Premier League game at Derby. Manchester United were the visitors and Brian, Gaz Birtles and myself were commentating and analysing the game. It was a bitterly cold day, I can remember that, because I was togged up from head to foot in warm gear.

I had big boots, woolly hat, scarf, big coat and jeans on. The reason what I had on becomes relevant is that immediately after the game, Cloughie decided that he was planning an impromptu visit to the Pride Park boardroom and insisted that I accompany him!

'Hey, come on son. We'll go and have a drink in the boardroom,'

I looked down at my totally unsuitable attire and the fact that I was carrying a load of heavy equipment and pointed out it might not be such a good idea.

'Brian, I'm not going to get in the boardroom with all this clobber. I've got jeans on for a start.'

'Hey, you will with me son, c'mon.'

He wasn't taking no for an answer and so off he marches with us two behind him looking quizzically at each other and shaking our heads.

The thing was, not one single person on any of the doors we went through made even the slightest motion to stop him or question what he might be doing. Can't say as I blame them to be honest, but after years covering football matches, stewards can be formidable things to try and get past. Perhaps, unsurprisingly, Cloughie didn't seem to have any such problem. It was like a hot knife going through butter. Any bloke on any given door just seemed to step aside.

So, we get to the boardroom door and by now I'm kind of trying my best to hang back a bit, uneasy that any minute now I'm going to be entering a boardroom full of people dressed the part, looking like the Yeti. Well, Cloughie has breezed through the door and, like I said, it was like a scene from a movie, where the villain enters. The entire place went deathly quiet. Total silence. By now we are in the room and all eyes are on us.

'Get yourself a drink son,' he said and so I politely and indiscreetly as I could helped myself to a glass of wine. Lionel Pickering was the owner of the club at the time and Cloughie has spotted him over the other side of the room.

'Chairman!!! We've come to see ya,' he bellowed.

'Oh, right Brian,' came the slightly anxious reply.

The Manchester United directors looked on with an air of expectancy – and they weren't to be disappointed because by now Cloughie has spotted none other than Derbyshire MP Geoff Hoon, who just also at this time happened to answer to the title of Defence Minister.

'Geoffrey!!! You owe me son,' Brian yelled.

The Right Honourable Secretary of Defence looked slightly startled and tentatively acknowledged us.

'Hey, I got you in son. I campaigned for you and you owe me!'

Mr Hoon mumbled something and must have wondered whatever was coming next. He needn't have worried.

'Come on son, we're finished here,' he said and motioned a quick about turn.

It was just bizarre. But I do know one thing for sure. He obviously felt he had a point to make – and he made it.

❝ Stuart Pearce doesn't wear pants and that's braver than his tackles. He goes horse riding for a start ❞

Respected national sports writer DAVID LACEY soon knew he had upset Cloughie when he received a telegram from the disgruntled boss letting him know exactly what he thought about a report he had written in his newspaper.

93

TELEGRAM SLAM

DAVID LACEY

I still have a less-than-complimentary telegram from Cloughie after one of my very first meetings with him . . . but more of that later.

I must say that after that rather awkward start, we got on absolutely fine. I guess he was just trying to make a point in his own inimitable way.

I didn't have to work with him on a regular basis but I would often come up from London to cover matches and went on countless European trips with him.

He could be engaging, very pleasant and highly amusing on occasions. A number of us from Fleet Street would come up from London for big matches and pile into the Midland Hotel in Derby.

He would sometimes come in after a big European match and order champagne for us. My, how times have changed. Can you honestly imagine Jose Mourinho or Sir Alex Ferguson doing that?

I always recall meeting at the airport before one foreign trip to somewhere in deepest, darkest Romania and seeing Cloughie roll up with a squash racket in his hand!

'What are you doing?' I said.

'Hey, you never know, there might be a court there!' he exclaimed.

I think most people who crossed paths with him over the years would remember him and his antics with affection. But, as I said, I hardly got off to the best of starts with him at all.

I'd been up to see him, or his team, and written an article which obviously hadn't met with his approval.

The next day, I received a telegram saying something to the effect of: 'Your newspaper has always enjoyed a reputation for a high standard of journalism, but this morning I think you fell well below that standard. Brian Clough.'

❛ I believe I have been good for football. I don't tell many lies; I'm not too big a cheat and I don't pay lip-service to influential people ❜

Former West Ham and England star SIR TREVOR BROOKING was given a warning that Cloughie had slated him in a newspaper column. He gave the perfect response with a Wembley winning goal and reveals how the manager made amends.

94

WIN DOUBLE

SIR TREVOR BROOKING

A couple of days before the 1980 FA Cup final I took a phone call from Peter Watson, the sports editor of the Daily Express. Cloughie did a column for the newspaper on a Saturday and Peter had given me a courtesy call to tip me the wink that what was to appear a couple of days later was far from complimentary to both myself and West Ham. It was nice of him to do that so I didn't get taken totally by surprise on the morning of the match.

Basically, Brian was having a go at the fact that a Second Division side like West Ham had got to the FA Cup final yet just missed out on promotion. He was saying in his own inimitable way that we would have been far better off concentrating on getting promotion.

At least when the article appeared, it was no big surprise. Obviously, history tells you the game went well for us and we beat Arsenal 1-0 courtesy of a real collectors' item - a Trevor Brooking headed goal!

Because of the circumstances of the win, a lot of people were asking me afterwards whether Cloughie's outburst played any part.

It wasn't the case at all. It had nothing to do with it and if anyone was interpreting it that way then they were way off the mark.

The fact that I scored didn't vindicate me or prove him wrong in the circumstances. I think people judge you on a season or a career, not just 90 minutes of a Wembley final.

I hadn't thought any more of it really. I had seen him at one or two functions, but there was no kind of conversation between us.

Anyway, it must have been a good seven or eight years later, I was working for the BBC at an FA Cup match at Crystal Palace.

Barry Davies had gone to the TV gantry and I said I would hang around for a while. I was standing in the corridor at Selhurst Park when Brian poked his head out of the dressing room door. There was no one else around. He saw me and I nodded to him. He came out, closing the door behind him and came right up to me before speaking.

'Young man. A few years ago just before the FA Cup final I did an article in a newspaper which I shouldn't have done. I was wrong and I'm sorry!'

Wow! Was this really the great man himself admitting for once that he had made an error of judgement? As quick as a flash he did an about turn and went back in. Our brief exchange couldn't have lasted more than 20 seconds, but I have always respected him for that.

The ironic thing about it all was that he made moves to sign me in the early 70's when he made a typically audacious bid to try and get myself and Bobby Moore to join Derby. It was much later that I heard about it. I think Bobby was actually the key to all that and I think Ron Greenwood our boss at West Ham said he would leave the club if that were to happen. It certainly would have been interesting, I'm sure, but there was never a chance of Ron agreeing.

By coincidence, it was Ron of course who then got the England job when Cloughie was right at his peak and a cult figure with the public.

He could well have got it because he was the much-heralded people's choice. But I think there was understandable wariness from the FA, given the circumstances that had seen Don Revie leave, and they took a safer option.

Years later our paths crossed in a sad and completely different way when I attended his memorial service at Derby's Pride Park. It was a fitting tribute to a man who had really captured the public's imagination not only with his incredible achievements but also with his magnetic personality.

He was the first really outspoken TV pundit of sorts. Anyone who knew anything about the game, knew what a tremendous manager he was, but there was more to him than just that whenever he appeared on TV. You were just never quite sure what was coming next.

In fairness to him, his record is right up there with the best of them. To take provincial clubs like Nottingham Forest and Derby to league titles and then win the European Cup twice is truly remarkable.

So while he was, quite rightly, proud of his own footballing doubles, I had one that has to be just as unique – an FA Cup winning goal and an apology from Brian Clough!

❝ My dad was a football fanatic and he worked in a sweet factory. What else does a boy need? ❞

*Forest keeper CHRIS WOODS says that Cloughie never tired
of reminding him just what a great goalscorer he had been
in his day and frequently tried to underline it by
firing shots at him on the training ground.*

95

FINISHING SCHOOL

CHRIS WOODS

'Hey, I might be forty and fat but I can still stick the ball in the net, young man,' the gaffer would exclaim with his trademark modesty.

Brian Clough's larger than life personality and legendary status as a soccer manager sometimes overshadows the fact that he was goalscorer of the highest calibre.

Such is his astonishing management record, the fact that he scored 267 goals in 296 appearances for Middlesborough and Sunderland before his career was cut short by injury, sometimes goes unnoticed that's not to say I didn't get the odd rollicking here and there – but tell me, who didn't!

And he didn't mind showing his goal touch in training either with me the man on the receiving end more times than I can remember.

Forty and fat or not, you could tell what a fantastic player he had been. His eye for goal and his finishing touch was there for all to see as he enjoyed blasting balls at me - and past me - in 20-minute sessions at the training ground.

He really was superb and I'm sure he would thank me for that observation! He could still knock the ball in without difficulty and made sure you knew about it.

On or off the training ground, he was a man who kept you on your toes at all times. I was lucky in that I really got on with him very well and have nothing but fond memories of him. That's not to say I didn't get the odd rollicking here and there.

I remember one occasion having had a good game and feeling pretty pleased with myself I headed for the shower. I had thrown my keeper's top and an undershirt on the floor and Cloughie picked me up on it immediately.

'Hey, young man, get over here and sort that out!' he shouted.

❛ We had Larry Lloyd and Kenny Burns at the centre of our defence and they could scare people – nobody messed with those two ❜

157

Daily Express journalist JOHN WRAGG got closer to Clough than most and travelled the world covering Forest. And here he reveals that there was never a dull moment when coming into contact with the unpredictable soccer boss.

96

PLANE UNPREDICTABLE

JOHN WRAGG

You never knew quite where you were with Brian Clough. Some days he'd smile and chat as though you were his best mate. Other times on hearing a well-intentioned 'Good morning' he'd bark ' Don't you good morning me!' Other times he'd say wait for him. And he'd just never turn up.

GOOD BRIAN: We were on the back of a plane flying somewhere for a European game. Midway through the flight he walks down to the back of the plane where about half a dozen of us are sat. 'Hey, can we work?' he says giving his thoughts on the game and the world in general. We were right by the engines and could hardly hear a word. Even Cloughie bellowing - and he could bellow- didn't help.

He finally gave up. 'Hey, lads, tell me please. Do you pay to be on this aeroplane?' We told him we did. 'Hey, on the next trip you lot can sit at the front of the aeroplane and the shit-house players can be at the back.' And they were.

FUNNY BRIAN: Forest were in Barcelona playing a pre-season friendly. Diego Maradona was playing for Barcelona at the time. For some reason I was in the tunnel area of the Nou Camp with Clough when Barcelona ran out for their warm-up. Brian clocked Maradona. He walked over to him, grabbed him by the balls and said: 'Hey, I want no trouble from you.'

ACID BRIAN: Ronnie Fenton, Brian's assistant manager, tells this story. Three of us, Hughie Jamieson, from The Sun, David Moore from the Daily Mirror, and me were on a pre-season tour with Forest in Sweden. They were playing very low key games against the equivalent of non-League teams. Ronnie said: 'Brian saw you three come out of three of the portable toilets. He turned to me and said "Hey look, Ronnie, three shit-houses coming out of three shithouses."'

> **❛ If you sort out the small things, the big things won't bother you ❜**

Veteran football reporter DENNIS SIGNY OBE first crossed swords with Cloughie when he was boss at Hartlepool and recounts how he got off to a bad start by daring to suggest that no one from the south should be made to go to the North East at Christmas.

97

POOL SPLASH

DENNIS SIGNY OBE

I first met Old Big 'Ead Clough on Boxing Day, 1965, during my time at Brentford. I was general manager at the club and we had just played Hartlepool and managed to get a 2-2 draw.

I had spent the previous weeks in print, castigating such a stupid computer system that would pair a London club with one from the frozen North East at Christmas. In my eyes it was such a ridiculously long trip to expect people to make over the festive period and let my feelings be known in no uncertain terms.

Cloughie was very much the 30-year-old new kid on the block and in his first management job. From memory, he called me 'Young Man' even though I was years older than him, and gave me a dressing down for even daring to suggest in headlines that no one wanted to travel to Hartlepool at Christmas.

When Hartlepool won the return game at Brentford 3-1, Cloughie wound up the crowd to such an extent that he was booed off the pitch. It was all part of an unknown Brian Clough establishing himself as a larger-than-life character many reckoned should have managed England.

He always remembered that first meeting and when we saw each other regularly over the years at games or hotels prior to matches he would always greet me with 'Come and have a whisky, young man!'

He would insist on telling his companions that I was one of the powers of a Fleet Street mafia who wrote exclusive but rubbish stories in The People under cover of a made up by-line. I quickly gave up explaining that I wrote for the News of the World for 17 years under my very own name!

One stunning trick I recall him pulling was something few, if any, managers would survive to tell the tale. Well, they might but they would be out of a job!

Mrs S and I organised a series of tribute evenings at The Savoy to mark outstanding contributions to football. When Cloughie was due the honour, Nottingham Forest organised two tables for the prestigious event and arranged for their party to travel to London as one group by coach.

Just before the dinner, Mrs S discovered Fred Reacher, then the Forest chairman, looking somewhat lost and bewildered in the reception area and clearly all was not well.

'You should be in the VIP room,' she told him.

'But I haven't got a ticket,' he replied.

Indeed, he hadn't . . . it turned out Cloughie had generously handed the chairman's tickets to the coach driver and his wife!

'When I first went to Derby all the fans thought I was a cocky bugger, but we started winning things and they put up with me '

Old Trafford legend STEVE BRUCE skippered Manchester United to their first title win in 26 years. He recalls how he was on the receiving end of an unexpected piece of Cloughie 'revenge' when he made a trip to the toilet.

98

TACKLE FROM BEHIND

STEVE BRUCE

Cloughie was one of the main instigators of getting the tackle from behind outlawed. So it was little wonder he once caught me by surprise when I was certainly in no position to defend myself.

I was just coming towards the end of my playing career and was at the PFA awards dinner in London when our paths crossed.

I can't say as I actually knew him that well but inevitably having played many years for Manchester United we came up against Cloughie's Forest teams on numerous occasions. I think it's fair to say there was no real love lost between the two clubs in those days and there was a real sense of rivalry between the two managers – Sir Alex Ferguson and Cloughie.

To be fair, they are both greats of the game. While Sir Alex would win hands down in terms of trophies amassed over the years, no one can argue that Clough's success with provincial sides like Forest and Derby was truly astonishing. One thing is for sure – it will never be repeated.

And while many people only remember him as a manager, coming from the North East as I do, you don't need to go too far to be reminded of what a legend he was as a goalscorer either.

And he showed he hadn't lost his touch for stealing in on the blind side and catching a defender unawares the night we bumped into each other.

I was standing in the toilets at the awards night having a pee when suddenly I felt someone boot me from behind.

I lurched forward and almost wet the front of my suit trousers as I turned to see who it was.

'Hey, that's for what you've been doing to my son for the last 10 years,' said the instantly recognisable voice. It was Brian.

'No problem,' I replied.

And with that he just smiled and walked away!

❝ Football always attracts a certain percentage of nobodies who want to be somebodies at a club ❞

Former Manchester United star ROY KEANE was one of the most feared midfield warriors of his generation. But he reveals he was lost for words in the Forest dressing room when furious Clough dished out his own special brand of teaching.

99

FIST OF FURY

ROY KEANE

I am probably the last person Cloughie would have expected to ever become a manager because it is fair to say my off-field life wasn't exactly perfect at the time I played for him.

I meet other players who played under him and we all have our own stories, but he was a genius – an absolute genius. He is certainly the best manager I played under without a doubt. Some of the lads would hide and had a fear of him, but I just had the greatest respect for the man.

Nowadays people think I am over the top with players but I'm not. I think I am very fair. Sometimes, as a player, you need an arm putting around you, but sometimes you have to learn the hard way.

I remember once making a mistake in my early playing days at Forest and Cloughie smacked me in the mouth. And he was dead right! It was the best thing he could have done to me to make me learn.

It was an FA Cup match at Crystal Palace. We had battled for a 0-0 draw in the away game. In the replay at the City Ground we were 2-1 up when I under-hit a back pass to our keeper Mark Crossley with disastrous consequences. Mark managed to hook the ball clear but only to John Salako, who chipped him from 50-yards. 2-2. Fuck.

When I walked into the dressing room after the game, Clough punched me straight in the face.

'Don't pass the ball back to the goalkeeper,' he screamed as I lay on the floor, him standing over me. I was hurt and shocked, too shocked to do anything other than nod my head in agreement.

Dressing rooms can be hard, unforgiving places. Being knocked down by Clough was part of my learning curve.

❛ Burns was a bit wild, a rough character. He was startled when I said to him: You're going around like a bloody tramp ❜

162

*Former FIFA ref CLIVE THOMAS reveals a fish and chip supper
washed down with champagne took a turn for the worse when
he dared suggest to Cloughie that he thought the game
he had just reffed was a particularly poor one.*

100

FISH & CHIPS

CLIVE THOMAS

Some people might find it hard to believe, but I was invited into Brian's office after EVERY match – no matter what the result or what had happened during the game.

I recall one occasion when Forest played Middlesbrough who were managed by Jack Charlton at the time. They were an effective side, capable of grinding out results. But, to put it bluntly, they were boring.

Anyway, after this particular game, Brian said 'Come in and have a drink before you go home.'

I told him that it was a bit awkward because I had a couple of friends with me – just normal punters – but he just said to bring them along too.

So, we went into the office where Brian held court and his son Nigel was there – he'd only be about 10 or 11 at the time.

'Go and get some fish and chips Nige,' Brian said as he opened up a bottle of champagne.

'Now then . . . the match. What did you think?' he asked.

'Well, I have to say, I wasn't very impressed with the game,' I replied.

'What do you mean?'

'I thought it was very poor football,' I said, a little too candidly for his liking.

'Did you now?' he replied, looking somewhat perplexed.

'I wasn't asking you about the football. Don't start telling me about football,' Brian exclaimed, putting me right in my place.

You couldn't help but like him because he was so astonishingly forthright in the way he spoke. But I'll tell you one thing, being out there on the field, you could see the impact his presence had.

I NEVER ever heard a player shout back at him. I don't think anyone dared. Rule by fear? Who gives a damn? The end product was playing entertaining, disciplined football and few would argue that his teams didn't do that.

❛ When the FA get in their stride, they make the Mafia look like kindergarten material ❜

Even by Cloughie's bizarre standards substituting a player before the kick-off takes some beating. But as legendary Forest star LARRY LLOYD reveals, the day he was told to pull his socks up provoked another angry exchange with his boss.

101

BLIZZARD WARNING

LARRY LLOYD

I received a severe Blizzard warning in Canada even though the mercury was rising on a boiling hot day in Toronto. I've been involved in some pretty bizarre incidents during my career, but I can't think of one crazier than when I was substituted during the warm-up!

To me the only thing that truly mattered were competitive games. Give me a game with something hanging on it and I will put everything on the line. I always did struggle with friendlies or exhibition games.

The bigger the game, the better I was. So you can imagine that for a pre-season game with Toronto Blizzard, I was really struggling to get my mind on things.

Proceedings hadn't started well when the organisers arranged to have the teams walking out in two lines for the national anthems, trying to create the impression that it was a really big match. It was really hot and for that reason I trudged out with my socks rolled down.

Up went the maple leaf flag for the Canadian national anthem and as it did the referee slowly came across to me and told me to pull my socks up.

'Hey dude, would you mind showing some respect for the flag – pull your socks up.'

'Are you taking the piss?' I asked somewhat less than diplomatically. It wasn't my national anthem after all and anyway, somebody telling me to do something like that was red rag to a bull at the best of times.

The referee went over to the dug-out to have a word with Cloughie and I assumed it would be all sorted out. And it was. Up went the board – come in number five! I was being substituted before the kick-off. A new record surely?

The crowd were going mad while my sympathetic team mates thought it was just about the funniest thing they had ever seen and were absolutely pissing themselves.

' My mom's old mangle serves as a reminder of the days when I learned what life was all about '

Cloughie certainly made waves beside the seaside when he turned up at Brighton. Local reporter JOHN VINICOMBE reveals that although the manager was only in charge for eight brief months, it was a time when the club was rarely out of the headlines.

102

GOLDSTONE GOLD

JOHN VINICOMBE

Clough's time at The Goldstone might not have lasted long – eight months to be precise - but to say it was an exciting time would be something of an understatement. Suddenly, Brighton and Hove Albion Football Club was in the news and at the centre of attention like never before.

Personally I have never known a time like it and have so many memories of his short but eventful stay. But as time has passed, I would definitely say he wasn't given the credit for what he did. The Clough era was unbelievable and people still talk about it to this day, well over 30 years later.

I think people could see what he was doing and that was stripping out the dead wood and getting things down to the bare bones to rebuild again.

He was immediately suspicious of people or players he suspected were phonies. He could be cruel with his remarks and observations, but I genuinely found him to be a kindly man.

I once went into the dressing room on a horrible night up at Walsall and there he was on his hands and knees helping a player get his boots off. The look of surprise must have been etched on my face but he just turned to me and offered his explanation.

'This young man's played very well tonight. It's wet and horrible and I'm just helping him untie his laces.'

That summed him up – give him your all and he would ask no more. He was fascinating.

There was a warmth about him that the people of Brighton – a notoriously fickle crowd – picked up on. You have to bear in mind that the Brighton public couldn't be compared with any from an industrial northern town where the football club was the centre of everything.

Overnight, Goldstone gates had swelled to an astonishing 16,000 when they had been down to five or six thousand. The Press descended on the place and gobbled up his every word. I had copy coming out of my ears, yet for the local freelances, Clough's arrival was a bit of a nightmare. Suddenly, the national papers sent staff men to the matches to feast on the offerings at Clough's table.

He breezed in, ordered most of the players to get their hair cut and set about putting right all that was wrong.

He saw players in black and white and quite rightly came to the conclusion that Brighton had been struggling because they had a lot of bad players. Such was his standing on football matters and such was his record as both player and manager that it was incredibly difficult to question him.

And I was lucky enough to get to see it first hand. These were bygone days when the local reporter could get close to the manager, no matter how big his name.

Because he didn't spend a lot of time down on the South Coast in the week, he would invite me up to his house to fill my notebook – and fill it I did.

Despite the best efforts of the chairman Mike Bamber, who Cloughie has openly said was the best he ever worked for, he spent very little time at the club in the week. When he did he would stay at The Courtlands Hotel, which is one of the better addresses in the area. Generally he would turn up latish on Thursday night in his silver Mercedes and generally at about ten to six on a Saturday, he was making his way back up to the Midlands.

But it wasn't just football that he could captivate you with, he could talk on any manner of subject.

One of my fondest memories of him was travelling by train to an away match at York. I was sat next to him for a journey that was going to be quite a long haul.

It was about 9am when one of the train staff came down the gangway and said: 'Good morning gentlemen. Coffee?'

'No, no, bring us a bottle of champagne!' he said. That was just typical of him and my life was all the richer for the experience.

‘ I have tasted the two extremes of football. I have been to the very top and I have had the sack ’

Former Forest keeper STEVE SUTTON tells how a quick escape to the loo was foiled by the angry Forest boss. Cloughie was far from happy and he was in full flow. But his furious outburst had an unexpected effect on his terrified player.

103

TOILET HUMOUR

STEVE SUTTON

The gaffer could be so scary that he could make you NOT piss yourself. I'm serious . . .

I remember one occasion when we were losing at half-time and the boss was going absolutely ballistic. My changing spot was right by the toilets and I was desperate to go, but obviously not while he was giving us all a right dressing down.

Suddenly, it went quiet for a moment and I assumed he had finished, so I half got up in a bid to make a sharp exit for the loo.

'Hey, where the fucking hell do you think you're going?' he screamed.

I sat down and he started ripping in to me. I had let two in and I was this and that etc, etc. I had to just sit there and take it and when he had eventually finished tearing me to bits he granted me permission to leave.

'Now you can go to the toilet young man.'

The rest of the lads in the dressing room just fell about as I meekly offered my reply.

'I don't want to go now!'

That is the effect he had on you but all of us who were lucky enough to come under his wing will all agree that we will never see his like again.

I was fortunate in that I got on really well with him – most of the time. Yes, he could be an awkward cuss when he wanted, but everyone knew that.

The one thing that I have noticed about him is that even players who he let go or didn't particularly get along with, all have positives to say about him. You don't get that with too many people in a game where slagging someone off goes with the territory. How many players have you ever heard slagging Brian Clough?

❛ I wrote to the FA sometime afterwards politely asking if I could have a loser's medal. They said they only provided medals for the players. I found that incredible ❜

167

*When Liverpool's Graeme Souness was running the game at Forest,
Cloughie laid into his players for letting the midfielder boss
them around so much. As PETER DAVENPORT recalls,
the angry manager had a simple solution.*

104

CHOP SOU-EY

PETER DAVENPORT

Cloughie never hid his admiration for truly great footballers. Liverpool's Graeme Souness would definitely come into that category, but there was a nasty edge to him that ruffled the gaffer's feathers. Cloughie admired him as a footballer, but I know for a fact that he struggled with the Liverpool midfielder's combative style.

Take nothing away from Souness, he was a brilliant player who quite rightly goes down as one of the legends of Anfield. That's no mean feat in itself, given the glittering array of talent The Kop has been treated to over the years. But . . .

Souness was Liverpool's midfield enforcer in those days, a self-styled hitman who took great pleasure in stamping his authority on a game. If you let him boss things, he would and it drove Cloughie mad if he saw the Scot starting to conduct the orchestra. Souey loved the physical side of it all.

He'd scream: 'Hey! That fucking Souness is parading around in MY centre circle like he owns the fucking joint! Sort it!'

Easier said than done, but the gaffer was having none of it. He'd demand we got close to him and move him about. He'd urge us to try and make it hard for him to play. I'm sure he respected his ability but he always had an aversion to the hatchet-man types. Souness was a marvellous footballer but he did have a fearsome side to him and, just to make matters worse, seemed to revel in it.

He was top man, but I do remember one occasion when we had him spitting feathers after he was at fault for the goal in our narrow 1-0 win against them.

He was just inside their half when he didn't quite manage to control the ball and I nicked it off him. He tried to 'do' me with a flying tackle, but I jumped it and charged off towards goal.

Bruce Grobelaar, their keeper came out to make the angle as difficult as possible but I sent it in between Grob and his near post to score. Souness was going berserk! I had done well not only to nick it away from him but to then somehow clear his knee-high challenge on me. And the angle I had to get the ball in from was unbelievably tight to say the least. The gaffer would be pleased with that one, I imagined.

'What did you try there?' he enquired.

'It was such a tight angle that I aimed for the post,' I explained.

'You what? You aimed for the post? What did you do that for?'

Was it really worth explaining? To cut a long story short, I tend to get a bit of drag on a left foot shot from an angle so I compensated for that by aiming for the post.

'So I aimed for the post . . .'

Clough yelled: 'He's fucking mad that Davenport. He was aiming for the post, not the goal.'

It was something he would not let me forget for quite some time. We could be in training, or trying something out and he'd never fail to amuse himself.

'He's crackers that Davenport. He's the only striker I know who doesn't aim for the goal, he aims for the post.'

6 Sir Alex took me into his office and gave me a drop of sherry. I told him I didn't think they were still making thimbles 9

While the outspoken Clough might have revelled in his controversial, fearsome reputation, he wasn't afraid to wear his heart on his sleeve at times. GEORGE EDWARDS was there when the Derby boss openly sobbed in public watching a moving TV report.

105

HEART ON SLEEVE

GEORGE EDWARDS

Brian was a quite incredible man and had qualities few would see or even know about unless they observed him from close up.

For all of his bluster and swagger, he was a man who wore his emotions very much on his sleeve. He could be a very caring and emotional person and was also given to wonderful acts of kindness. It was a trait that manifested itself in some quite remarkable ways as I was lucky enough to witness at times.

On a number of occasions I saw him pay for an old person's groceries in the supermarket. He wouldn't make a fuss or do it to impress others, he would just motion quietly to someone working on the till that he would sort out someone's bill and wave them quietly on their way.

He was certainly no ordinary person, but in some ways that's exactly how he wanted to be seen. So there was no barging to the front of queues or thinking he should be afforded special privileges like some celebrities are easily prone to do. If ever we stopped for fish and chips on the way back from somewhere he would make a

point of waiting his turn and it was the same in the pub if we went for a drink.

But what he would do on occasions was pay for a few people's fish and chip suppers once he had got to the counter and leave before they even knew they had been treated. He would have left the shop before an unsuspecting customer would know they were in for a free supper or have time to thank him.

I found out also, but not from him I should add, that he quite often dropped off baskets of fruit at the Derbyshire Children's Hospital in North Street on his way home from the ground.

But one of the most extraordinary times his sensitive nature burst through to the surface happened when we were sitting together in the TV room of a London hotel. It seems hard to believe nowadays, but back in the early 70s, hotels had one large TV for guests set aside in a separate room. The days when every room had a television were still some time away.

One Friday night before a game, I recall being with Brian sitting among a large number of guests in the TV room of the Great Western Hotel, next to

Paddington Station.

We were all watching the early evening news which was carrying a particularly distressing report about the famine in Biafra. The pictures coming back at us were particularly poignant and could not have failed to affect anyone.

The report was illustrated by heart-rending newsreel footage of pot-bellied starving children close to death and mothers clutching babies covered in flies.

There was much coughing and hard swallowing from the gathering of strangers as they watched scenes of abject misery, but there was no such stiff upper lip from Brian.

He just sat there with tears streaming down his face muttering quietly 'terrible, terrible,' over and over again.

It wasn't as if he wasn't known at that time – far from it. The people in that room would have been well aware who he was – the big mouthed, opinionated so-and-so they had seen on the TV. But they witnessed another side of the man that night.

It was quite touching and yet just another example of one of the many facets of his complex and intriguing character.

❛ Turning back the clock is just impossible to do – this was the nearest I could hope to get to it ❜
– on unveiling his bust

Trying telling renowned hardman Dave Mackay that sherry's for girls! ALAN HINTON lets up the secret of Clough's unusual pre-match preparations and how he would always treat his trusted skipper to his favourite tipple.

106

MACKAY'S SHERRY

ALAN HINTON

If anyone thought sherry was a bit of a poncey drink, they certainly didn't air such a view in the Derby County dressing room.

Our hard-as-nails skipper Dave Mackay was partial to a drop of the sweet stuff. And if it's good enough for him, then none of the lads were going to question his choice of tipple!

We'd go to the Midland Hotel in Derby on a Friday night prior to a home match and Cloughie would bring in a crate of beer for the lads and a bottle of sherry for Mackay.

'Have what you want, but be careful,' was all that he would say.'

Mackay was an extraordinary player and man. Everybody adored him. He was very funny and such a popular figure who also had total respect. He was tough as old boots.

He had a real winning mentality which rubbed off on the rest of the players. Mackay wanted to win and, just as importantly, he knew how to win. He really got us all going. What he did for Derby out on the pitch is quite rightly recognised.

He was a leader of men. When his chest was puffed out and he was out there alongside you, it made you feel good.

He only not had moral and physical courage on the pitch, but he showed a lot of balls when he took over as manager amid all the fuss and controversy of Clough's resignation.

I admire him for that because he had the guts to take it when a lot of people didn't want him to. He went on to take them to the title. Like I said, that man knew how to win.

He probably toasted that with a small glass of sherry and I'd bet every penny I have that no one ever had the balls to tell him it was a girlie drink!

' Derby should have become as big as Liverpool, possibly even bigger and there's only one man to blame for that not happening – Brian Clough '

Christmas certainly came early the day Cloughie dropped the bombshell that he would come out of retirement to take up management again. NICK LUCY saw the office festive celebrations put on hold while the agency he worked for broke the news.

107

XMAS COMES EARLY

NICK LUCY

Brian Clough was big news no matter what organisation you worked for. When Cloughie spoke, the world listened. His forthright views and willingness to express them meant you were never short of a story if he decided there was something he wanted to get off his chest.

I was now working for the Lawson and Bowles freelance agency after my years working on the Nottingham Post. John Lawson was very close to Cloughie to such an extent that apart from the odd exclusive for national newspapers here and there, everything else went via John. Him and Cloughie had been friends for years and kept in regular contact even though by this time – Christmas 1995 – the great man had long-since retired.

Anyway, on this particular day everyone was hurrying about some routine chores in the morning before going off for the office Christmas lunch. It was to be a relatively quiet morning followed by some hard-earned revelry from midday onwards. But the minute John put the phone down having just spoken to Cloughie, we sensed that lunch might be delayed a little while.

Former England boss Graham Taylor had been sacked by Wolves, which was of little concern to an agency in Nottingham ... until Cloughie put a different slant on it.

'Hey, I'd come out of retirement to help a great club like Wolves,' he told John. It was a great story, but one that we could have done without just an hour away from our office Christmas 'do.'

The phones were suddenly red-hot as we bashed out the story and started sending it all over the place. All the national papers took it because, like anyone knows, he was pure gold whenever he spoke – retired or not.

Ah well, that was the office lunch paid for anyway . . .

❛ We spent the week prior to the European Cup final in Majorca – doing absolutely bugger all ❜

The goals were going in thick and fast for Middlesborough striker HUGH McILMOYLE and comparisons with Clough were doing the rounds. But the striker was soon put right on that when he bumped into someone who had a different take on the matter.

108

WELL DONE SON

HUGH McILMOYLE

When I joined Middlesbrough there was still a lingering feeling of bitterness at the club about the way Clough had departed to join local rivals Sunderland. The £55,000 transfer fee was a record at the time and you do wonder what figure such a devastating finisher would have commanded in today's ridiculously inflated market.

People told me that as a player he was abrasive, self-centred and opinionated. Pretty much the same as he was as a manager then, I guess!

He was never quiet. He was the sort of bloke who just had to say something. He couldn't walk by. If he saw an old woman crossing the road he'd have to help her along, chatting away from pavement to pavement. And if he saw someone doing wrong, he'd be just as quick to tell them off. I liked him.

When Clough was managing Derby, I went down there as a player with Carlisle in 1967 and we beat them. In the tunnel afterwards, there was no need for him to speak to me, but he turned around and said 'Well done, young man. You gave our young centre-half the run around today and that's

no mean feat because he's going to be England's centre half sooner rather than later.'

He was right, of course. That young man was Roy McFarland. Clough must have been disappointed having just been beaten at home, yet he still found time for a kindly word for an opposition player.

The next time I met him is probably the funniest and shows just what a direct and intriguing character he could be. It was at the Scotch Corner Hotel where the A1 meets the A66. I was a Middlesbrough player by this time and I'd got off to such a cracking start there that the local newspapers had begun doing the odd article comparing me with Clough.

The routine was that I would drive to the hotel from home to be picked up by the Middlesbrough team coach. On this particular day, Derby County were meeting there as well. I was sitting alone, drinking a cup of coffee when Clough presented himself bang in front of me and said:

'I've been reading in the papers that you are a better player than I ever was. Let me tell you, you will never be as good a player as I was and you'll never score as many goals as I did!'

I said: 'Well, you are probably right Mr Clough,' to which he replied. 'I know I'm right, young man. On both counts.'

No sooner had he arrived, than he'd gone. In the normal course of events, you would expect someone to introduce themselves, exchange a pleasantry or two and then say whatever it was that was on their mind. Not Cloughie – he was straight in there.

That's the way he was. He'd come out with these one-liners and people would be so taken aback that they didn't have chance to respond.

I think he was just a complete one-off. He was so good a manager that his playing career is rarely mentioned. But when you consider that he scored 204 goals in 222 games over a 10-year period at Boro, then he has to have been just about the best striker Britain has ever seen. That record almost defies belief.

❝ Shilton won me the championship. We thought if we scored, we'd win because no bugger could get the ball past him ❞

National Union of Mineworkers official GORDON BUTLER reveals how the picket lines were given a huge lift when Cloughie decided his Derby players should be given a reminder of just how lucky they were with a trip to meet striking miners.

109

NEW STRIKERS!

GORDON BUTLER

During the 1972 miners' strike I was at Spondon Power Station near Derby on picket duty when out of the blue a big car pulled up followed by four or five more cars and a minibus behind it.

The passenger door flew open and there was absolutely no mistaking who it was – out came Brian Clough in his trademark green jumper.

'Who's in charge here?' he asked. I told him I was and he happily informed me that he'd drafted in some support.

'I've brought some of my Derby County football team to join you on the picket line,' he said.

Then he turned to the players and said: 'I'm going to show you lot what these men have to put up with. But the big lesson that you have to learn is just how good football is going to be to you in comparison with being down the pits with these lads.'

He asked how long we were going to be there and at that particular time we were manning the picket line 24 hours a day in shifts. So he said to the boys: 'I'll send the bus back for you when I think you are ready,' and off he went.

The players stayed with us all day and we took some of them with us as we approached lorries on their way into the site.

Brian Clough was a true socialist who supported the miners' cause and said he thought we were paid a pittance.

He brought the other half of his team to do the same the next day. Afterwards he sent us a load of free tickets and we took 30 or 40 people to one of Derby's home games.

6 They make me smile . . . these players who think they can take off their boots one day and put on their suits and become a manager the next. They couldn't be more wrong 9

*Former Wolves and Everton striker WAYNE CLARKE was one
of the ones that got away. He decided not to sign for Forest
as a kid and reveals that years later when their paths
crossed again, Clough certainly hadn't forgotten.*

110

THUMBS UP

WAYNE CLARKE

Being the youngest of the five famous footballing brothers it was inevitable that scouts had been beating down the door for some time, when the great Brian Clough threw his hat into the ring.

I was only 14 but already the interest was great largely because of my brother Allan who was the Leeds and England international.

Funnily enough, Allan knew Cloughie quite well, having been one of the very few people who had backed him up during his torrid 44-day spell at Leeds. Cloughie had a great rapport with Allan and so when my brother heard of Forest's interest in taking me, he was fully behind it saying he hadn't a single problem with his former boss.

Me and my parents went over to Burton where we had been told we were going out for a meal with the Forest boss. But when we got there he was standing at the bar with his squash kit, swinging his racket and clutching half a lager.

He came over and apologised for not being able to make the meal, but said he needed to shoot off and take a shower. He put us in the hands of Liam O'Kane, who was the club's youth development officer at that time.

'Look, I want you to come to us,' Cloughie assured me. Truth is, I would have loved to have played for him and I'm sure he could have improved me greatly.

He was one of the greatest goalscorers of all time and had it not been for the fact that I was a bit of a homebird, I think the two of us could have got on just fine.

But the simple fact of the matter is that when it came to deciding my future, it was a bit of a no-brainer when Wolves came in for me.

I had been down to Arsenal for trials and Leeds while Liverpool and Everton were keen on taking me. But I preferred to stay nearer home and so that was that.

But our paths were destined to meet some years later and there's a nice twist to the story.

I was playing for Manchester City at the time when a Christmas fixture took us down to Forest's City Ground in 1990.

When I say I was playing, I was actually substitute and no doubt desperate to show boss Peter Reid I should be in the starting line-up.

Anyway, I came on at half-time and as I was making my way out of the tunnel, I felt a sharp nudge in the back accompanied by an unmistakeable voice.

'Young man, you'd have been a better player than you are if you had come and signed for me!'

I smiled and made my way onto the pitch. Mid-way through the half I scored with a diving header to clinch victory and seconds after the ball hit the net, I turned towards the dug-outs.

I don't know exactly what made me do it – more than likely I was making a point to Reidy that there was plenty more where that came from if he would only play me from the start.

But as I glanced across there was Cloughie giving me his distinctive thumbs-up as if to say 'Great goal, son.'

It didn't matter that I was actually playing for the opposition or that at 3-1, his side had now almost certainly lost. I thought that was a magnificent gesture and coming from someone who knew a thing or two about scoring goals, I still regard it as the greatest of compliments.

❛ Bill Nicholson used to say a pat on the back isn't too far from a kick up the backside. He was right ❜

When ANDY GRAY was a striker with Wolves he scored the goal which sunk Forest in the League Cup final at Wembley. But Cloughie had spotted the raw-boned striker might be a bit special a few years earlier when he was starting out at Aston Villa.

111

WORD OF WARNING

ANDY GRAY

Cloughie once made a point of paying me a wonderful compliment and it's only a shame that I wasn't there to actually hear it from the great man himself.

Our paths crossed most famously at Wembley when I scored the only goal of the game in the 1981 League Cup final to give Wolves victory over Nottingham Forest.

I guess my name might have been mentioned in the Forest dressing room that day as well, though perhaps I was better off missing out on that particular conversation!

I was also there at the Midlands' Player of the Year awards night when he famously ticked off Trevor Francis for standing there with his hands in his pockets! The thing about that was that this happened in the days before Cloughie forked out £1m to land Trevor, so he wasn't even his player when he had a go at him that night!

So, while I met him at various gatherings over the years, in a way my contact was mainly from a distance. But, there was just that one time when something he said was relayed back to me and made me immensely proud.

Unfortunately, I never had the pleasure of playing for him – boy, would that have been fun! But I did come to his attention sometime before that Wembley winner in a game at Villa Park.

I would have been around 20 or 21, just starting to try and carve a name out for myself in England after moving down from Dundee United. The goals were coming thick and fast and in this particular home game against Forest, I recall having a really good game.

After the match, four or five of our apprentices went into the visitors' dressing room to start cleaning it out. Cloughie was hanging around and started chatting to the youngsters.

So he asks this one kid his name and the lad tells him and Cloughie then asks: 'And which position do you play son?'

'I play centre-forward, Mr Clough,' came the reply.

'Do you now! Well, it could be quite a few years before you get in the first team young man!'

Typical Cloughie, but I thought that was really nice. It was a massive compliment to me from a man who was no bad judge of a player and particularly a striker. He was a goalscorer who was second to none in his day and so for him to say that, is something that I will certainly take with me to the grave.

He was box-office as a player and he was TV dynamite as well. I recall those days in the 70s when he was never off the box and was THE pundit of all soccer pundits.

Imagine if he had been in his pomp now. I doubt anyone could have afforded him! He was an absolute one-off who just had so much self-belief and certainly didn't sit on the fence when it came to putting his views across.

But it is what he got out of players that will be his lasting legacy and, let me tell you, what he did at two provincial clubs will never be repeated.

A few years ago it would have been nigh-on impossible, but now with the new money levels that clubs like Chelsea and Manchester City have brought to the game, it simply is impossible. It CAN'T happen now, which is a shame. But you can say categorically that even if someone pumped £200m into a club like a Nottingham Forest or a Derby, it still would not bring the kind of success Clough delivered.

His legacy is one that will last forever and is not going to be repeated.

❛ If a player continues to get booked, fine the manager. Sir Alex Ferguson is so tight, he'd soon stamp down on that ❜

Interviewing Clough could be a nightmare if he just wasn't in the mood. BBC radio reporter MARTIN FISHER recalls how he had a tricky time of things when the Forest boss seemed far more interested in perfecting his skills at cap-throwing.

112

CAP THAT

MARTIN FISHER

The thing with Brian Clough was that if you expected him to do one thing, you could absolutely guarantee he would do the opposite. Trying to second-guess him was just impossible. A couple of examples of that spring to mind.

I was working for BBC Radio Nottingham and although I had a reasonable relationship with him, he was at a stage in his career when he wasn't forthcoming at times. I went down to the City Ground one day to try and get an interview for a big piece I was doing on 'The Clough Years.'

I got my questions all sorted so I was well prepared and I was armed with a full tape to record the great man's pearls of wisdom as they came spilling out.

But as soon as I sat down in his office, it became vividly clear to me that this might be a fruitless mission. I asked a few questions and I knew from his answers that I wasn't getting anything. He knew it too. My tape was whirring away, time was ticking on and every question I asked was met with answers of no more than a couple of words. To make matters worse, he was doing a sort of James Bond impression trying to throw his cap over a hat-stand in the corner of his office.

He was trying to get the cap to stay on there and Carole, his loyal secretary, was returning it to him when it missed – as it inevitably did. I just wanted Carole to stop returning it, him to stop throwing it and maybe, just maybe, give me a couple of useable answers. But I was struggling. He knew exactly what he was doing. He didn't want to do an interview in the first place and he was just being his stubborn best – or worst! I walked away thinking he hated me, the world hated me and that I was probably just useless at my job. He could get you that way!

Conversely, a few days after that, I went to do an interview with him when he was receiving the Freedom of the City.

I didn't actually realise that the interview I was doing would go out 'live' to the many members of the public congregated outside.

'Mr Clough . . .' I said.

'Son, call me Brian.'

'I'm sorry . . . I thought you only let

me call you Mr Clough,' I said.

'Well son, because I'm in a good mood today, you can call me Brian.'

That was brilliant for the radio piece, so I set about asking him how he was finding it all.

'How has your day been, Brian?'

'Very nice, thank you.'

'Has it been a bit of a hassle because I know you have been chased around by journalists everywhere today,' I said.

'Journalists?' he countered and I immediately sensed he was on the attack.

'Journalists? Hey, you are one of them. You've been pestering me all day as well!'

Then he gave me an absolutely love-ly interview about how honoured he felt and that it was fantastic to be recognised in that way.

He had a warm side, make no mis-take, but sometimes it took quite a bit of getting through to it.

He was without doubt the most fas-cinating character I have ever had the pleasure of interviewing and I can't see that changing either, to be honest.

He was unique and I would simply have loved to see him handling some of these multi-millionaire superstars of today's game. That might have been lively.

‘ There's nowt wrong with a place being run by a dictator – just so long as that dictator is me ’

*Forest star IAN BOWYER enjoyed a trophy-laden career under
Clough and knew to always expect the unexpected. But when
a man dressed as a clown ran on to the pitch, he could hardly
believe his eyes when the boss decided to tackle the problem.*

113

CLOWNING AROUND

IAN BOWYER

The next bizarre moment was never too far around the corner when you spent so much time in the company of the incomparable Cloughie.

But even by his standards the episode of the clown who failed to make him smile takes some beating. It was back in 1982 and we were playing Graham Taylor's high-riding Watford side at the City Ground.

Suddenly a guy dressed up as a clown ran onto the pitch and while my very first instinct was to laugh, I could see the boss in hot pursuit and looking far from amused.

I could see from the expression on his face that this particular clown wasn't tickling his funny bone and everyone just looked on in amazement as he chased the offender.

Eventually he caught him, gave him a cuff around the ear and manhandled him away to the delight of the crowd.

But the strange upshot to it all that very few people know about is that Cloughie and the clown went on to be big mates!

I know for a fact that after the incident the clown came into the club on at least a couple of occasions – having abandoned his circus outfit, of course. He met up with the gaffer and they had a bite to eat together in the old Jubilee Club at the ground.

I think the two of them felt kind of guilty. Cloughie realised that he perhaps shouldn't have taken the law into his hands and given the guy a clip, while the clown man was sorry for going on the gaffer's sacred pitch in the first place. So out of that, an unlikely friendship was born.

It was the time Cloughie was kissing everybody so the clown got a couple of smackers and everybody went home happy!

Fancy that, Cloughie giving a supporter a whack and then getting them to come into the ground and apologise to him!

**' I don't know why it is that clubs always
want me when I'm in work '**

114

FOOD FOR THOUGHT

PETER THE GARDENER

Brian loved all of the creatures that visited his garden – well, with some exceptions. I remember him getting quite hot under the collar one warm summer's morning when a few thousand unwelcome visitors decided to pay a visit. It was a Saturday and because Brian was preparing to fly off to Majorca later that day he didn't want to be disturbed.

So I was busying myself with some gardening duties when I noticed a large swarm of bees overhead which alarmed me a bit. They had settled on one of Brian's trees, right by the house. I quickly ran to the back door and informed him about them.

Brian walked down the garden and inspected them and because he was leaving shortly, was keen to get the matter sorted so he wasn't left worrying about it while he was away. He asked me what I was going to do about it.

'Me? What can I do?'

'Well if you can't do anything, find some bugger who can!'

'They'll move on shortly,' I assured him.

'Like when?' he asked anxiously.

'I don't know.'

Brian went out of the room and came back with the Yellow Pages.

'Here, find someone,' he said.

I ended up ringing a gentleman from Derby who told me that the bees were probably just travelling through and would disappear before too long. I told Brian exactly what he had said.

'Get him up here,' he insisted.

I told the man the situation and he arrived an hour or so later. He donned all his gear and we directed him in the direction of the tree. They'd gone! I popped back to the house to tell Brian the swarm had gone and that the man had wasted his journey.

'He's nearly as good at his job as you are at yours,' Brian laughed. He gave the man £10 for his trouble and went away on holiday without having to worry about his unwanted visitors. He'd never have done anything to harm them because he was an avid wildlife fan.

One of Brian's passions was bird life. He was extremely knowledgeable about the different types and varieties, which stems back to when he collected birds' eggs as a youngster.

He used to get a fantastic amount of pleasure from feeding the birds in his beautiful gardens. He would always make sure there was an assortment of food out for them, particularly when the cold started to bite. Sunflower seeds and nuts were all on the Clough garden menu and he would even make-up his own fat balls for them with scraps from the table.

He loved attracting birds to the garden and he knew every particular type that ventured into his patch.

At the back of his garden he had a big, old veranda where you could often spot him leaving bits of this or that for the grateful visitors. Because of its location, you would occasionally get the odd pheasant or fox nipping in to see what snacks might be available and they were rarely disappointed.

He derived great pleasure from walking in the countryside or just observing things from his own garden. You could tell it was one of his ways of unwinding. Strangely enough, I remember a conversation I had with him once over a cup of coffee that best summed it all up I suppose.

He always used to go on to me about the pressure involved in doing what he did and the constant scrutiny he was under and seemed to think that someone like a humble gardener was exempt! In his eyes there could be no greater way to earn a living than working outside doing gardens. I often explained to him that while I was, indeed, lucky to earn a living in such a way, it wasn't pressure free and the pay certainly wasn't as good as being a top football manager either!

Anyway, one day we were chewing the fat over something or other – probably how different our jobs were – when I recall the conversation going something like this.

'Pressure? You work out in the open air and you've got no one looking over your shoulder. You don't know what pressure is,' he exclaimed.

As we spoke, a robin was hopping about just to the side of us looking for worms in the frozen soil.

I said to him: 'If that little fella doesn't find any worms, either he or his family will starve to death – now, that's what I call pressure wouldn't you?'

'Hey, you've got a point there,' he said with a smile, wagging that famous finger.

I dwelled momentarily on a point well made, but I should have known the glory wouldn't be mine for long.

'I'll leave that with you then,' he said, heading off back for the warmth of the house.

'Sorry?'

'Well, you'd better get digging and turn some soil over for the poor little bugger then!'

❛ I've decided to pick my moment to retire very carefully . . . it's in about 200 years time ❜

Arsenal legend CHARLIE GEORGE spent a brief, but memorable, time at the City Ground. He loved working under Cloughie but reveals how he always remained a proper Charlie in the name games the Forest boss loved to play.

115

NAME GAME

CHARLIE GEORGE

It never fails to amaze me that for all the things I've done in the game, people continually ask me what it was like playing for Cloughie.

It says something about the man that people still ask me what he was like, yet I only played for him for one month on loan from Southampton and that was over 30 years ago.

The one thing that still makes me smile when I recall my time spent under Cloughie was how he'd continually refer to Kenny Burns as 'Kenneth.' It just cracked me up. Kenny was a great player, but by his own admission hardly a male model. He could scare Christopher Lee when he took his teeth out.

'Now then Kenneth . . .' Cloughie would say, and it's something that always has me chuckling all these years later.

Strangely enough, although I was christened Charles, he never went down that particular route with me. I played just four games for Cloughie,

though I helped him win the European Super Cup with a goal against Barcelona, so I did make some kind of an impression.

The thing that I did like about him was that he didn't over-complicate things. He didn't insult players who could play by trying to fill their heads with mumbo-jumbo. I think in that respect he was something of a pioneer.

He would come up to the training ground brandishing his squash racket and Peter Taylor would be there with his dog. Slightly bizarre, but they kept it simple.

He was a great, great manager who I absolutely loved working with. The one thing that did impress me about him was his reaction when I told him I wouldn't be staying. Some managers can get quite narky or hold it against you, but not Cloughie.

'If there's any time I can help you, then don't you hesitate to give me a ring,' he said. I thought that was absolute class.

❛ If you're not sure what to do, do nowt – sleep on it ❜

When Stoke's no-nonsense defender DENIS SMITH asked the Forest boss if he would be the speaker at his testimonial dinner, he didn't realise just what he had on his hands. A black market developed for the hottest ticket in town.

116

BLACK MARKET

DENIS SMITH

Cloughie was once at the centre of a black market tickets frenzy – and it was all down to me!

Let's start at the very beginning . . . Cloughie had tried to sign me on a number of occasions. There was a point where he was speaking to my missus more than I was. For one reason or another, nothing ever came of it. One of the main reasons was that being at clubs in those days was unrecognisable from nowadays and my gaffer at Stoke, Tony Waddington, was having none of it.

But Cloughie did manage to get my old mate Peter Shilton to Nottingham Forest – even if it did take a record sum of money to do it. Nevertheless, I think Shilts was just what Cloughie needed and, I have to say, that is particularly true the other way around too.

Shilts was a fanatic for training and getting himself in peak condition to the extent where I honestly believe he over-trained. If there had been floodlights on the training ground he would have been back in the evenings. Brilliant though he was, Shilts had become a bit of a lump of wood because of his obsession with training.

It was Brian who got him to relax a bit more and I think that was the making of him to some extent.

Don't get me wrong, it is difficult to fault a guy who is just so focused on being the best and fittest in the business that he can just see no other way. But Cloughie also knew the benefits of taking it easy every now and then.

Apparently, the first morning after he'd signed for Forest, he reported for training and Cloughie took him for a walk down the banks of the Trent and said: 'That's it for you, see you Thursday!'

'Gaffer can I come in tomorrow and do some training?' Shilts asked.

'What for?'

'I want to do a bit of work on my crosses boss.'

'Hey, I didn't pay over two hundred grand for you to go around dropping crosses. Now, fuck off.'

I once agreed to look after a young player who was coming across from Ireland for a trial at Forest. My sister asked if I could take him under my wing and I agreed to get him over to Forest. Surprise, surprise, I had my leg in plaster at the time so myself and my brother-in-law took him over there.

Brian was out on the pitch with the players and as I went up to the touch-line, he motioned for me to come across.

'When any of you lot can defend like this man then you'll be a player,' he said, smiling in my direction. I'm not so sure that Kenny Burns and Larry Lloyd would have agreed with him on that, but it was a nice compli ment all the same.

So, taking all that into considera-tion, our paths had crossed on more than the odd occasion when I asked him if he would consider doing a speech at a testimonial dinner that had been organised for me at the North Stafford Hotel.

Bear in mind this was just prior to Forest reaching the 1980 European Cup final, so I knew they would be having a pretty busy time of things.

'I'll do it. Leave it with me – and I'll bring Shilts as well,' he said.

I was chuffed to bits. Just one would have been great – but I knew that if I could get Brian and a former Stoke hero as well, it would prove to be a great attraction.

They both came and the thing that will stick with me forever was the sight of men fully decked out in dinner suits waiting outside and in the recep-tion area, desperately trying to pay over the odds to buy tickets for my dinner.

It was the hottest ticket in town and it was unbelievable to see people wait-ing there on the off chance that they would be able to get fixed up.

No one should forget just how pop-ular Brian was and when he spoke, people listened. He was quite brilliant that night and never asked for a penny for doing it.

I felt honoured and privileged that the game's biggest voice and one of the most colourful characters in the country, never mind football, had agreed to do that for me.

How often would you get a black market for dinner tickets? That's what you call real pulling power.

❝ When I first won the League Cup in 1978, I stuck the trophy on the telly and just sat there eating fish and chips and gazing at it ❞

*It's DARREN FLETCHER revealing how Cloughie weaved
his magic yet again at a meet the fans evening. The master had the
audience eating out of his hand but just what made him completely
crack-up when he was asked to sign an autograph?*

117

APOLLO MISSION

DARREN FLETCHER

Brian was the special guest at a dinner we attended in Sheffield. There had been a question and answer session which Cloughie and Garry Birtles had done and it had been a brilliant evening. I had been the compere and tried to ensure things went smoothly but with the main man himself in great form, it was hard not to go down a storm.

After the dinner, people were invited to go up to the top table and get an autograph, picture or whatever and Cloughie was lapping it up. Punters just love him. You had to be there to appreciate the love and respect they had for him.

Anyway, this old guy who must have been pushing 80, comes up and says: 'Hi Brian, lovely to meet you. Could you sign this to Max please?'

'Son, I think you'll find that your mother had you christened Maximilian!'

And so, he signed it 'To Maximilian, Be Good. Brian Clough.'

The best was yet to come. You couldn't make it up. The next fella comes up to the table, exchanges pleasantries and asks Cloughie if he would be kind enough to sign something for him.

'What's your name young man?'

'Can you sign it to Apollo?'

'Apollo?' Cloughie spluttered.

Well that just absolutely floored him. I was sitting to his right and Gaz was on his left. He grabbed my arm and was killing himself laughing.

'Hey, have you heard his bloody name? He's called Apollo!'

The guy is just loving it in fairness, which was just as well, because Brian certainly wasn't finished.

'Where are you from son? The moon? You don't look like a space rocket to me, son."

Anyway, he duly signed it to Apollo with his trademark 'Be Good,' and all the way home he couldn't stop chattering about someone actually being called Apollo. It had made his night.

> 6 **The ideal director raises money, manages it and then passes it on to me to spend as I see fit** 9

Photographer TREVOR BARTLETT almost caused an international incident when he got lucky on the roulette table in Bulgaria. Here he reveals how Cloughie came to the rescue over trying to get his money out of the country.

118

YOUR NUMBER'S UP

TREVOR BARTLETT

Brian Clough is a pretty handy man to have around when you are in a spot of bother. The number of times just the mention of his name has helped iron out a potential problem are countless. But when you are facing a 'mafia' hit over a perceived roulette sting in a casino, you would think it might take more than even Cloughie to come up with a solution.

Let me explain, although this story is all the more incredible because I'm not even a gambler. But try telling that to the less-than-impressed owners of the Bulgarian gambling joint I appeared to wipe out with one lucky bet.

It's so funny looking back on it, but at the time things got quite serious and I was genuinely worried for my safety. Not without good reason I can tell you, after a series of veiled threats from shady-looking Bulgarian gangsters.

Forest were playing CSKA Sofia and in the early 1980s the Bulgarian capital was as far away from a holiday destination as you could imagine. This was Eastern bloc, Iron Curtain territory and it was a drab, dreary place where everyone was genuinely suspi-cious of a group of journalists and photographers in the first place.

Anyway, we did find relief from the boredom one night when someone pointed us in the direction of a hotel which had been set-up to cater for those with more capitalistic leanings. The added attraction of the place was that it paid out in American dollars rather than the local currency which would be rendered completely useless the minute you were out of Bulgarian airspace.

The odd thing about the whole story as it is about to unfold is that I had never even been in a casino or gambled up to that point. I was a complete novice and so the term beginner's luck certainly springs to mind.

Now that's a tag that couldn't be applied to Forest's legendary England keeper Peter Shilton who was known to like a flutter. Even he couldn't have believed what was about to happen as I stepped across to the roulette table.

I had cashed in some money for a few chips and lost most of them on the blackjack tables when I decided to have one last flutter on the roulette wheel.

The other gamblers, including Shilts, were spreading chips all over the place hoping to strike lucky whereas I decided to put all my remaining chips on just one single number – I think it might have been 30 or 31. The croupier actually handed me one chip back because it would have exceeded the house limit in the unlikely 36-1 AGAINST chance of it coming in.

The ball popped in and out of seemingly every number before the wheel finally slowed to a halt and the ball nestled snugly in my number. Bingo!! Or whatever phrase I might have used at the time. There was just stunned looks from the staff as what seemed like millions of chips were counted out.

The croupier shoved them over with a transparently false smile and I scooped them all up barely able to believe my luck. I decided to quit while I was ahead and cash in – then the problems started.

It turned that I had won around 1,700 US Dollars – a small fortune back in those days. I was laughing and joking on the bus back to the hotel when a mysterious-looking guy asked me why I hadn't carried on playing. I told him I wasn't really a gambler and that the money would come in useful.

Ominously, he said something to the effect of that I hadn't left the country yet!

I became aware of various people seemingly taking an interest in my movements and appearing to put pressure on me and told Brian about my fears.

'I'd best look after it,' he said. 'If I've got it, you should be all right. They won't give me any bother. I'll give it back to you back at the City Ground and you can take your bairns away on holiday with it.'

As the time came nearer to flying home it became clear that the casino mob thought I had pulled off some kind of sting. For a complete stranger to just stroll in, place all his chips on one number and then win and walk away with the house jackpot was not their idea of a good night out!

Now I don't look like Paul Newman and I certainly don't gamble like him either, but my new-found status as some kind of big-time hustler was wearing a bit thin.

Despite being asked about the money again by a man at the airport, we eventually got out with it safely thanks to Brian – the only 'untouchable' man in the party.

When we got back, he handed over my wad of cash and I took the whole family on a surprise holiday to Spain!

❛ I was told: 'Don't ever forget that directors never say thank you' and it was good advice ❜

Pal HAROLD ROOME saw many sides of Clough that were off-limits to the general public. Here he recounts how the generous Derby boss offered a helping hand when a friend was put in a tight spot with car problems.

119

A CUT ABOVE

HAROLD ROOME

For many years the man responsible for many of the Derby County players' haircuts was a barber called Frank Reader whose shop was close to the old Baseball Ground.

Brian wasn't a fan of long hair and was pretty old-school in that respect. Frank's shop was very much of its time – a proper old barber's shop.

Eventually, the business got to the stage where it had seen better days. Fancier, unisex salons had started to become the norm and the recession had taken its toll on a lot of people at that time too.

He had made provision to retire and decided it was time to call it a day. But he hit an unforeseen snag when he smashed his car and was left without wheels.

'What's happening on the car front, Frank?' Brian would ask him.

'Well nothing really, I can't afford another one,' he would reply.

'I'll get you one,' Brian assured him.

Frank insisted there was no way he could afford to buy another car and wasn't going to be able to get into any sort of agreement, no matter how well intended, because he couldn't afford any repayments.

One day, a man arrived at Frank's door in a new car and asked him to sign for it. After much argument with the bemused delivery man, Frank reluctantly signed for it, knowing who was behind it all.

Frank immediately went to Brian's and said the car would have to go back.

'If it's worrying you that much, you can pay me back what you like when you like,' Brian assured him.

Frank insisted he wanted a proper agreement drawing up but told me much later that what he had ended up paying back wouldn't have bought the ashtray!

❛ A good goalkeeper can save you 18 points a season. That's like a striker scoring a winning goal every six matches ❜

When Forest fell foul of a dodgy referee in Europe, the manager was offered the chance to take the matter further. But striker PETER DAVENPORT reveals that even in his darkest hour, Cloughie decided to take it on the chin.

120

DARK MOMENT

PETER DAVENPORT

Anyone can be magnanimous in victory, it is how they react when they have just been served a sickening blow that can be the true test of someone's character. I was playing for Cloughie at Forest when we were cheated out of a place in the UEFA Cup final and to this day I can't believe how gracious he was given what had just happened.

Paul Hart, our big and experienced defender was crying because I think he realised it might be his last shot at it, while the rest of us were just shaking our heads in utter disbelief. But what I remember even more vividly is when an elderly gentleman in a tweed suit came into our dressing room at the end of the game.

What he said to the gaffer is still clear in my mind even now. I doubt his words will ever leave me. It actually took well over 10 years for it to be proved that something dodgy went on that night, but we didn't need any convincing at the time that something stank.

Forest were playing Belgian side Anderlecht in the semi-final of the competition. It was the second leg and we were defending a 2-0 lead from the home tie. In the return game, everything that could go wrong did – and it was far from coincidental. Anderlecht won 3-0 and Harty had a late goal disallowed for 'pushing' when TV replays showed there was nothing wrong with it at all.

I played on my own up front that night because we knew exactly what we had to do and were two goals to the good so there shouldn't really have been a problem.

Fairly soon it became apparent that something very odd was going on. Anderlecht's players were clattering into me from behind – and yet the free kicks were being given against me! Things just went from bad to worse and we were dumped out of the competition.

The rest is history – 13 years later the Anderlecht president admitted that referee Emilio Gurucetta Muro was paid a £27,000 'loan' after the game. The Spanish official was killed three years later in a car crash.

But, as I said, the thing that almost haunts me now, all these years later, is the visit of the mystery man in the

193

tweed suit.

He turned out to be the UEFA delegate at that game and he came in to our dressing room and said: 'There's something not quite right here, Mr Clough.'

He went on: 'Something has happened. Do you want to complain? What do you think?'

The gaffer's response said more about the man than anything. Bear in mind he had been the victim of dodgy practices when he was in Europe with Derby.

'Just leave me alone with my own thoughts in my own big head. I've been in this game 26 years and I have never complained about referees. I'm not going to start now."

The old guy bowed and made his way to the door. It was one of the strangest things I have ever seen.

❛ I always appointed brave captains – Mackay McFarland, McGovern, Pearce – all courageous men, who led by example ❜

If Clough decided a player just wasn't going to cut the mustard then he wasn't slow in addressing the problem. STEVE SUTTON recalls the day when a caustic remark from the manager let everyone know that a big money striker would soon be on his way.

121

CURRIE'S OFF

STEVE SUTTON

The gaffer's sense of humour is legendary but if he did want to cut you down to size or get a point over, his delivery could also be astonishingly cutting.

He was a genius in dealing with people. He knew when to wield the stick or offer the carrot. The trouble with him was that if he made his mind up about you and didn't like what he saw, then the exit door beckoned.

I think he took the view that it was a boss-employee situation and if he felt someone wasn't up to the job there was no point beating around the bush. The only times this became a little confusing was when he had forked out good money for a player in the first place.

Cloughie signed a striker called David Currie from Barnsley for the then not inconsiderable fee of £750,000.

The gaffer was never afraid to show that he felt he'd made a big error.

Currie hadn't been at the club very long at all when one brief exchange clearly signalled he'd come to the end of the road at Forest.

Dressing rooms can be cruel places. You have to sink or swim and that goes whether you are a youngster or the most seasoned pro. Currie was no kid and had come for a big fee, but he wasn't exempt from the sharp end of the gaffer's tongue.

The dressing room is a unique environment and when someone else is being slaughtered, the nature of things is that the rest of the boys can find it highly amusing. There might not be any noise but you can see the shoulders shaking as players try to stifle their giggles. Clough teed up his target with his usual precision. Only this time you sensed he wasn't joking.

'Young man, have you bought a house up here yet?'

'No gaffer,' Currie replied.

'Hey, well don't fucking bother!'

❛ My terms of employment are simple – if someone wants to employ me, they take me as I am ❜

TV football legend JOHN MOTSON reveals a secret that he shared with Peter Taylor. The Forest boss never got to know about the help his assistant was given coming up with a book title – which is probably just as well.

122

TITLE DECIDER

JOHN MOTSON

My BBC colleague John Rowlinson and I collaborated on a book about the history of the European Cup from its inception in 1955 to 1980 – the year Forest won it for the second time, beating Hamburg in the final.

We set about interviewing the key figures who had shaped the competition. And I arranged to sit down with Clough and Taylor.

'Compared with some of the other managers who have won it, you don't seem to spend much time coaching on the training ground,' I ventured.

Clough took a large gulp of champagne and gave me a look of pity. 'John, I coach every time I open my mouth,' he said.

Seat-of-the-pants stuff was typical of Clough and Taylor. Nobody knew what to expect from one moment to the next - least of all the players.

One Friday night at the Hendon Hall Hotel in north-west London before they played in the League Cup final at Wembley the following day, Clough walked into the lounge with a crate of beer and insisted all the players had a drink until it was empty.

I was sitting on the other side of the room with Taylor, who asked me whether I thought he should write a book.

'If you do, you will have to link it with Brian somehow,' I said. Although I knew how much of a part Taylor played in the partnership, the public at large identified only with Clough.

'What should I call it then?' asked Taylor.

'Well, something like With Clough, by Taylor,' I suggested.

When Taylor brought out his autobiography later, that was what it was called. Clough was far from pleased at its publication, though at least he didn't know the title was my idea!

❝ Stealing Archie Gemmill from Derby was definitely an imprisonable offence. He was that good a player ❞

Clough's bizarre ways of helping to bond his players in training sessions is the stuff of legend. Former Forest and Manchester United star ROY KEANE recalls how hitting the back of the net was all part of the fun and games

123

BACK OF THE NET

ROY KEANE

Brian Clough and I did not always see eye to eye, but he was a genius, an absolute genius and certainly the best manager I played under, without a shadow of a doubt.

I meet other players who played under him and we all have our own stories but he was such a larger than life character.

He was a really generous man. I went to a charity night with him and some young players and at the end of it he just gave me £50 for going. He didn't have to. It was the first time I had ever seen one of those!

His training was simple, five-a-sides and sprint competitions. He made us all get in a five-a-side goal one day which I thought was brilliant.

We were all crammed in this goal for absolutely no reason at all. So you had the whole Forest first team all squashed in there like a big game of Twister.

If someone did that today, you would be thinking how has this fella got his 'A' or Pro Licence?

But it was brilliant and I used to love the fact that when he came down the training ground, he'd bring his dog. You always knew when he was in because you would see Del Boy.

The thing with him was, he was hard, but fair. I had one or two incidents under him, like in Jersey on tour when I was sent home.

It was a drinking session with a female hockey player, who I think was married. To cut a long story short, an argument happened and there was an incident.

I was only defending myself, but Cloughie had something for me . . . my boarding card for the flight home.

' That Brazilian lad will be fine at Newcastle for a week or two. But I'm not so sure how at home he'll feel when he's knee-deep in snow. Does it snow on Copacabana beach? '

197

Forest strike star GARRY BIRTLES got to know Cloughie better than most and frequently met up with him long after he had retired. But such was the awe in which he held his former boss that that there was one request he couldn't go along with.

124

CALL ME BRIAN

GARRY BIRTLES

There were one or two things I called the gaffer over the years but . . . I could never call him Brian.

I felt strangely honoured when he gave me permission to do just that some time after his retirement.

But I never even attempted it. It didn't seem right and I know John Robertson felt exactly the same way.

I was still in touch with him and the family long after his retirement from the game and he invited me to call him 'Brian' rather than 'Gaffer.'

The same honour was bestowed upon Robbo as well, but we just found it impossible. He was always 'Gaffer' to us and always will be.

I guess the only way I could have even contemplated such a thing was if he had been called 'Sir Brian.' Now that would have been a different matter. The fact he never was knighted, to my mind, is a travesty.

He famously never won the FA Cup but there are a couple of other things that eluded him which remain little short of scandalous really.

How he never got the England job was an absolute disgrace for which the FA should be ashamed. .

He was the top man – the outstanding candidate. He plucked me from obscurity and turned me into an England player with two European Cup medals. If he hadn't done that, I'd probably still be laying floors.

And why the hell he was never knighted is absolutely beyond me. The likes of Trevor Brooking, Alex Ferguson and Bobby Robson were.

Perhaps it was because he threatened to take on the establishment but if that's the case then how come Mick Jagger got a gong as well? It is ridiculous and something that gnaws away at me to this day.

❝ One of the worst crimes you can commit, not just in football but in life, is to ask people to deliver something they haven't got. That destroys them totally ❞

Ex-Forest star STEVE CHETTLE spills the beans on how the manager showed his truly generous side over a bonus dispute. When the players got a call to meet the gaffer after another cup success at Wembley, surely it could only mean one thing?

125

IMPERFECT TEN

STEVE CHETTLE

While I'd be the first to applaud Cloughie's generous side, he could be a stickler when it came to cash – just ask our skipper Stuart Pearce.

In the late 80's and early 90s, we had some success in Wembley cup competitions that were just slightly left of centre when it came to being recognised as mainstream tournaments. We landed the Simod Cup in 1989 with a 4-3 victory over Everton and also lifted the Zenith Data Systems Trophy in 1992, beating Southampton 3-2.

Because they weren't on the same radar as the FA Cup and League Cup there had been no provision made for any win bonuses in the players' contracts.

After realising the implications of that with our Simod Cup victory, the players decided the matter was worth exploring. After all, the club made good money from such a cup run which ended with a healthy gate at Wembley, so why shouldn't the players get some payback?

Pearcey, the skipper, was the man who went in to see the boss and was somewhat surprised by his reply.

'Hey, I'll tell you what. If you win, I will personally give you all a tenner out of my own pocket.'

Pearcey couldn't get any sense out of him on the matter but we felt that we had made our point which hopefully had registered.

And it had!

After beating Southampton, our hearts skipped a beat when we were told the gaffer wanted to see us in the club's trophy room. What kind of surprise could be in store?

As we streamed in, we were met with the sight of 16 boxes of chocolates, each with a crisp ten pound note stuck to the top.

Was this a joke?

Cloughie smiled: 'Hey, well done. The tenners are for you and the chocolates are for your wives and girlfriends!'

'Dave Mackay was Derby County . . . he was better than Bobby Moore'

Top commentator MARTIN TYLER reveals how being really prepared for a meeting with Clough badly backfired. The manager had his own special ideas of how to best protect the TV man's voice and he wasn't going to take no for an answer.

126

ICE CREAM STORY

MARTIN TYLER

I was lucky enough to meet Brian on many occasions and have a number of stories about meetings with him. One of the main reasons I got close to him was because he was very big friends with Brian Moore, the legendary television commentator. I was working for ITV and London Weekend Television in particular and Cloughie would regularly come down in the week to do broadcasts with us.

I found him absolutely wonderful but that certainly didn't mean I was exempt from his masterful displays in what I can only describe as reverse psychology. I think he invented that phrase before it actually became a recognised part of the English language.

I remember once having to interview him immediately after a 2-0 home defeat against Liverpool. We were literally doing it on the hoof, straight after the game had finished. I only had time for a couple of questions so there was no time for messing around. It was seat of the pants stuff and you had little time to collect your thoughts.

I said something like 'Well, Brian, I know you are a big admirer of Liverpool and the Liverpool way, so does that make this defeat a little bit easier to take?'

'Tell me, young man, what is the Liverpool way?' he countered.

Obviously it wasn't the right question, or if it was I hadn't phrased it quite to his liking and he wasn't going to let me get away with it. I stumbled a bit, but squeezed my next question in.

'Well, you haven't scored today, but you've got a young striker playing in your reserve team with a very famous name. Is it time for him to get his chance?'

The young striker in question was none other than his son Nigel, of course, and he wasn't going to take the bait on that either!

'Absolutely no chance!' he insisted.

However, I think if you look it up, young Nigel made his debut very shortly after that.

As I said, he was very good friends with Brian Moore. They were really big buddies who had similar leanings politically it must be said.

Brian Moore and myself were guests of Cloughie's for the infamous

FA Cup match against non-league Walton and Hersham during his brief spell in charge at Brighton.

I'd only just joined the network and the previous season I had played in the Isthmian League for Corinthian-Casuals. I was still very much something of a young lad and very proud of non-League football. Walton won 4-0 and Brian Moore had to tell me to keep calm as the underdogs handed out a real humbling.

One thing is for sure – he was a fascinating man. What he used to do was always keep you on your toes. If, for whatever reason, you thought you were in his good books, it could be dangerous. If you arrived and said 'Brian, we're ready for the interview' he could keep you waiting for hours just to keep in your place. But if you went there in trepidation, which we often did, he could make you feel the most welcome person in the world.

In my numerous times in his office I have had legendary players like Peter Shilton and Trevor Francis making me a cup of tea. I had an apprentice come in and clean my shoes, which I was more than a little uncomfortable about, but had no choice in the matter. What had happened was, I had been walking around the outside of the pitch which was covered in a kind of shale.

'You can't go home with your shoes in that state,' he said.

He made me take them off and dispatched one of his young players to get them cleaned up before returning them to me.

But, my funniest story without any shadow of a doubt came about in the late 70s when Cloughie's Forest side were playing the first leg of a League Cup semi-final against Leeds. Because of getting to know him through his big mate, he invited me to join him prior to the match in the Victoria Hotel in Sheffield which a pal of his ran. My instructions were to get there some time after lunch.

I was driving up and so because I didn't want to be late for a meeting I felt privileged to be having, I made sure I got there with plenty of time to spare. I ended up getting there at around 12 noon and made the conscious decision to treat myself to the biggest lunch possible because I knew that with meeting Brian afterwards the chances were that I would probably not get to eat again until extremely late. So, thinking ahead and making sure I was totally prepared for what the day could throw at me, I found a place which fitted the bill and duly feasted until I could eat no more.

Satisfied it was now time to catch up with Brian, I got to the hotel only to find him still at the lunch table. The message was quickly relayed to me that Mr Clough was expecting me and I was beckoned to join him.

'Right young man, you have got a very important job tonight with that voice of yours.'

I probably nodded and wondered what was coming next. I couldn't possibly have guessed that's for sure.

'Do you know what's very good for your voice?' he asked me.

I waited . . .

'Ice cream – that's what. Waiter! Get my friend some ice cream please.'

Now, as I explained, at this point I am still absolutely full having eaten like a horse and couldn't have eaten another crumb. What was I to do? There was point telling Brian that I couldn't tackle it. Ah, what was one scoop of ice cream anyway? I'd get on with it. Well, you can imagine. Because the waiter is aware the ice cream is at the special request of you-know-who, he walks in with the biggest plate of it you have ever seen.

'Eat that, young man,' he said.

'Ermm . . .'

'I'm telling you – it's good for you.'

So, I pretty much demolished what amounted to a vat of ice cream while he was kindly informing me what his team would be for that evening's game.

He sent me away with all the information I needed, an extremely full stomach and a memory I will cherish for ever.

❛ I'd spotted a girl in there with a smile as wide as Stockton High Street. Little did I know then that my future wife had been brought up so close to where I lived - just on the other side of Albert Park ❜

– on meeting his wife

*Nottingham Evening Post photographer STEVE MITCHELL had
good reason to suspect the worst when he found himself in the
Forest dressing room. And Cloughie let him know there
could be dire consequences if he didn't turn back.*

127

SOPPY FILM

STEVE MITCHELL

It had been a day of tension and drama. Forest in the 91/92 Rumbelows League Cup semi-final second leg away at Spurs. The match was all-square at 1-1 after the first leg at the City Ground following some controversial offside decisions - Wembley awaited for the winners at White Hart Lane.

As kick off approached, police announced that the stadium was to be evacuated as a bomb threat had been received. Supporters packed the streets and pubs as we waited for news. No-one knew if the match would even go ahead.

The game eventually kicked off almost two hours later in lashing rain, by which time the atmosphere in the ground was incredible.

Roy Keane's goal won the tie. I can still remember the distinctive whoosh of the water that had built up on the net hitting the ground as he smashed his header home.

At the final whistle I managed to get round to the players' tunnel, grabbing a picture of Brian Clough shaking Stuart Pearce's hand and getting Keane and fellow scorer Lee Glover together for another shot. In the confusion I somehow managed to actually get down the tunnel where I eventually got the nod to go into the Forest dressing room.

When Forest had beaten Bristol City in the 1989 League Cup semi-final second leg, I was unceremoniously dumped into the team bath by the players. Luckily. I'd managed to stay on my feet as I hit the water with camera in hand, so I felt easy enough to join in the general amusement at my expense - until I

realised that all my rolls of film from the day were in my waterproof pocket just above the waterline.

So when I was ushered into Tottenham's away dressing room, I was more prepared for the inevitable dunking. The players were celebrating in the tub at the back and Brian was sitting on his own in the main area. I asked his permission to go through for pictures.

'Well, you can, but you know what'll happen,' he said with a knowing grin.

With my films safely in my camera bag, I disappeared into the steam. This time the ambush was more successful.

Nigel Clough whisked my camera off me and I disappeared full length under the waves. As I surfaced I remember a lot of raucous cheering and laughter and Stuart Pearce saying: 'You'll catch your death - do you want a Fisherman's Friend?'

I got out of the bath, weighed down by my sodden clothes - all I had with me for the long, cold drive back to Nottingham - and emerged to a blunt assessment from Clough.

'You bloody prat! I told you, didn't I? Now get stripped off and get that lot on - all you're short of is shoes.'

He pointed over to a neat pile of hot towels, a pair of socks, tracksuit bottoms, t-shirt - and one his famous green sweaters.

I thanked him profusely - he'd probably saved me from certain pneumonia. As I got dressed I looked over and was amazed to see Brian Clough, the victorious manager who had just got his team to a Wembley final in dramatic circumstances, trying to undo the knots on the shoelaces of my soaking old Doc Martens.

Two days later, Forest were back in the capital at Crystal Palace. With the green sweater duly washed and ironed, I handed it all over to Liam O'Kane.

'You daft bugger, you could have kept that as a souvenir,' he said cheerily as he disappeared into the dressing room with it!

Imagine that – one of Cloughie's very own green tops all of my own.

6 **When you open your big gob like me you are a target. I've got to be a winner or they'll cut me to shreds** 9

Nottingham Forest's official club photographer JOHN SUMPTER has spent well over 30 years with unrivalled access to Clough and his players. But here he reveals how such a long-standing relationship didn't get off to the best of starts.

128

FIRST AND LAST

JOHN SUMPTER

I hardly got off to the best of starts with Brian but I must have done something right – 33 years as Forest's official club photographer would suggest that!

The very first time I became aware of him was shortly after I had started in 1978 when I was summoned to the trophy room to do a picture with his secretary who had just had a baby.

I set things up and got everyone into place only to discover to my horror that just when we got to the crucial moment, I hadn't switched my camera on!

'Hey, I told her you were a professional,' he said shaking his head in disbelief.

As I'm sure you can imagine, over 30 years of taking pictures for the club's programme has provided me with some magic moments. Cup successes at home and abroad, were all dutifully recoded on my camera.

But, oddly enough, my first excursion on the Cup glory trail ended up with me being banned from the team bus by Cloughie for having too much to drink!

I had actually travelled down to the Wembley Littlewoods Cup final clash against Luton on a coach laid on for the commercial department of the club.

Victory meant everyone was cock-a-hoop and I was in the dressing room immediately afterwards recording the celebrations.

After getting a load of fantastic shots, Cloughie asked me how I had got down to the game and so I told him.

'Hey, come back with us!' he insisted. 'Get yourself on that coach.'

I took him up on the offer and I was given a seat immediately behind the jubilant manager near the front.

The champagne had been flowing in the dressing room and then continued on the coach and, gradually, I started to get a bit too chatty for the boss' liking.

'I don't want to hear your voice again, young man,' he warned me.

'That's the last time I want to hear a peep out of you.'

Eventually, as he made it clear he was getting more and more irritated, I thought it might be wise to move out of his earshot.

'Can I go to the back and take some pictures of the players with the Cup?' I asked.

'Hey, you're not lifting that cup,' he said sternly, clearly worried I might drop it.

I knew I had had enough to drink. The motorway was heaving and it was as much as I could do to make sure I didn't follow suit.

By now I was at the back with the players, which was separated off from the front few seats by a curtain.

When we eventually pulled up, Cloughie appeared at the curtain and fixed his eyes on me as I sat with Steve Hodge one side of me and Stuart Pearce the other.

They had a match with Southampton on the Tuesday so Cloughie informed the players of the arrangements and I thought I'd got way without hearing any more about it. But at the ground on the Monday, he collared me.

'You were a bloody disgrace on our coach – that's your first – and last – time, I'm telling you!'

And it was . . .

There was no long term harm done. I enjoyed a good relationship with him over the years and one thing he often said to me, has stuck with me all these years.

He really appreciated the importance of photographs and was more often than not happy to pose or stunt pictures to suit the occasion. He could turn a smile on like a politician. I've had to fix up pictures when he wasn't in the best of moods for whatever reason, but suddenly, his face would light up for the camera.

'Photographs are for evermore,' he would say. And, as usual, he was right. That phrase has stuck with me.

❛ I wished there had been a local by-law prohibiting Gascoigne from ever playing at Wembley again ❜

Top freelance journalist NEIL HALLAM reveals how it was him Clough turned to when he wanted to break a massive story. The trouble was he was in the pictures at the time and hadn't prepared for the mystery and intrigue that was to follow.

129

KELLY'S HEROES

NEIL HALLAM

I never did get the money that Brian Clough owed me for two cinema tickets and it was several years after I went to my local fleapit to watch 'Kelly's Heroes' before I found out whether Clint Eastwood, Donald Sutherland and Telly Savalas managed to hijack a huge consignment of Nazi gold. How come?

As the film moved towards its denouement, the screen suddenly flickered and the action was interrupted by a message which read: "Would Neil Hallam ring Brian Clough at the Midland Hotel. URGENT."

There were disgruntled mutterings as I picked my way along the row of seats and made for the cinema manager's office to make the call and more mutterings when I went back to tell my girlfriend that Brian had asked me to get to the hotel immediately. 'Don't worry,' he said. 'I'll give you the price of the cinema tickets and you'll make enough money out of the story you'll flog when you get here to pay for the best seats every night for ten years.'

We hurtled down the A6 to Derby and as soon as I walked into the hotel, I realised what he meant. There with Brian and Peter Taylor was Ian Storey-Moore, the Nottingham Forest winger who was just about the most coveted player in the English game at that time.

'Bloody hell,' I gasped. 'I thought he was supposed to be going to Manchester United.'

'Aye, so did he,' said Brian. 'And so did Forest,' added Peter.

In those days I was sports editor of Raymonds News Agency, whose head office was in Derby, and Brian and Peter were keen to have it all over the morning papers that Storey-Moore had opted to pull out of a transfer to United and sign for the Rams instead. They hoped that this would force Forest, United and the Football Association to accept that the move to Derby was 'fait accompli.'

My first thought was to offer the story to the Mirror – then the biggest payers in Fleet Street - as an exclusive but Brian and Peter wanted everybody to have it. The more coverage the better.

'Forest and United won't like it but if the papers are full of it there's not much they can do about it,' reasoned Taylor. 'Apart from get us banned sine die for kidnapping,' said Clough.

I mobilised the agency to whip the story out to the nationals and the major broadcasting channels and then returned to the bar to say my goodbyes and head home, job done. Fat chance.

'We've booked you a room,' Brian informed me. And then, pulling me out of Storey-Moore's earshot, he added: 'You're in the next one to him. Any sign of him clearing off and you ring me immediately, whatever the hour.'

'Is there any danger of that?' I asked, slightly alarmed to be appointed the player's keeper. 'I thought he wanted to sign for Derby.'

'He does,' said Brian. 'But Matt Gillies (the Forest manager) and Frank O'Farrell (the United boss) are camped out at his house and they keep getting his wife to ring up and plead with him to go home.'

Brian was clearly nervous about the whole business and, it transpired, with good reason. While Derby had transfer forms bearing the signature of Storey-Moore, they had no agreement, written or otherwise, from the City Ground. United, on the other hand, had forms signed by Forest and con-senting to a £200,000 transfer to Old Trafford.

I awoke the next morning to discover, with some relief, that Storey-Moore had not bolted from under my nose and that the story was plastered all over the back pages of the nationals and was told that he would be introduced to Derby fans as a new signing that afternoon, before the kick-off against Wolves.

'Make sure it gets on the telly,' urged Brian. 'Make sure everybody has got cameras there.'

He and Peter were still convinced that the FA would 'not have the bottle' to veto something presented as a done deal but, rarely for them, they were completely wrong.

Storey-Moore did go home. He was persuaded to sign for Manchester United and the FA did have the bottle not only to ratify that transfer but also to fine Derby heavily for as blatant an attempt at hijacking as the game is ever likely to see.

On the other hand, as I discovered much later, that other hijacking attempt by Clint Eastwood, Telly Savalas and company worked a treat.

❛ Sometimes you win football matches in unusual places – like before you have even set foot on the field ❜

Top sports journalist DAVID MEEK was well-connected at Old Trafford as the Manchester Evening News' United reporter for many years. Here he recalls how Cloughie couldn't resist giving him a message for the United directors.

130

UNITED MESSAGE

DAVID MEEK

I went to cover Forest's European Cup final victory over the Swedish side Malmo in 1979. The game took place in Munich – a city with special significance to anyone with a Manchester United connection. That certainly applied to me, as I covered United on a daily basis for the Manchester Evening News.

I'd met Clough before, in fact the first time he rather unnerved me by saying: 'You've not been in this game very long have you?'

I informed him that I had been in it for quite a few years, upon which he said I looked too smart and fit to be a journalist!

I don't know whether it was the fact that I looked smart and fit or that he didn't think I was very experienced which unnerved me, but something did.

Anyway, bearing that in mind, I kind of felt I knew him but wasn't sure he would place me amid all the excitement of that night in West Germany – how wrong can you be?

Cloughie gave his after match press conference and when that had finished I wondered if I might get something a little extra and a bit different by following him out of the room and trying to get a quick word.

He got into a lift to go down to the dressing rooms a few floors below and I asked him something. He came back at me, quick as a flash . . .

'Hey, you tell those Manchester United directors that if they had had the courage to appoint me as their manager, it could have been Manchester United winning the European Cup tonight!'

Typical of the man – even in his hour of glory, he just couldn't resist having a dig.

❛ If any footballer is under the illusion that a manager's job is NOT to replace him with someone better, then he hasn't been properly educated ❜

209

When Clough decided to bring firebrand STAN BOWLES to the City Ground, it always promised to be a fiery relationship. The former QPR striker reveals how one row too many signalled the beginning of the end of an unlikely pairing.

131

STORMY RELATIONSHIP

STAN BOWLES

Cloughie must have had something special to achieve what he did – but I haven't a clue what it was. I never saw it.

Cloughie was alright – when he was asleep! I guess you could just say that when it came to me and him there was a clash of personalities.

When the reigning European champions came in for me it was the greatest day of my career. I got a £15,000 golden handshake from QPR and the same from Forest.

I remember him standing in the dressing room one day and saying 'Rome wasn't built in a day laddie, but I wasn't on that particular job!'

He was quite amusing at times. But when you see Clough on the telly – it wasn't an act. No, he really was that arrogant . . .

People go on about what a great manager he was and to win two European Cups is staggering. But . . . he never took training and he didn't come into the dressing room until five minutes before the kick-off, so you tell me how he won them.

To be honest we got off on the wrong foot. He said: 'You Cockneys are all the same.'

I said: 'Excuse me I'm from Manchester. Then I told him I had loads of 'O' and 'A' levels and when he found out that was bollocks he went mad.'

Of course my biggest row with him came when I stormed out of the European Cup final in 1980 because he wouldn't select me for John Robertson's testimonial. John was a big pal of mine and Clough said: "You're turning down a European Cup medal for that!'

'Yeah, fucking poke it!' I fumed. We never spoke again.

'European Cup winner's medal?

I just got the hump. I do things on instinct. Robbo was my best friend at Forest and Clough left me out of his testimonial. It sounds stupid, but to me it wasn't and that was it.

❛ Teddy Sheringham has got bigger dimples than Shirley Temple ❜

When former Forest defender STEVE CHETTLE was laid up after fracturing his cheek, he was handed a generous rest cure by Clough. Was the extrovert boss really planning to send him out to the West Indies? Well, not quite.

132

SKY HIGH

STEVE CHETTLE

Football fans the world over can remember something special that happened in Forest's home game with Manchester City back in 1990 – but it sticks in my mind for a completely different reason.

To most, the abiding memory is of Gary Crosby's cheeky match winner when he came from behind City keeper Andy Dibble, headed the ball out of his hands and scored to the disbelief of everyone – none more so than poor Dibble!

My recollection of it all is slightly more blurred mainly because I had taken a whack in the face from City's big Scottish defender Colin Hendry in the first half and had to be taken to hospital.

I had to leave the field in the first half with what turned out to be a fractured cheekbone. The gaffer hadn't realised how badly I was hurt and was desperately trying to get me back out to play. But I ended up being carted off to hospital and needed surgery to fix the problem.

After I had come out I was feeling a bit down in the dumps as I realised I would need to take it easy for quite some time while my face healed. Out of the blue, the gaffer got in touch.

'Do you like cricket son?' came the rather unusual enquiry.

'Yeah, I love it boss,' I replied.

'Would you like to watch the West Indies and England Test series?'

For one fleeting moment I wondered if he was going to tell me to pack my bags and jet off to the Caribbean – but no such luck.

But what he was offering was a fantastic gesture to a young footballer feeling a little bit sorry for himself. He arranged to have Sky TV fitted at my new house and paid for it all himself so that I could convalesce in a bit more comfort.

I thought that was a magnificent gesture.

❛ Robert Maxwell had an ego bigger than his yacht – perhaps that's why he fell overboard ❜

Former Forest youth team coach JOHN PERKINS came up with his own solution when one of his youngsters was getting just a touch too big for his boots. But he was a little bit worried when Cloughie came to watch and noticed his star player wasn't in the team.

133

YOUNG BIG HEAD

JOHN PERKINS

The gaffer was quite proud of his 'Old Big 'Ead' nickname, but he always insisted it was because he used it as a reminder of him not to become one. He had no time for anyone who he felt was getting too big for his boots as I was to find out one day.

I worked for him for over six years as his youth team coach at Forest. I still feel it was a great honour and privilege to have worked for such a legend of a manager. There is not a day goes by when I don't think of him and I will be forever grateful for the opportunity he gave to me to coach at a professional level. I have now been coaching in the game for twenty five years, and I owe that all to him. Despite the demands of running the first team, he always wanted to know how the young players were progressing and whenever possible he would watch the youth team on a Saturday morning.

There was one particular Saturday I recall, on a pitch in the middle of nowhere, when I was genuinely worried that I might really have upset him.

We had a very promising young player who had just gained his first England Under-18 youth cap. His name was Stephen Howe, but was better known as Bobby. We had a youth team game against Chesterfield away which was something of a geographical nightmare. Chesterfield's home ground for youth team games was in the middle of nowhere and exceptionally hard to find. The joke was that if the Russians ever invaded these isles then you could do a lot worse than go to Chesterfield's youth ground, because they would never find you there. For this particular game I had named Bobby as a substitute in an effort to just bring him down a peg or two. The previous week he had been with the England squad, and performed very well. But on his return his training and general attitude to the staff was very poor. For the want of a better word he was going round the club being a bit big-headed. So he was being left out of the side for these reasons and that was something he did not agree with.

So there we were in a remote part of Chesterfield and the match had been going for ten minutes. All of a sudden I heard a very familiar noise. Yes, it was the sound of the gaffer's dog Del

Boy, and just behind him walking very briskly along was his master. I couldn't believe my eyes, although I shouldn't really have been that shocked.

He walked very slowly towards me, with a big smile. As he got closer he said: 'Good morning Grimshaw (a pet name).' 'Can I have a quiet word with you, pal?' he added. So we walked 20 yards away from everybody and he asked, very assertively:

'Why have you left my England boy out of the team?'

I don't mind admitting I was a little apprehensive as to telling him why I thought it had been necessary to make a point on this particular issue – star player or not.

'Gaffer, he came back from his England trip with a bit of a bad attitude, and was basically being a big head, so I named him as a sub and told him to make the drinks at half-time.'

There was at least a minute's silence, long enough for me to wonder exactly what was going through his mind, before he replied. I admit, I was getting ready to duck or prepare myself for an ear-bashing. He then said in a very loud voice:

'Well done, pal, I would have done exactly the same thing.'

He then called Bobby over and said: 'Son, I would like you to take my dog for a walk for 10 minutes . . .'

'Hey, and by the way Bobby, there's only one big head around here AND THAT'S ME!!'

❛ I never froze a player with fear in my life. I sent them out thinking they were the best since Stanley Matthews ❜

134

THE GENTLE TOUCH

DAVID BALL

I think the best way to describe Brian's relationship with our club was that he touched it gently. He lived just yards away across the road and we would see him occasionally, but he was never in our face.

I think that although he loved sport, he had enough of it in his life not to want to get too involved. He loved his cricket and was a vice-president here, supporting us occasionally. He'd sit on a bench in the far corner over there and watch us now and again. That was his corner.

He became very friendly with our groundsman Steve because he would walk his dog around the ground early in the morning when no one else was here. The two of them would often have a chat.

I do recall one evening he wandered in to a committee meeting thinking it was a quiz night. I don't think Brian and committees were ever a good match and once he'd realised it wasn't a quiz, he kindly left a £20 donation and promptly left!

But the one thing that absolutely stands out for me was one occasion in the close season when we were working hard to remove some undulations on our pitch.

Brian wandered across and a few of the kids including my youngest son Christopher were having a kickabout. He played a bit of football with them and then after chatting to us, asked if he could take the children across to his house so he could give them a bar of chocolate.

Off they went, Brian making sure they crossed the road safely and he duly gave them all a chocolate bar before marching them back!

❛ Long ball game? The only thing I've ever seen catch a ball on it's nose from 14 feet was a seal I watched as a kid at Blackpool Tower circus ❜

Singing legend Frankie Vaughan steadfastly refused to ever sing without a proper pianist to hand. But here, former top ref CLIVE THOMAS recalls a night when he was forced to make an exception as Clough decided he fancied a croon.

135

GIMME THE MOONLIGHT

CLIVE THOMAS

Brian might have been a massive fan of Frank Sinatra, but it was singing with Frankie Vaughan that led to him getting one of his biggest rounds of applause.

I count myself privileged to have been there that night when my big pal Frankie, Brian, myself and Kenny Lynch brought the house down with a rendition of Gimme the Moonlight.

One bit of background to this unlikely musical foursome that I will explain says more about the persuasive powers of Brian Clough than anything he has ever done on or around a football pitch.

Frankie was a very close friend of mine and, I can assure you, he would NEVER sing at any function unless he has a proper pianist. He sang this night – he had no option - and the four of us came off to rapturous applause.

The dinner was a special one for me because I was picking up a Sportsman of the Rhondda Valley award putting me in a select bunch alongside legends like rugby union star Cliff Morgan and ex-Swansea and Manchester City footballer Roy Paul.

Brian came down to do a speech and stole the show of course. Like on so many occasions, he came along to give his support without any renumeration.

I've lost count of the times Brian did me the honour of coming all the way down to Wales for charity functions, or whatever, and never charging a single penny. He wouldn't ask for anything towards the petrol and was just as generous with his time.

One time he came down to an event for Boys' Clubs in Wales and we ended up raising about £15,000.

I asked Brian if he wanted anything and he just said I needed to look after his friend and former Derby director Mike Keeling who had driven him.

'Make sure Mike's got a few sandwiches for the way home and that'll be fine,' he assured me.

❛ We were arrogant at the bottom and we were arrogant at the top – that's consistency ❜

*Former Ipswich Town PRO MEL HENDERSON found himself
in a tight spot over a promise to his young son. Would Clough
come to his rescue? The Forest boss did more than that
as he gave the youngster a real day to remember.*

136

MASCOT MAGIC

MEL HENDERSON

There's no shortage of Cloughie fans who think he is a miracle worker. Well, I've got to say that on one particular occasion, he certainly worked one for me.

Picture the scene . . . I'm the public relations officer at Portman Road and on this particular Saturday morning, I'm off up to Nottingham for a Sixth Round FA Cup clash between Forest and Ipswich Town. It was March 7, 1981 and little did I know that morning that I was going to witness an absolutely classic match. The *Observer* headline the following day simply read: MATCH OF THE SEASON.

My son Derek was six at the time and his favourite footballer was Trevor Francis. As I was just about to leave the house, Derek asks if he can be the mascot for the game!

I, of course, had what appeared to be the perfect get out of jail card in that the match was over at Nottingham and that was a long way for a little boy to go etc, etc . . . .

Anyway, I explained with daddy working at the football club, it wouldn't have been fair on all the other girls and boys who wanted to be mascots.

I'd wrongly assumed that he wanted to be Ipswich's mascot but Francis was his favourite player and he wanted to be Forest's mascot.

I rashly promised him that if the game was a draw I would ask Brian Clough if he could be mascot.

Sod's Law, the game finished 3-3 and now I've got to try and make some serious inroads into seeing if there is any way my boy can be a mascot at the replay. I had no relationship with Cloughie, but because I was the PRO for Ipswich it meant I did have access behind the scenes.

About an hour after the final whistle of an absolutely thrilling game, an official pointed me in the direction of Brian's office.

I knocked the door somewhat hesitantly and there was no answer. My second knock was met with a faint 'Come in.'

I opened the door and the first thing I noticed was that the room was almost dark. There was no light on and the great man was just sitting there apparently collecting his thoughts.

I apologised and said I hoped I wasn't disturbing him and explained who I was and then told him the story. To my astonishment, a big smile came to his face and he said:

'You bring him to us at the Copdock Hotel at about 5pm and we will look after him.'

I could hardly believe it. I thanked him profusely and made my way out of his office. The Copdock was a favourite haunt of visiting teams. It was about three miles out of Ipswich and was favoured by some teams because there was a grass pitch to train on nearby.

I couldn't wait to get home to tell my young son. When I had, Tuesday just couldn't come quickly enough. He had the Forest kit and his little boots on and I took him along to the hotel in good time where Cloughie said: 'Leave him with us, we will look after him.'

I thought they would just give him a few minutes of their time but they were actually going to take him in on the team bus!

I went down to the ground and said to a mate on the gate: 'Do me a favour and give me a shout when the Forest bus comes.'

I was quite lucky really because at Ipswich there is a long driveway the team bus has to take on the approach and it has to crawl at about 5 mph along the way.

I got the nudge and made my way out of the main office block and you can imagine the lump in my throat as the Forest coach came towards us.

There was Cloughie at the front and there, perched on his knee in his full Forest kit, was little Derek. I couldn't believe it, so heaven knows what he must have felt like.

He was taken into the away dressing room and re-appeared for the pre-match knockabout where his hero Trevor Francis looked after him. He got to kick a ball past Peter Shilton just for good measure and later told me that he had actually sat with the players for the pre-match meal!

He went up to the centre circle to meet the Ipswich mascot and join up with skippers Kenny Burns and Mick Mills and even got a mention on TV!

ITV were broadcasting highlights of the game and commentator Gerry Harrison commented: "The Forest mascot today is actually the son of the Ipswich PRO!'

My son has never forgotten that day. He was so infatuated with Trevor Francis that he even switched his allegiance from Forest to Manchester City when the striker moved on. He remains a City fan to this day.

I've got to say that Cloughie's generosity and kindness that day is something that has stuck with my son for life. And guess what . . . he still has his lucky 10p coin that the referee gave him!

❛ He can now retire overnight at the age of 12 ❜
– on giving his medals to his grandson

137

SWEET GESTURE

HAROLD ROOME

My dear wife June used to work for Brian and would run him about quite a bit. Every Sunday she would pick him up and take him down to the newsagent's shop at Bramcote, just outside Nottingham, and on many occasions he would come out of the house clutching a pot of tea.

One of the funniest memories I have of him is over a stunt he used to pull when when we went to watch Burton Albion together. My wife got into the habit of making sure she had a large bag of sweets at the ready waiting for the inevitable question.

'Juney? You got any sweets?' he would ask before taking one himself and then handing them around to any of the children who were close by.

Where we sat at Burton was up with the directors but the position of the seats mean that people could walk right by him and have a chat or ask for an autograph. It was quite astonishing how much you could feel the love for the man.

Punters loved the fact that they were in such close proximity and some of the things he came out with had them in stitches.

Kids would walk past with pie and chips or whatever and Brian would say 'gizza chip.' It was all so up close and personal considering what a legend he was and people seemed to really appreciate the fact that he just sat there watching his son's team like any proud dad. To see him you would never have guessed that here was a man who had built teams that had gone on to conquer Europe and was widely regarded as having one of the most astute football brains of all time.

Brian's generosity is pretty well known to those who were close to him. When I first retired in 1986 through ill-health, he often used to urge me to go and spend some time in his apartment in Cala Millor free of charge.

'Piss off and get some sun on your back,' he'd say, even offering to pay for the flights if that was the problem. We never did take him up on that, but we knew he would have.

I mean to say, we are talking about a man here who once gave us the surprise of our lives one Sunday afternoon.

As I said, June used to run Brian to Bramcote. We had a Datsun, but it was a bit of a rot-box if the truth be known and was getting to the stage where we really needed to be doing something about it.

'Have you done anything about your car yet, Juney?' Brian would ask.

One Sunday afternoon he rang us up instructing us to go over to his brother's house in Mickleover.

'Get over and see our Baz, he's got something for you.'

And there it was . . . a brand new Ford Fiesta Ghia.

Brian's only personal insistence in cars was that he didn't like people driving like lunatics. He had an absolute hatred of that. I recall one day when a group of us were being driven back home in his Merc by his close friend Mike Keeling. Mike was driving extremely fast and Brian asked him to slow down. In the end his patience snapped and Brian ordered him to stop the car so he could get out.

He got out of the car and started to walk. Mike drove on a little further before asking the rest of us if anyone else had a problem with his driving and would like to get out. We all said yes and he duly stopped to let us get out. Brian eventually caught us up and was falling about laughing. We asked him what was so funny.

'What the hell did you lot get out for? You don't need to worry about me, I can get a lift anywhere!'

❛ Me and Taylor were the first to introduce the two-man job – now everybody's copied it ❜

219

*Former Leeds and Liverpool star GARY McALLISTER reveals
how a bizarre meeting with Cloughie over a £1m transfer
to Forest from Leicester persuaded him that maybe he
would be better off taking his services elsewhere.*

138

PASS MASTER

GARY McALLISTER

I came so close to signing for Cloughie, but in the end I became the one that got away. I was a massive fan of his and to this day I can't help wondering how it would have worked out between us. I'm sure I would have been good for him and the style of football he liked to play and I'm equally certain he would have been great for me. As it happened, it wasn't to be and, much to his annoyance, I chose to go in a different direction to him! Well, Leeds, the club where he was famously sacked after 44 days.

I was at Leicester when Forest came in for me. It was the time when they had players like Stuart Pearce, Des Walker and Nigel Clough and were noted for their excellent, exciting brand of football. I'm sure their style would have suited me down to the ground.

David Pleat came and told me that Forest wanted to talk to me and we arranged to meet at the Sandiacre Post House hotel. There was no love lost between Cloughie and my agent Jon Holmes. Jon had fixed up deals that took a number of good players out of Forest - the likes of Peter Shilton and Tony Woodcock to name just two.

Because of my agent's connection, I was well briefed on Cloughie's often unorthodox style, so perhaps I shouldn't have been shocked by the way our talks went.

He surprised me for a start by choosing to conduct them in a public bar. I'd expected that Forest might have fixed up for a private room somewhere.

First off, he started on Jon, by telling me: 'This guy representing you is a shithead!'

He quickly followed that up by insisting that he wasn't really and asked one of his assistants: 'Send Jon's wife some flowers and chocolates from me!'

As we tried to get talks under way, there were frequent occasions when Cloughie found it necessary to acknowledge the intrigued stares of passers-by.

'Yes, you're right, it is Brian Clough!' he said.

Then he took me by surprise, asking his chief scout Alan Hill: 'Tell me, have I watched this boy play before?'

Alan reminded him that he had

which came as something of a relief considering he was about to pay around £1m for me.

'Ah, yes, I remember,' he assured me.

'You don't like tackling do you?'

I just shrugged my shoulders and waited to see what came next. I didn't have to wait long. He eyed me up again.

'Ah, yes, and you don't like chasing back either do you? And you don't like to head the ball do you?'

I was beginning to wonder just what I could do that might appeal to him, when he revealed all.

'But I tell you what you do do well. You pass the ball and I LIKE THAT,' he said exaggerating the last three words.

Then he informed me that there was something else he wasn't particularly happy about.

'Now then, the money you are asking for. I've got the England captain in my team and even he doesn't get that much. But I'm going to give it to you!'

Then, he started on my dress sense, picking out a smart pair of gentleman's boots I was wearing. He referred to them as cowboy boots and they clearly fascinated him.

'Young man, what are those? If you sign here, you must buy me a pair of those - they're wonderful.'

It was getting more bizarre and in the end I told him that I had two or three other options and needed time to think things over.

The following day I spoke to Leeds and when Cloughie rang me back it was with slight trepidation that I felt obliged to tell him I had chosen to go to Elland Road. Leeds? Brian Clough? I didn't know what he would think about that. I quickly found out.

SLAM! The phone banged against the receiver and I quickly realised that any move to Forest, was now well and truly dead and buried.

6 Not only did I do my knee, but I banged my head. A lot of people have put that down to the way I've behaved for the last ten years 9
– on career-ending injury

221

Favourite snapper TREVOR BARTLETT reveals a touching story of how he jumped to the front of the queue and beat Fleet Street's finest to the pictures everyone wanted after the legend called time on his extraordinary managerial career.

139

PICTURE PERFECT

TREVOR BARTLETT

When it was suddenly announced that Brian was to retire from the game it seemed like every photographer in the United Kingdom and beyond was camped outside the The Elms – the beautiful family home in Quarndon.

Suddenly that lovely house where I had been so often was surrounded by photographers from everywhere hoping to get a shot of the great man. There were lenses of all shapes and sizes wherever you looked.

The Elms wasn't the easiest of places to stake out because it could only be approached by the front and that was fairly well protected by established trees and a huge hedge.

Brian guarded his family privacy with a vengeance and had always been fiercely protective of that throughout his career. How handy that hedge was now a pack of paparazzi was camped outside waiting to get a shot.

They might well have got a shot they weren't expecting in times gone by when Brian was at his bristling best! But this was different. The fact that someone who many felt was the greatest football manager of all time was bowing out was a massive story. He knew that better than anyone. Believe me, no one had to tell Brian what was or wasn't a picture opportunity.

He knew exactly what photographers wanted. In just the same way he instinctively knew the requirements of radio reporters or the written press. And when he was in the mood, nobody did it better. The fact that they were now camped outside his house in numbers might have irritated him a little but, believe me, he would have been more surprised if they hadn't been there!

When I got there, the normally restricted view was now non-existent. Many of the photographers had steps to try and by-pass the assorted shrubs and foliage and it was as much as you could do to squeeze into a decent spot. Those who were there for the national daily newspapers had all day to try and get their picture while I didn't have that luxury. I was there for the Nottingham Evening Post and with every passing minute would come one more bead of sweat. I certainly hadn't got forever and a day to come up with something and because of my relationship with Brian I wasn't about to start poking a zoom lens in the direction of the house. Here was a man who I had been to many different parts of the world with; a man who I had shared a drink and a laugh with and a man who had helped me out more times than I could remember.

Whether or not he was looking out for me or not, I don't know. But somehow he spotted me from an upstairs window and got a message to me to come to the door. The other photographers could only look on enviously as I made my way to the front door and was ushered in.

'Fancy having a big hedge like that Brian, I'm only a little bloke you know?' I said. He laughed at that one.

'Come on in,' he said.

He was absolutely brilliant with me and I took pictures of him and Barbara, his lovely wife. They got me to take pictures of him with the children and some of the grandkids. It was fabulous stuff and needless to say I was the envy of, well, every photographer in the country really, as I made my way to the office with a lovely set of exclusive pictures for my paper.

You obviously have sympathy with some of the other lads camped outside there hoping to get lucky. But my 'luck' was the culmination of many years working with Brian and having his trust. It hadn't come overnight. They would have quite happily paid a lot of money for what I had in my camera that day.

❛ I'd tell players if they couldn't get into work by 10.30 in the morning then they weren't worth bothering with ❜

223

Burton Albion chairman BEN ROBINSON reveals how Cloughie offered his congratulations over an FA Cup giant-killing act only to quickly put him in his place when he suggested that maybe son Nigel had inherited his star quality.

140

PURE GENIUS

BEN ROBINSON

I must be one of the few football club chairman never to fall out with Brian. Without question Brian and his son Nigel put Burton on the map as a footballing town.

The brilliant job Nigel did as manager is well documented and there, gently coaxing him on in the background, was his dad. The one thing I would say is that Brian never interfered. He hardly missed a home game and watched us in a couple of away matches too.

He was a legend and the fans loved him. People used to love having their picture taken with him and he'd always be coming out with the odd quip. Lots of excited fathers would bring their sons to meet him and would introduce him as their hero. He was a legend.

When Nigel took the player-manager's job in 1998, Brian became a regular visitor to the club and he actually bought a vice-president's ticket.

The one thing I genuinely regret was that I never asked Brian to become our club president. It was a mistake really, albeit one made for all the right reasons. I didn't want to impose on

him, or make him think that because Nigel was the manager that it might be something he was obliged to take on.

I just know that he enjoyed his times watching Burton so much. He had his seat there and we'd take him a cup of tea and a biscuit at half-time. To all intents and purposes he was just another supporter watching on from the stands.

Of course, he was very much more than that. But for all his experience and knowledge he would never shout out anything other than the odd observation.

But odd quips, from the master, were inevitably lapped up by those around him. He had a very special presence. He could silence a room when he walked in, such was his charismatic personality.

The one story I always remember came about when we played at Torquay in an FA Cup game. Because it was such a long way and they were league opposition, it was decided to stay overnight. We ended up winning the game.

On the team coach on the way back, Nigel's mobile rang and after a short while he turned to me and said: 'It's dad – he wants a word with you.'

'Hello, Brian, how are you?'

'I'm fine Mr Chairman. I just want you to know that you should take a lot of credit for this victory.

'How do you work that out?' I replied.

He said he thought it had been very important that the players had been allowed to go down the night before and prepare properly rather than having to make such a gruelling journey on the morning of the game.

So, I said to him: 'Well, I think that proves you now have two geniuses in your family.'

Quick as a flash, he replied: "Hey, well when you find the second one, do let me know!'

❛ When I retired, one or two of the directors wives wrote to me, but not the directors themselves. Strange isn't it? ❜

England legend Tommy Lawton had been to hell and back after turbulent times. But close friend and former Nottingham Post editor BARRIE WILLIAMS recalls a night when Cloughie stepped in to make him feel ten feet tall again.

141

TWO GIANTS

BARRIE WILLIAMS

My years as editor of the Nottingham Evening Post brought me into contact with some true sporting giants and they don't come bigger and better than Brian Clough and Tommy Lawton.

And my story of a memorable night when they were both centre stage is best prefaced with a beautiful insight into the man regarded by many as the best centre forward ever to play for England.

The schoolteacher in charge of a kids' team was sprinting up and down the touchline like a demented greyhound.

'Run, run, run!' he was bellowing at his young charges. 'Move, move, move!'

An elderly man watching this pantomime could stand it no more. He walked up to the teacher.

'Look mate,' he said. 'Never mind all this run, run, run. Get them to dwell on the ball; to play the ball; to love the ball; to think.'

'Oh yeah,' replied the teacher. 'And who the bloody hell are you?'

'Nobody, son,' said the man softly. 'Nobody at all.'

The 'nobody' was Tommy Lawton, the greatest centre forward England ever had and he despaired at the way these lads were being 'taught' to play football.

Tommy told me that story, among countless others, in many an hour I spent with him enjoying a pint and a fag and talking football.

I never saw the great man play. He was from my dad's era. But coming, as I do, from a family with strong Liverpool connections (Everton supporters, all of them) I had heard endless stories about Tommy's days at Goodison Park. I had seen many pictures of him in 1950s soccer albums; the slick Brylcreemed hair with what looked like a half-inch parting; the descriptions of the 'giant', 'fearless', 'strong', 'brilliant', archetypal old-style centre forward. I had read about his incredible playing record – a career spanning 20 years with Burnley, Everton, Chelsea, Brentford, Arsenal and Notts County; 231 goals in 390 league games; 22 goals in 23 England appearances; 24 goals in 23 unofficial war time international matches and an astonishing war time scoring record of

337 goals.

I had heard old boys in pubs drooling about how Tommy headed a ball harder than most men could kick it. I had read Bill Shankly's account of how Tommy's headed winning goal in the England v Scotland match played at a packed Hampden Park in 1939 . . . 'As the ball went home like a bullet, the swish and ripple of the soaking net made a sound that frightened me. 'Pick that one out,' said Lawton and it was like a knife going through me.'

I knew that Tommy made Burnley's first team at the age of 16; that only 25 games later he was transferred to Everton for £6,500 (millions in today's money) to replace living legend 'Dixie' Dean; that he became the leading goalscorer in the land while still in his teens; that even though he was as hard as nails and built like the proverbial brick outhouse he was such a sporting player that he was never once sent-off and was never even booked.

Then, in Nottingham in 1984, I went looking for him. At that time Tommy was a man sadly and badly disillusioned with football. The game had used and abused him, picked him up in his teens and dropped him cruelly from a great height in his 40s.

When his playing career ended, Tommy managed Notts County for a while. They sacked him.

He kept a pub, which failed, due in no small measure to hangers-on who knew what a soft touch Tommy was for free drinks and open-ended loans.

Hopelessly in debt, he took a poorly-paid job selling insurance, got tempted into fraud in a clumsy bid to end his money-worries and ended up briefly, but devastatingly, behind bars.

The mighty had fallen as far as it was possible to drop. He was ashamed to open his front door. The hangers-on disappeared. People who owed him large sums of money, crossed the road to avoid him.

The erstwhile super hero of English football was broken and virtually penniless.

Tommy had in some respects been his own worst enemy. He had, in many ways, been the George Best of his day. Jack-the-lad around town, particularly when he was with Chelsea, he had lived as hard as he had played. He had always been generous to a foolish fault and, if all those who had borrowed money from him had paid up, he would have been a very rich man. As it was, the international superstar who had graced the world's biggest soccer stages, sailed on yachts with millionaires, had an audience with the Pope and appeared in films with Lupino Lane and Diana Dors, stood hunched and alone in the pouring rain at bus stops in Nottingham; that famous, feared head bowed; those great shoulders stooped, unrecognised or shunned and disowned by people who had once lined up in sycophantic file to shake his hand and plead for his autograph.

My own interest in Tommy Lawton at this time was purely and unashamedly journalistic. This was a great story. I tracked him down in order to let my newspaper publish his life story. At first he was sullen, uncommunicative and deeply suspicious of me – and who could blame him?

Many journalists could be counted among those who dumped him in the gutter. Eventually, but still reluctantly, he agreed. Then, with every meeting that followed, he became more relaxed and the real, cheeky, confident, funny and plain-talking Tommy began to emerge.

My newspaper duly told his incredible life story and I then signed him up to become a soccer columnist. Tommy Lawton was back.

Throughout the years that followed Tommy was one of my dearest friends. Tommy Lawton was a gentle man and a gentleman and I consider it an honour to have been granted his friendship.

Writing the soccer column for my paper really put Tommy back on top. Not long after taking him on, I took him as my guest to a 'do' at Forest's Jubilee Club where Cloughie was speaking.

Cloughie had the audience in the palm of his hand – nothing unusual in that. But what moved me and the rest of the audience to the brink of tears was what came next.

Cloughie said: 'Hey, I was a bloody good centre-forward was I not?'

Up went the cheers and acknowledgements for the man who was unexpectedly about to move out of the spotlight.

'But, I tell you what. There's a bloke here tonight who was a bloody darn sight better than me . . . the great Tommy Lawton.'

Tommy adored Brian. He had a broad smile as he took up his invitation to go on to the stage and when he got there he raised Brian's arm like a referee would in a boxing ring.

Cloughie planted a huge kiss on his cheek. 'You were the best,' he said. 'You were the best.'

It was a wonderful occasion and as Tom walked back to our table suddenly the rainy days at bus stops seemed a million miles away.

There was almost a swagger about him. He looked ten feet tall again – and it was all down to Brian Clough, the second greatest English centre forward!

' Harry Storer told me: 'When you become a manager and you are leaving for an away game, look around the team coach and count the number of hearts. If you are lucky there will be five. If there aren't, turn the coach around and go back '

AND FINALLY . . .

Almost 300 stories later . . . and all good things must come to an end. I'm staggered there ended up being anywhere near so many. And someone somewhere will be saying 'and you haven't got the one about . . .' Ah well, hopefully you feel you know Cloughie that little bit better. In the words of the great man himself when doing radio interviews, you need an 'out' and so this last little tale seemed to thrust itself forward as a candidate.

Away from the spotlight, Clough enjoyed a quieter and more sedate existence. In the final story, groundsman Steve Hollis tells of a friendship which developed over many early-morning chats on the outfield at Quarndon Cricket Club. The picturesque village club was almost directly opposite the Clough family home in the leafy Derby suburb.

Cloughie had a passion for cricket, wildlife and nature in general and his early morning walks with his beloved dog Del Boy managed to combine the lot.

In the following story, Steve recalls how a friendship developed tackling odd-jobs around the cricket ground. And so the collection concludes, quite fittingly, with . . .

THE CUTTING IN THE HEDGE

Local cricket club groundsman STEVE HOLLIS shared a unique relationship with the former soccer boss. And the Derby fan wraps up this collection of stories with moving memories from beyond the boundary at the club right opposite Clough's former home.

142

THE CUTTING IN THE HEDGE

STEVE HOLLIS

'My work is done, Steve.' Five short words delivered with such stunning certainty that there was no point seeking clarification. And, anyway, who was I to argue with the legendary Brian Clough as he stood there in front of me just hours before one of the biggest matches of his life? If a few overs of cricket in the nets was his way of preparing for it, then I was more than happy to go along with it.

Even when I tell the story now, it sounds unbelievable. But I know the story is 100 per cent true and I also know I was lucky enough to see the great Brian Clough in some of his most private moments. Times when he couldn't have been further away from the madding crowd and the pressures he would often find himself under.

On this particular day back in 1991, Forest were playing West Ham in the semi-finals of the FA Cup at Villa Park. I certainly hadn't banked on seeing him when the familiar figure popped through the cutting in the hedge and came over to where me and a pal of mine were having a net.

'Can I have a bat?' he asked.

'Course you can,' I replied. How could I have said 'no' anyway?

I bowled a few balls at him and you could certainly tell he had played to a good standard in his time.

'How about that, young man?' he said proudly, as he straight-batted one back. I could hardly believe what was happening.

It got to about 12.30 and I started to wonder if he shouldn't be getting over to Villa Park for the big game. An idiot would have known the FA Cup was the one big one that he had missed out on in his glorious career.

'Excuse me, Brian. But you've got one of the biggest games of your life in a few hours. Shouldn't you be getting over there?'

'Don't you worry about that. Keep bowling,' he insisted.

Another short while passed and he still seemed quite happy knocking a few balls back to us.

'Brian, are you going today?' I asked a short while later.

'Don't you worry. In about 10 minutes there will be a big blue Mercedes arrive to pick me up and take me to the game.'

He stopped, told me that when he

got to the ground he would just put a ball on a towel in the middle of the dressing room. He'd tell them that the towel was the pitch and all they had to do was keep the ball on it and play.

''My work is done, Steve,' he assured me.

You don't forget things like that do you? He still had his shorts on when the Mercedes arrived and off he went. Forest won. A few hours later, he was there on the telly! Cloughie was in the FA Cup final and I'd been lucky enough to be part of his rather unusual preparation for one of the biggest games of his career. And over the years I was lucky enough to become his friend and get a unique glimpse into some of the things that made him tick.

Brian would often have a chat with me inbetween walking his dog around the outside of the cricket ground which has been such a big part of my life for well over 30 years as both player and groundsman.

Sometimes you could tell he just didn't want to talk and was best left - on other occasions he was more than happy to chat. I've had so many conversations with him over the years, but some stand out more than others.

'I tell you what Steve, this ground looks like a dump!' he said bluntly one day. I explained to him that with a shortage of money and manpower, sometimes things were difficult.

'We need a skip for a start,' I informed him.

'Well how much is a skip?' he asked.

'Oh, probably sixty quid,' I replied.

The next time I saw him he reached into his pocket and slapped sixty quid in my hand.

'Here, get yourself a skip and tidy the bloody place up,' he said with a cheeky smile.

Another time, a couple of us were starting to top-dress the square when he ambled over and asked if we wanted him to do anything. He wasn't at his best because his dodgy knees were playing him up terribly. We had 160 bags of loam to get down and I didn't think lugging bags around was the ideal thing for him to be doing.

'I tell you what, I'll open the bags up for you if you go and get me a pair of scissors,' he said.

So, me and a lad were wheeling the loam around when my labourer made the mistake of starting to open a bag. Brian gave him a right bollocking.

'Hey, that's my job! Leave it alone young man,' he yelled. That was just typical of him.

On another occasion he invited me over to his house and we were sitting in his kitchen.

'Would you like a drink?' he said.

'What are you having?' I replied.

'Well, you ought to have a Diet Coke if you ask me, because you are putting some weight on!'

He was a bugger like that, but I got on really well with him and, for me, just a normal bloke who loved his football, it was really something special to enjoy such close contact with a legend who fascinated most people.

Sometimes when he sat there in the corner, I could tell he was feeling under the cosh. I'd just leave him to himself and his thoughts when he looked that way.

I never knew when I'd catch him. Sometimes he'd come through that little cutting of his at around 7.30 in the morning and walk the dog around the boundary. To be honest, he was more often than not happier talking about the wildlife, the nature or cricket as he was football. I think it was his way of unwinding and getting away from things.

We'd have some right laughs at times. On occasions he would come over and have a cup of coffee in the pavilion.

'Get your sister to make me a nice cup of tea, Steve,' he'd say. She'd make him one and he would ask how much it was.

'Nowt, you daft bugger - you can have that,' I'd say. Once he handed a £20 note over and told us to put it in the club funds.

Another time, we went over to the house and he kindly offered to show me his trophy room. I couldn't believe it. It really opened me eyes.

'I'm not clever, you know,' he'd say. 'But come in here and have a look at all this.'

For me, just a normal Derby fan, to be taken somewhere so special and so personal was just fantastic.

There were medals – the lot – in there. League Cups, European Cups, Watney Cups, countless Manager of the Month awards and the like and right in the middle of them all was a lifesize picture of Geoff Boycott.

Those are the memories I will treasure for ever and I feel proud and privileged to have shared them with him.

I still think about him sometimes when I'm doing jobs around the place. The funny thing is the little cutting in the hedge he used to come through has gone now. It has long since grown over since he stopped using it.

I miss him and it would be nice to think we would see him come through it one bright spring morning.

Brian Howard Clough died on September 20, 2004. He was 69.

‘ My work is done . . . ’

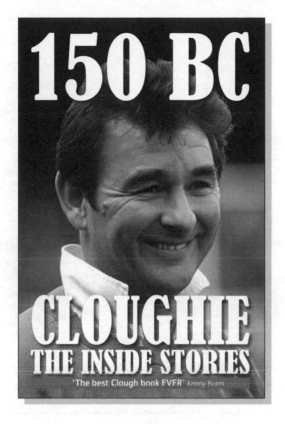

'**Brilliant collection**'
Oliver Holt, Mirror

'**Magic stories**'
Daily Mail

'**Wonderful stories**'
Henry Winter, Telegraph

'**Will crack you up**'
The Sun

'**The best Clough book I've ever read**'
Kenny Burns

'**Funny, touching and revealing. A unique take on Clough**'
Steve Nicholson, Derby Telegraph

Also by Dave Armitage

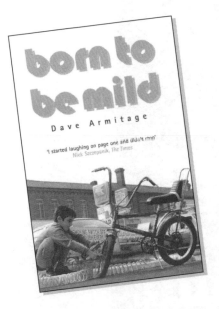

BORN TO BE MILD

It's Christmas, 1969 . . . a pint of bitter is 2s.4d(12p) and a new Ford Escort costs £703.13s.11d. Paul Dunn is 11 and more important issues lie ahead - like getting a good signal on Radio Luxembourg and the beautiful, but out of reach, carnival queen Belinda. Santa has brought him a Chopper and Dunny takes a rocky ride through the 70s
- Pan's People, puberty, Slade and T.Rex.
Thirty years later he meets Belinda and she's available, but so much has changed since those days. She is the size of a house, Donny Osmond is a grandad and Gary Glitter is facing the firing squad for something other than his records.

'Stingray, sex and the 70s . . . superb' - Daily Mirror.

'I started laughing on page one and didn't stop' - The Times.

PAST AND PRESENTS

A self-made billionaire receives a shock 50th birthday present - a photograph relating to the blackest day of his life when he was 16.
Could this now be the best present he's ever had? As he thinks back
a fascinating and funny story unfolds as he recalls all of his birthdays - past and present.

'Outrageously funny' - Daily Mirror.

'Laughtastic' - The Sun.